THE
UNDISCOVERED
COUNTRY

THE
UNDISCOVERED
COUNTRY

conversations
about death & dying

Mary Brown

Published by KCA Training

www.kca.training

First edition published

This edition published 2018 by KCA Training

Copyright © Mary Brown, 2018

The right of Mary Brown to be identified as the author of
this work has been asserted by her in accordance with
the Copyright, Designs and Patent Act 1988

Printed by IngramSpark

Contents

Preface

When Mary Brown began her work on this book it seemed far removed from the work of KCA. This was to be a book drawing together conversations about death and dying, and KCA is a training organisation providing professional development for people who work with children and families. We are concerned with the beginning of life, and Mary and her contributors with the end of life. Yet as the research progressed and themes began to emerge it became clear that this was a book that KCA would be honoured to publish. Not only is it of value to everyone who works with, or whose life is touched by, the realities of death and dying but it also, we have realised, is an immensely valuable resource for those who work with children and families – because children and families also face these issues of mortality and grief.

KCA exists to improve the lives of vulnerable people by changing the practice of those who work with them. We do this by sharing transformative knowledge, encouraging deep reflective practice, and empowering individuals and organisations to make a difference. The transformative knowledge we share is based on research and theory around attachment, trauma, and resilience, underpinned by the insights offered by current neuroscientific research on the development and function of the human brain and nervous system.

The knowledge which KCA exists to share makes it clear that from the beginning of life connectedness with others is a deep human need. Connected relationships with safe adults provide children and young people with the vital emotional nurture that feeds their developing brains and nervous systems. These connections are deeper than words, involving the human capacity for both compassion and reason.

Adults who can adequately hold this centred space provide our young with the mindful co-regulation and co-learning that builds young brains. This is the formative power of attachment relationships. When we are unable to self-regulate and maintain compassionate reason we experience toxic levels of stress which switch our brain and nervous system into survival mode and disconnect us from our own reasoned functioning and from our social network. This is the disintegrative power of traumatic experiences. Yet such disintegration can also be a point of growth and creativity when those around us connect or reconnect with us and hold us safe as we make the journey to recovery from toxic stress. This is the transformative power of resilience.

The contributors to Mary's research make it clear that in their experience connectedness with others is the most pressing need when facing the end of life for ourselves or for those we love, and that in our society this can be the very time when others disconnect from us. These are stories both of the wrenching pain of such disconnection and the transformative power of connected relationships. It becomes clear in reading this book that attachment, trauma and resilience are lifelong elements of human experience and human need.

It also became clear to us that this book is not just addressing themes at the very heart of the work of KCA, it is also directly a resource adding to the knowledge base we share. Children are not only concerned with the beginning of life but also face issues around its end. They, or those who matter to them, may die or face mortal illness. Publishing the stories of these contributors is directly adding to the knowledge that can enable those who work with vulnerable children and families to reflect on these experiences of disconnection and the power of connectedness so that they become empowered to make a difference in their own practice environment. And we hope this reflection and transformation can be extended to every practice environment in which people deal with other people at points of vulnerability.

And finally, KCA (Knowledge – Change – Action) is committed to telling the stories of those who are willing to express openly their experiences of human vulnerability. Knowledge is most effectively shared when it engages compassion as well as reason. Change happens when we can reflect deeply on the meaning of this for our own lives. Action follows naturally as we review and revise our ways of being with others. The contributors to this book have opened themselves to this exposure of their vulnerability in telling their stories. Some of them have told Mary that being able to share their stories has been transformative for them. Listening to the contributors has been transformative for Mary. We owe it to them, and to her, to read their stories with care and tenderness, and to transform ourselves – and therefore our society – in response to their courage.

Kate Cairns, September 2018

To everything there is a season, and a time to every purpose under the heaven: a time to be born, and a time to die.

(Ecclesiastes 3)

1 Choosing life

'I call on heaven and earth this day against you, that I have set before you life and death, blessing and cursing: therefore choose life, that both thou and thy seed may live.'
(Deuteronomy 30:19)

This book is about death. Why would anyone want to read, let alone write, a book about death? Death is the great unmentionable. We all know that we one day will die, but until then we seem to prefer not to talk or even to think about it, almost as if this makes death less likely. This conspiracy of silence around the subject is very different from earlier times when death was accepted as a part of life, commonly witnessed in the home, freely discussed, acknowledged, and mourned with appropriate rituals. Today our deaths are sanitised, hidden away in hospitals and mortuaries; yet at the same time death is all around, a trivialised picture of death as entertainment in films and television programmes. The BBC appears to think that at Christmas what most people want is a juicy murder, with close up scenes of horror. Why? Such programmes appear popular. Caroline, in one of the conversations that form this book, said, 'we are bombarded by material through soaps, horrible films, all the rest of it, by just that: hideous car crashes, drownings and murders – it's all done through films, and people seem to do it vicariously, not directly.'

At the same time, there is almost a cult of celebrity death. In 2016 the deaths of David Bowie and Terry Wogan, very close to each other, dominated the media for days. Caroline also said, 'When Princess Diana died there was an opening of flood gates – the number of men, who'd never known her, who were putting down flowers in honour of her in floods of tears.' Does this suggest that things are changing? Are we becoming more able to talk and to think more freely about death? I believe, rather, that these celebrity deaths sustain us, and comfort us, in the view that death happens to other people. We can contemplate the deaths of celebrities: they are not like us, they die. We admire them from afar: we are not like them, we will not die. Yet even this grieving for celebrities, grieving vicariously, at second hand, is perhaps better than not acknowledging death at all.

The ubiquity of trivialised death on our screens may distance us from the real deaths that matter to us, particularly our own and those of people we love. I hope this book may help to bring some light to a subject that currently seems shrouded in a guilty darkness, to return death to the sacred, perhaps rescue it from its current profanity. Most importantly I hope it may help us to realise that we, too, will one day die, and we need to think about how we will spend the precious time we have until we do.

What does 'choosing life', which Deuteronomy's God advises, mean? Is it that we should deny the reality of death, and live as though our lives could (perhaps should) go on for ever, refusing to talk or even think about death? Or does it mean that we should make the most of our lives while we can, live them as fully as we are able. I am so sure that the second was what was meant, and that our current culture of the denial of death is not healthy for individuals or for society, that I have spent several months talking with a variety of people, who agree that death should not be denied, but thought about, talked about, discussed. This book is based around 45 conversations I have had with people who are not afraid to talk about death.

I believe that there are many good reasons for writing, reading, talking and thinking about death which are more powerful than reasons not to. Fear is, I think, one of the reasons for not wanting to contemplate it. Many fear death. We fear the unknown, and death is, in Shakespeare's words, 'the Undiscover'd country, from whose bourn no traveller returns.' (Hamlet Act 3 Scene 1). Could bringing death back into the open make us fear our own deaths less?

Many contributors to this book who have witnessed the death of another, either in the course of their work or the death of a loved one, say that through this experience they have lost any fear they had of their own death, although one said, 'I wouldn't be as arrogant as to say that I am not afraid.' So acknowledging death could make it less fearful.

The second reason is very practical: many people die without having discussed what they would like to happen after their deaths, so that relatives do not even know if they want to be buried or cremated; more than half of us have not even made a will. When people are asked where they would like to die, 70% say at home, but in fact over half die in hospitals. Only 6% of us have an Advanced Directive, telling relatives and medical staff what we want. If we would prefer to stay peacefully at home rather than being subjected to intrusive interventions to keep us alive for a few more days, or perhaps weeks, we need to have made this clear, so that we might be able to die where and how we wish. Another very practical reason is that if we talked more about death, more people might sign up to donate their organs, and fewer families might prevent such donation: talking about death could save lives.

Perhaps the most important reason, which has come from these conversations, is that those who have been bereaved say they need to talk about their loss, but find it hard to find someone who is prepared to listen. If we were more able to discuss death, we might be better able to help the bereaved. Contributors told me that people think they 'don't know what to say', when actually they don't need to say anything, beyond 'I'm sorry', or just a hug. Silence is acceptable. It is the bereaved who want to talk, we need only listen. In quiet listening, in silence, we can be united in some mysterious but very meaningful way with our fellow human beings. Death unites for we will all die; in a sense, all lives are lived on 'Death Row.'

I have another, very personal, reason for writing this book: a few years ago I nearly chose death. After living over 70 years, mostly as a very healthy and active person, I became worryingly short of breath and unnaturally tired. Leaking heart valves were diagnosed, and I was told I would need open heart surgery. Did I really want, or need, to go through all that this would involve? Would it not be simpler just to allow myself to die? My GP told me that if I did not have the operation I would get more and more breathless, until I could no longer breathe at all. It sounded peaceful, unlike surgery.

About a year before this, I was very ill and had been taken to hospital unconscious; I would have died if friends had not broken into my home and found me. I remember no near death experience, only a deep peace, from which I was dragged. I remembered that perfect peace, it seemed inviting. I had to choose.

I debated with myself whether I really wanted to go through with it. I think I had almost decided that I had lived long enough, that my life was complete. I had had more than my biblical three score years and ten. I had retired, even, when I became ill, from voluntary work which I loved. I had seen my four children grow up and had eight grandchildren. Perhaps it was time to say goodbye to them all?

However, one day I was in a Quaker meeting, hoping perhaps to find some clarity about my decision, when one of the Quaker 'Advices and Queries' (number 27) was read: 'live adventurously. When choices arise, do you take the way that offers the fullest opportunity for the use of your gifts in the service of God and the community? Let your life speak.' I realised I had to choose life. How could I live adventurously, or serve God or the community, if I chose to die? I had the operation: gave my life a chance to speak.

My final, and to me the most important, reason for talking and writing about death also comes from Quakerism. I am a Quaker, a member of the Religious Society of Friends, a universalist rather than the Christ-centric Quaker. The Quaker 'Advices and Queries' number 30 asks: 'are you able to contemplate your death and the death of those closest to you? Accepting the fact of death, we are freed to live more fully. In bereavement, give yourself time to grieve. When others mourn, let your love embrace them.' I chose life, and am alive and freed to 'live more fully,' which I try to do. One of the things I decided to do with the time I have, was to write this book about death.

Nicola, a counsellor, told me how the death of her father made her realise that she would die. She had known this before, but now she had what she called 'deep knowing',

> 'Well you can know it intellectually, from quite a young age, but to really get it on a cellular level, really get it, to really realise that we are going to die, enough to really make the most of our lives. To value the sacred element of our life, all life is sacred, and the more we value the sacred element the more we value life and make the most of it. When our body knows it's going to die, deep knowing that how special, how amazing it is to be alive. I realised I really am going to die, it's an amazing way of seeing my life, it's really precious... The more I think about death the more I want to live.'

Maybe this is the knowledge of death that we need 'to live more fully'. I hope these conversations may contribute to fuller lives.

This book is based on conversations with a random group of people. They are not random in the statistical sense, of each having an equal chance of being chosen, rather haphazard: they were people who were available to me, and were willing, even happy, for a variety of reasons, to talk to me about death. This makes them unusual, atypical. They are not celebrities, they are ordinary people like us all; they speak as one of us. If it is important to talk about death, then hearing what those who are willing to do this have to say to us may help others feel more able to discuss, and contemplate, their own death. Listening to these sometimes untold stories, these truths, these sadnesses which were shared with me because the contributors want me to share them with you the reader, I was moved, sometimes almost to tears. Reading the transcripts later I sometimes felt unwell, exhausted, wondering whether I should give up the whole enterprise. However, I knew I must carry on for the sakes of the contributors. I am privileged to have heard what they have to say. More than one told me this book 'needs to be written.' So I have persevered.

These are conversations not interviews. Each person who talked to me had their own unique perspective on death, so the questions I asked were few, different for each individual and changed slightly as time went on. Sometimes, when I was reading all the conversations, I found topics and themes emerging and wondered what earlier contributors would like to say about that topic, so occasionally I emailed or phoned and asked them; most seemed pleased to help again. I hope these conversations were more informal than interviews. I was told by more than one contributor that talking to me had been helpful. I was slightly uneasy about this, as that was not my aim. I am using (perhaps even abusing) what I was told for my own purposes; this is very different from a counselling conversation, however much some might have seen it as that. I tried to make this clear. The conversations did not lead me to a final truth: the undiscovered country remains undiscovered. This is a collection of thoughts, ideas, dreams about death, which a number of people have been willing to share. I am deeply grateful to them for their contributions and hope I have done them justice. As far as possible I have used the words that I heard, keeping my own contributions to a minimum, in the hope that you can hear their voices. They deserve to be heard.

My original idea in writing this book was to talk to people I knew who, I was sure, would be happy to talk to me about death. I thought of someone who became a GP in part, perhaps, because both her parents died when she was a child, and who would like one day to work in a hospice; I thought of a friend whose daughter killed herself. I even thought I might not need to record the conversations. However, not long into the first, aborted, conversation, I realised that I needed more detachment. I decided not to use friends, though one or two conversations were with acquaintances, and I have got to know some contributors quite well after the conversation.

I recorded each conversation, sometimes in the contributors' homes, sometimes in mine. Three I met in public places, cafés or pubs, which was not ideal, as my recorder picked up a lot of the background noise. Two I met outside, and we were disturbed by aeroplanes. Four I spoke to on the telephone as they lived too far away for us to meet, or I only wanted a brief talk. When I had written up each conversation, I sent my transcript to the contributor to check. I had done this in previous research, and it seemed to work well: most people returned the transcript promptly, with few if any changes. This time it was different: some people took several weeks to get back to me, and then had very many changes they wanted made. I realised that this was a sign of just how important the subject is. They wanted to be quite sure I had got them right. It was, literally, a matter of life and death. Some took hours doing this, and I am so grateful that they thought it worth their time. Some went to immense time and trouble to rewrite my account of our meeting, some offered poetry or art work. Appendices two and three give two full rewritten stories. J and Sarah are two of those who took the greatest time and trouble to make sure that I had what they told me exactly right.

Most contributors had experienced bereavement; some of those who worked with the dying in some capacity also spoke of personal bereavement. The deaths of loved ones which I heard of, some recent, some as much as 20 years ago, were all very fresh in the minds of those who talked to me.

All contributors are anonymous: I have used names which each chose for themselves. Some kept their real names, others chose a pseudonym, some an initial. Some changed their minds, after thinking about it. When I told M5 that I already had an M, but she could be M1 or M2, she choose M5: 'my favourite motorway'. When I found I had two Sarah's, Sam kindly agreed to go by that name. Jean, a carer, emphasised the vital importance of confidentiality, 'it's about respect... confidentiality goes on after death; that's what carers stick to.' She had discussed with her sister whether it would be acceptable for her to talk to me.

Some contributors I met through the local death café. The growing popularity of death cafés, where people meet, usually monthly for tea and cakes and to talk about death, suggests, on the one hand, that things are changing, there are people who want to talk about death; but, on the other hand, the fact that they need to go to a death café to do this, suggests that we have a long way to go before we can discuss death as part of a normal conversation.

Pammy organises the local death café, through which I also contacted Jean, James, Julie, Annabel, M, Nicola, Paul, Christine and Hannah. James is a funeral director ('with a difference'). Julie is a Marie Curie nursing assistant, whose partner died six years before our conversation. M is a nurse who now works with her husband, a vicar, with the newly bereaved. Nicola is a counsellor, involved in bereavement counselling, who worked with Cruse in the past. Annabel and Hanna are both retired nurses who have worked in hospices; Annabel also worked in a Rudolf Steiner nursing home, Hannah also as a Marie Curie nurse. Jean is a carer, whose work involves her with dying people, and, in the past, with those living with AIDS/HIV.

Isabel, Gill, E., Chris, Jenny and the chaplain all work or volunteer at the Welcome Hospice (again a pseudonym, suggested by Isabel). Swami S and Sister Ally both belong to the Community of the Many Names of God, a multi-faith monastery in a remote Welsh valley. As well as receiving many thousands of pilgrims each year from all over the UK, mostly with their origins in the Indian subcontinent, the monastery runs a hospice. Swami S described himself as 'passionate about hospice care, end of life care'; sister Ally works as a carer in the hospice, and loves her work.

R lost his mother at the age of 15 and his wife three years before our conversation, and is now a Cruse volunteer. Corinna is an end of life doula. Anne is a retired palliative care nurse who has worked in a hospice, and now writes to prisoners on Death Row in America. Phoebe took her father to Switzerland to die with Dignitas. Rosie told me of a course she had attended with William Bloom, called 'Passing Over', on preparing for death. She also told me of Jung's ideas about death, for which I am very grateful; Jung came to be a central theme in my interpretation of the conversations. Sam is a Samaritan. Eve is a follower of Rudolf Steiner, at 86 probably the oldest contributor, with six grown up children, 21 grandchildren, and eight great-grand-children. She and M5, who belongs to the Quaker Fellowship of After Life Studies, both told of continuing relationships with dead relatives. Violet told me of a remarkable experience following her mother's death. Tom's wife had six miscarriages, a still birth and a termination of pregnancy (on medical advice). One of his daughters had a miscarriage and the other a still birth, so this conversation was about death before birth, with its particular and very painful grief. SA is a homoeopath who had two near death experiences. Martin S ran a weekend workshop where participants could weave their own caskets for when they die. I heard of this when I had almost finished the conversations, so I only talked to him about the workshop.

Ellen, Caroline and J have all lost children. Ellen's son died of pneumonia just before his ninth birthday; J's son killed himself a the age of 33; Caroline's son was 22 when he suffered a horrendous alcohol related death that may or may not have been self inflicted; the coroner's verdict was inconclusive. Sarah's daughter attempted suicide just before her 24th birthday; she was saved but with serious brain damage. Sarah has lost the daughter she once had, now she has a toddler in her 30s. The GP is a family doctor who describes herself as 'slightly evangelical about the need to make difficult decisions about death and dying.'

C and Father P are Christian priests, belonging respectively to the Christian Community (Rudolf Steiner), and the Roman Catholic Church. Early on in my conversations both told me of the beliefs and ceremonies around death in their church. I also talked to John, a Humanist, about his beliefs (which do not include any religious faith) as well as about his support for the Assisted Dying Bill. Later I realised that as we now live in a multi-faith society I ought to talk to people of other faiths, so, late in the process, I added Kalsoom, GKP, Nimue, B and Rosa who told me respectively about Muslim, Hindu, Pagan, Buddhist and Jewish views of death. These conversations were briefer than others and form chapters ten and eleven, but some of their thoughts are also in other chapters. Some readers may prefer to leave out chapter ten, they may well know far more than I was able to learn in a brief conversation.

I also had the privilege of watching a film about a hospice in Scotland, 'Seven Songs for a Long Life', which has been shown on BBC2 Scotland. Amy Hardie, filmmaker-in-residence at the hospice, brought the film to the South of England to show on a wet, cold Saturday in January, to a hall packed largely, I think, by volunteers at the local hospice and those who go to the death café. It was through Amy that I was able to contact Iain, almost the last contributor I spoke with, who is a patient at that hospice. Until then, I thought that the one group I could not include was those who are dying, except in the sense that we are all dying. The hospices I visited, rightly, protect their patients, but Amy said she was sure that some of those who appear in her film would be willing to talk to me. So I was very grateful to Iain for the lovely conversation we had on the phone. Iain is probably unique among hospice patients, as he has been going there for eight years, and hopes to continue for many years more. He lives with the pain of Primary Progressive Multiple Sclerosis.

The final contributor is Helen, whom I met when I thought I had finished with conversations. I had seen her before a few times at meetings, but did not really know her. When I asked her how she was (I had no idea that she had been ill) she said, 'over a year ago I was given six months to live, but I'm still here.' I knew I must have one more contributor, and asked if she would be willing to talk to me. Until talking with Helen I had not been able to talk to anyone who was close to their own death. Helen's account of living with a 'death sentence' is particularly poignant; she said some things that were quite unique and do not fit completely with what others had told me. I am particularly grateful to Helen for providing this balance.

I actually had 46 conversations, but when I sent my transcript to one person, she decided that she would prefer me not to use it, although she is perfectly happy to talk about death, which is very closely related to her profession. So I have not used any of that conversation, although I may have unconsciously absorbed some of her ideas. I am fortunate that she was the only one to change her mind so radically.

Obviously, I have not been able to talk to anyone who has died. I heard very moving accounts of the deaths of others, and SA told me of his near death experiences, which were very similar to published accounts of such experiences.

These conversations ranged widely, each one covering a number of topics, so the same contributor may be quoted several times in different chapters. To make it easier to remember who people are, I will give a few words of identification the first time they are mentioned in a chapter. This may seem unnecessary to some: I got to know them first when talking with them, I knew them better when listening to and transcribing the conversations, and felt I knew them even better when I read them all, trying to pull everything into some kind of shape. I hope readers will similarly get to know the contributors: they are all worth knowing. Contributors are listed in appendix one.

All these people talked to me of their personal experiences and thoughts about death and gave me permission to use what they told me. Those who worked with or volunteered with organisations were speaking as individuals, not on behalf of that organisation, although I have the permission to use the name of the organisation where appropriate. Many contributors told me of books I should read, or more people to talk to. In the course of reporting the conversations I will mention various books, TV and radio programmes where these seem relevant to what contributors are saying. While we may be reluctant to talk about death or grief, we seem to want to read about it, and writers to write about it. Perhaps it is because we cannot talk, that we share grief at second hand, through books. These books are in the bibliography.

I will also share my experience of the deaths of my parents and my brother, and of being with a few others shortly before their deaths.

I could have had many more conversations, but I felt this was enough if I was to remember them all. I have tried to listen carefully to what each one told me and report it faithfully. I might not agree with all I was told; you may not agree with them or with me. We all have our truths. These are the contributors' ideas, their thoughts, their truths. Inevitably, this is also my interpretation of what they told me, but this is true of anyone using the ideas of others; however much social research may claim to be valid, or impartial, the ideas and interpretations of the researcher always impact on that research, if only in the framing of the hypothesis. Some may know, or believe they know, the truth about death. But we will never know if they, or we, are right or wrong until we die. The 'Undiscovered Country' will remain Undiscovered. Here I have no hypotheses.

I asked few questions, and let contributors talk for as long as they wanted, which ranged between 20 minutes and 1¾ hours. Most conversations lasted around an hour. In writing this, I have tried to let the contributors speak for themselves, quoting verbatim, sometimes at length, from what they told me.

Interestingly, of these 45 conversations only thirteen are with men. Obviously nothing can be concluded from such small numbers, perhaps it is just chance that, as a woman, I found more women to talk to. However, two of the men said they were not surprised: men are even less comfortable with the topic than women. Both said that their men friends were likely to suggest going out for a beer to comfort them in bereavement. Tom said, 'That's their tool-kit for dealing with another man in such a situation.' R said, 'They say "come to the pub and have a pint and forget about it".' Nicola, the counsellor, said few men came to her for bereavement counselling. 'For men, I think, the grieving process is often a bit more tricky, more difficult... Men don't acknowledge that they need help... needing help could be a sign of weakness. "'Big boys don't cry".'

I first thought that I wanted to talk to some people who, for whatever reason, feel it is not a good idea to talk about death, but I was not sure how I could contact such people: this would seem like talking about death. Someone who holds this view referred me to the poem by Philip Larkin, Aubade, in 'Poems that Make Grown Men Cry', where he writes of the fear of nothingness.

Ernest Becker in his award-winning book *The Denial of Death*, published 40 years ago, similarly claims that human activity is largely driven by our unconscious denial of our mortality. Our character and culture serve to shield us from our terror of death. Almost all of those who have talked with me, sharing a wealth of experience, would not agree with Becker. The exception is Helen. She is not someone who volunteered to talk to me; when I asked her she agreed but said, 'there is not much to tell', and I suspect others with her views might agree with this. I did not feel able to press her; I respected her wish not to talk any more about death. I realise now that had I found someone who did not want to talk about death, they might similarly think that there is not much to tell.

What have all these conversations taught me? I have learned that while death may involve horrendous pain and suffering, it can also be beautiful, a spiritual experience akin to birth: both events are hard work, and both have the power to move men to tears. We need not fear death.

Many talked about the wonderful last few weeks, days or, in one case, minutes before death. Pammy said, 'I would say Dad embraced life in that last month, he had some wonderful times, seeing all his friends.' Phoebe told me her father experienced something similar when all the arrangements were in place for her to take him to Switzerland.

Bereaved people told me of their desperate need to talk about their loss, and how hard it was to find people prepared to listen. Two Quakers, Tom and Caroline, said Quakers were the exception to this, and both found great support from those in their Quaker meetings. Caroline, however, said this applied only to the death of her son, not of her mother.

I learned that a hospice is not a place to go to die, rather a place where those towards the end of their lives are enabled to live as fully as they can, to the very end. Those whose work is with people at the end of life almost all used the word 'privilege' to describe their work. Julie said, 'I absolutely love my job, I really do, it's incredible. I believe it's as much a privilege to be with someone who's at the end of life as being a midwife at the beginning.'

Every death, every bereavement, is unique: the loss of a child, in the words of Ellen, '... is hell. It is one of the worst things that anyone can go through. Some people never get through it.'

Ellen lost her husband a few years after the death of her son, and said that this was a totally different bereavement. The day after he died she needed to be at work, whereas when her son died she completely fell to pieces. 'I was off work for some time, I wasn't functioning, I took to my bed. My boss from work used to come round and I answered the door in my pyjamas.'

The loss of the 97-year-old nun, which Sister Ally told me of, is different again, but still led to grief; all griefs need to be acknowledged and lived through.

Our lives, too, are unique; but underlying all our myriad ways of being is the truth that we all are one. What we share is more important than our individuality: in fact it could be what makes individuality possible. Is this a truth we prefer to ignore in our individualistic society? Could this be related to our denial of death? Sam told me that one of her aims in talking to those in despair is to help them to feel less alone. If the caller is determined to die, she will respect their wishes, and even stay on the phone so that they do not die completely alone, if that is what they want. She described doing this as a privilege.

Above all, the message that has come to me from these conversations is that death is a natural part of life: to choose life means to accept that we are not immortal, we need to make the most of our lives before we die, to savour its richness while we can. In the words of Hanna we must see life 'as it really is, in all its sparkling luminosity.' This book is about death, but, as it progressed, it seemed to be as much about life, for the two are inextricably connected.

The following chapters will go in more detail into the things I have learned: Chapter two will discuss the 'elephant in the room', our unwillingness to talk about death. Chapter three, 'Someone to grief with', will look at grief, and the importance for the bereaved to be able to talk about their loss. Chapter four is 'Life after death': nothing to do with heaven, hell or reincarnation, but the acknowledgement that life is never the same after a bereavement, but there can still be a life. Chapter five, 'When death comes,' looks at what contributors told me of what happens at the time of death.

Chapter six is 'Dissolving into love', looking at what, if anything, is meant by the phrase 'a good death'. Chapter seven, 'The Blossomest Blossom,' discusses the peace, contentment and depth of living that some can experience shortly before death. Chapter eight 'Going gently,' is about choosing death, and will look at suicide, assisted dying and advanced directives. Chapter nine is 'Oned in death': how death unites, and underlies the deep connections between all human beings. Chapter ten, 'In sure and certain hope', will look at different faiths' views on death. Chapter eleven is 'The cloud of unknowing', about the search for meaning, religious or otherwise, in death. The last chapter will return to the theme of this chapter: 'Living more fully.'

The next chapter looks at our 'culture where we're in denial of death,' as Hanna put it; or, in the words of Corinna, 'the elephant we don't talk about.'

*   *   *

Thank You

'Thank you', I said
When I saw your dead form
Such a strange thing to say
Given the torture we'd gone through
Yet deep in my heart
I still say thank you
Though how that can be
I simply don't know.

(Caroline)

2 The elephant in the room

'Whereof one cannot speak, thereof one must be silent.'
(Wittgenstein)

In this chapter I will look at our reluctance to talk about death: its denial seems to be part of our culture. After briefly suggesting possible reasons for death being the great unmentionable, I will look at why I believe this is not healthy for individuals or for society, and share what some of those whose work, both professional and voluntary, is with the dying and the bereaved have to say about the importance of acknowledging this 'elephant in the room'. I will then share some of what contributors have to say about changing this.

It sometimes seems that people find it difficult to even use the word 'death' or 'died', preferring euphemisms such as 'passed on' or 'passed away.' I noticed that Julie, the Marie Curie nursing assistant, tended to use such words rather than death, and asked her why this was, as she said she was happy to talk about death:

'I think it's habit – with people I go to, talking about death and dying is quite hard. It's in your face statements for someone when someone they know is going through that process, so yes, I tend to say someone passed away, rather than died; it's a friendlier way.'

I think that as a society we choose to deny the reality of death. Contributors supported this view: Phoebe, who took her father to Switzerland to die, said, 'It's strange how we pretend we're not going to die, the whole culture is based around that.' Corinna, end of life Doula, said, 'We live in this illusion that it won't happen to me.'

This denial of death seems largely a twentieth- and twenty-first century phenomenon. In the nineteenth, when sex was our elephant, death was seen as part of life: the bereaved wore black, or perhaps black armbands as some football teams still do if one of their number dies. I wondered when the custom ended, and found the question asked in Google, but no answers. In the past 'sorry for your loss' seems to have been an accepted greeting. (It is one of the phrases suggested to those who consult Google for how to give or to write condolences. I do not think the Victorians needed Google for this). The Irish novelist, Colm Tobin, in his novel *Nora Webster*, has the widow say that there is no reply to those words, and that the person saying them seemed in a great hurry to get away from her. So perhaps a set of words would not help.

Now that sex is so openly discussed, death has become a subject of shame. I wonder if this could be linked to the fact that we are now not only a secular society, but one that cherishes individualism, unlike the more socially cohesive societies of the past. In the nineteenth and early twentieth centuries, in mining communities, after the frequent disasters, distraught relatives would gather round the pit head looking anxiously at each face to emerge. Numerous novels describe this. There was no shortage then of people to share the grief. The solidarity and mutual support of mining communities lasted until the mines closed, but may have been largely lost along with the mortal dangers and inhuman conditions involved in working underground. Perhaps, if and when society changes again, so that we can once more admit that we all depend on one another, that there is such a thing as society, then we may also accept that our lives are finite: we do not live for ever, so must make the most to this brief and precious time we have together. Some contributors saw some signs of a change in this direction.

Caroline, who lost her son 14 years ago, said she thought that one of the reasons for our denial of death is our modern urban society. 'We're so cut off from nature and the natural world. That's a huge part of it. Take trees in autumn — the next part of life is already there, but there is the dropping off, and the dealing with that dropping off.' Annabel, a nurse who said there had been several suicides in her family, said, 'Getting very disconnected from nature isn't at all healthy.' She linked this to suicide. Hannah, retired nurse, told me she had worked on farms, and this was partly why she feels quite comfortable talking about death; but few grow up on farms, now. Pammy, the death café organiser, also grew up on a farm and saw animals die,

> 'I remember my dad once taking us to a slaughterhouse when I was quite young, and I remember a very big cow being shot – I'm a vegetarian now! So it seemed that death was all around. My brother and I spent time burying dead animals and birds, doing little funerals, digging graves and making little markers. I remember we once we dug a grave for ourselves, and we got in it, and I remember my mum being cross about that!'

Several people told me that there seemed almost an idea that death is somehow catching: if you talk about it, perhaps it is more likely to happen. The fear of death grows. Pammy said, 'Some sort of belief that if you talk about death maybe you'll bring it on, some sort of superstition or belief that for this reason it's best not talked about.' Could fear be a reason for not talking about death? R, the bereavement volunteer, said the bereaved sometimes fear for their own life.

> 'A lot of people who have been bereaved start doubting their own health issues. They start seeing things almost in a paranoid way, a fear that they are going to die as well. Because they've been touched by death, and therefore they think they are closer to it as a result… There is no reason to think like that, but they do.'

Hannah said death 'Is largely unfamiliar and unknown, and therefore it is dreaded or feared.' Eve, at the age of 86 said she wanted to talk about death because,

'I'm getting near to there myself, being 86. I don't think I've ever been frightened of it as such. Possibly the pain leading up to it, I'm not very good at pain, but we women suffer a lot of pain anyhow. I'm more interested in what happens after death, than death itself, I firmly believe that we will come back – reincarnate.

M, who supports the recently bereaved from her husband's church, said, 'I hope people learn to not fear death.' I asked her how they could, and she said: 'To talk about it, and to ask questions and to make sure that they live their lives as full as possible.' This seems the most important message from these conversations.

Nicola, the counsellor, said,

'I woke up the other morning, and got this feeling about fear of dying, but very quickly I realised I'm still afraid of life, not afraid of dying, once I got that, that it was a real wake up. The more I think about death the more I want to live. The more I want to cherish my life, every moment.'

Later, talking about counselling she said,

'It's also about bringing up their own fear of death – the fear of death, fear of life that can be really explored, that area of what do you want to do with your precious life?'

Phoebe said that once she had organised the trip to Switzerland for her father's death,

'The other thing that has happened to me is my whole relation-ship to death and dying has completely changed in that I don't feel at all frightened of dying any more, not at all. It definitely feels easier, the fact of my mortality is just a much more comfort-able thing now, having been with Dad through that. It's hard to quite say why, but perhaps because it's OK to die, really, because we're all going to. "We're all going to and that's OK", in a weird

*kind of way is how it feels to me about my own death; I can't
really articulate exactly why I think that... It's nothing at all to
do with not wanting to be alive, it makes life even more precious
because – here I am in this body, and it's like realising it won't be
for ever that makes it really precious to be in this body right now.'*

I asked if she had previously felt frightened,

*'I don't think I was frightened, but now death just feels the most
natural thing in the world. Even though it wasn't a natural death
in a way, it just feels like a really OK thing to happen... I can't
remember exactly, I just feel peaceful around the thought of my
own death now. In that situation I would do the same.'*

I was at first surprised at how many contributors said they had lost
their fear of death, although Hannah said to say this might seem 'presumptuous.' But if the fear of death is part of the general unwillingness to talk of death, then talking, as contributors do, should reduce
or remove fears. Pammy told me that fear of death is one reason for
some people coming to the death café. 'Some come to help them face
their fears, they're very frightened.'
E said of patients at the Welcome Hospice,

*'They talk about fears, fear of the unknown. There are two camps:
fear of the actual dying process, and those who are less well what
the end stage will be like, they don't always have an issue about
being dead. For others it's what will happen when they are no
longer here any more, what that means.'*

Yet, talking about his work in the hospice as a volunteer, Chris
said, 'fear does not seem to come over here.' I had asked him if
patients wanted to talk about their deaths, and he said most did not.
Gill, another hospice volunteer said she encouraged patients to talk
about death,

'Well, people will talk to you and say "I'm really worried", they may go to the social worker, and we do have a bereavement section. I've had people who've made their death plan, right through from first diagnosis to the funeral, and everyone knows, the family knows, and it's that person's wishes, and that's the important person. It is really wonderful. It's something we are all destined for, we can't escape – but we don't talk about it.'

The chaplain at the hospice said that the time of death is 'a time of great distress for some, a time of great uncertainty and a time of fear.' Yet talking about her work with the dying, Annabel said, 'sometimes some people just let go of their thoughts and get a different picture of what's happening when they are dying. Having been full of fear and distress, possibly around the not knowing of what will happen next, they may suddenly let go and find peace.'

Talking about the death of a 97-year-old sister at the Community of the Many Names of God, Sister Ally said, 'I think there was some fear, because letting go of the body is extremely difficult.' But later, describing the love that filled her room as she approached death, she said the room was filled with, 'not fear, not terror, not anxiety, just bliss.'

SA said, that after his near death experiences,

'I no longer fear death. From that very first time at 19 I no longer feared death. So much in life is to do with fear, and the biggest fear is fear of death, because it's final, finished, the end of a line. If that's what you feel or what your fear, then you want to hang onto it, with every last breath. You want to not risk that happening to you, you want to really hold on; whereas I'm quite relaxed about it… there was a rebirth, like being born again. You don't know what's round the corner, live for the now, don't be afraid of death, don't be afraid of dying.'

Another important reason for not talking about death is our lack of familiarity with it. Modern medicine has removed it from the home into the hospital. In the days before the NHS most deaths occurred at home and the coffin might rest in the front room until the funeral. Now death happens behind the closed doors of the hospital, and bodies wait with the undertaker. Death has been 'sanitised', according to E.

'People think they don't know how to do it: we see people from a distance afterwards, when they've been tidied up. So it's become distanced, not a normal thing. Medicine is now so fantastic we believe everybody should live for ever, if we were to believe what we see in media.'

Yet, despite the media, lives do end. Hospitals are in the business of saving lives, which may be why they, and we, are not comfortable with lives ending. It feels like failure.

Anne told me how she had been shocked as a student nurse at the age of 18 to see a dying patient moved into a side ward:

'I thought why can't he be in the ward with everybody else? Why is he isolated? And I saw the big chief, the consultant, come through, with his whole entourage behind him and I was a little minion – a first year student – and he looked into the room and walked on without entering. His attitude gave the impression that the patient had failed him because he was dying rather than recovering. I thought how terrible it was; it disturbed my 18-year-old brain because it went against my concept of what caring was.'

Anne moved into end of life care, first working in a nursing home, then in a hospice.

A very similar story of a consultant not going into the room of a dying patient is reported in the *Independent* newspaper in 2015 by a doctor, Katherine Sleeman. This happened to her in 1999 when she was a young junior doctor. But she says doctors still leave medical school as she did, ill equipped to deal with death and dying. Palliative care gets 20 hours in a five year course. She felt that this resulted in doctors who think that death means failure. She says the failure is not death, it's avoiding talking about it that is.

Another doctor, Mayur Lakhani, in a similar article in the *Guardian* entitled 'Medics must realise that death is an inevitable part of life, not a failure', says once again we need to have a national conversation about death and dying.

When my father died the doctor said he could not put 'old age' as the cause on the death certificate, even though he was 90. He said this was not allowed, implying that death has to come from some complaint, rather than being the natural end of life. I was later informed that this has now changed. So I asked the GP if she was allowed to put old age as the cause of death on a death certificate. She said, 'frailty of old age' was acceptable to the local coroner, but it could differ in other places. I googled 'frailty of old age', and discovered that it has been labelled an illness, because not all old people are frail. There are five 'symptoms'. So frailty of old age is still a complaint, which has not been successfully treated, not a natural end. I asked another GP on the other side of the country if she could put old age as a cause of death, she said she did if there appeared to be no other.

Another theory for death being a taboo subject is all the horrific deaths in the two world wars, which happened so far away that often no funeral was possible. When every family lost someone survivors just could not cope with the horror, and pushed it to the back of their consciousness. When men returned from the fighting they, too, were frequently too traumatised to share their experiences. Caroline shared this theory:

'What my parents went through in the second world war, their parents went through in the first world war: their grandparents

were going through loss of husbands, fiancés', partners in the first world war and then went through it again, losing their sons nephews and so on, only a few years later. How could they survive in any other way than blocking off? There was too much of it. It was happening everywhere, people were losing people, people were coming back different people than they were before, maimed or whatever; hideous things happening to them — if all that had penetrated into the core of people they couldn't have stood it. They would have had to put up that defence against that level of horror, and I think subsequent generations are suffering from that.'

Corinna said she did not think this refusal to acknowledge death helps the dying. She said

'The person who is dying is so sensitive, there is heightened sensitivity. They feel all of that, all these dramas and these wonderful processes that are going on in the room, the elephant we don't talk about. But they are huge in the room. Pretending doesn't work.'

Both B, the Buddhist, and Kalsoom, the Muslim, said that death was freely talked about in their cultures. Kalsoom told me that when Muslims pray five times a day, they pray for a good life so that they may have a good death. B said, 'Death is really important in Buddhist tradition. One thing people think about a lot in Buddhism are death and rebirth.'

Similarly, Father P, the chaplain to the Bernadine Cistercian nuns, quoted the rule of St. Benedict who said, 'keep death daily before your eyes'. He said this might sound morbid, but he went on to tell me that for a Catholic death is the final stage of our journey to eternal life: this life is only a preparation for that. He continued, 'in our secular culture we have no rites or rituals for death.' He mentioned the modern habit of putting flowers by the scene of fatal accidents, perhaps the start of a new ritual. The Catholic church has many rituals around death, which make it easier to talk about. I will look at what those of different faiths say they believe about death in chapter ten: a faith may make talking about death easier. Which again suggests secularisation as a cause for the denial of death.

Does this culture of the denial of death need to change, and if so why and how? I think there are very solid practical reasons, and other more emotional, perhaps spiritual, reasons for talking about death. I will look at the practical reasons first. The most important of these is that if we have never talked about our deaths, our relatives do not know what we would like to happen when we have died. Research carried out by ComRes for the Dying Matters Coalition (whose aim is 'to help transform public attitudes towards dying death and bereavement') found that in 2014 four fifths of the public believed that people in Britain are uncomfortable discussing dying and death. More than half of those with a partner (51%) said they were unaware of their end of life wishes. Only 35% of adults had written a will, while just over a third (32%) had registered as an organ donor or had a donor card. Only 21% of people had let someone know their funeral wishes. Meanwhile, just 6% of the public had written down their wishes or preferences about their future care, should they be unable to make decisions for themselves. 71% thought that if we were more able to talk about such matters, it would be easier for our end of life wishes to be met.

Dying Matters also found that 70% of people would like to die at home, but over half die in hospital. The GP said that the reason for this gross mismatch between what we say we want and what we get, is often because no one has asked a dying person such questions. Many hospital consultants, she felt, believed the most important thing is to keep people alive as long as possible. But 'trying to keep people comfortable at home and make sure they are dignified, comfortable and well looked after in a good place, if we can do that, that's our really important role.'

We need to be able to ask our loved ones these questions. On the BBC Radio Four programme 'Desert Island Discs' the American consultant and Reith lecturer, Atul Gwande, said, that people want other things in their lives beyond living longer. The ComRes poll found that 79% of the general public agreed that quality of life is more important than how long they live for. Of those aged 65 and over only 2% disagreed. Despite the fact that life expectancy is on the rise, only 6% of people aged 65 and over want to live to over 100. Things may be changing, as 64% thought it easier to talk about death and dying than it was ten years ago.

There may have been changes over the years that I have been writing this book, at least in the media. Radio Four has broadcast several programmes that deal with death, including two series of Joan Bakewell's 'We Need to Talk about Death.'

In 2017 BBC 2 showed a film called 'A Time to Live' which told the stories of 12 people who had been given terminal diagnoses. All said they had made the choice to make the most of what time they had left. The film, as its title suggests, was about living, enjoying life and loving.

In 2017 Quakers published a booklet called, 'Twelve Quakers and Death'. This is the eleventh in a series 'Twelve Quakers and ...' dealing with topics such as God, Evil, Truth. Quakers have no creed so it is impossible to answer the question, 'what do Quakers believe about..?' Different Quakers have different beliefs. The first of these booklets was published in 2004, so it has taken 13 years before one dealing with death. One of the twelve contributors says, 'Thank goodness we can now talk about death and dying!' But another writes of a 'conspiracy of silence.'

In 2018 there was even a Disney film 'Coco', based on the Mexican Day of the Dead. However, in an article about the film in the

Guardian, Danny Leigh says that the only thing we fear more than death is having to talk about it. With our children, we leave it to Walt Disney. Apparently he always tried to avoid funerals, yet made films which often include tragic deaths.

Death cafes are proliferating, but they do not seem to have become redundant. Things may be changing, but there is still a long way to go.

Another important reason for talking about death is organ donation. If more of us felt able to talk about the end of our lives, more organs might be donated and save more lives. Over 7,000 people in the UK need a transplant, and over 13,000 die while on the waiting list, or become too sick for transplant surgery. Organ transplant is one very real expression of the fact that humanity is one: we depend on one another for our very lives. The GP told me that it is never too soon to think about such things:

> *'My 13-year-old son said that if he was in a car crash he'd really want his organs to be used. That's the sort of conversation we should have as part of life.'*

Pammy invited a senior nurse involved with organ donation to come and talk to the death café. Death cafés do not usually have speakers, but this was specifically requested. This nurse brought someone whose brother had died without leaving any wishes.

> *'He decided that his brother probably would have wanted his body used and the result is that there are now four people living happily because of the donated organs.'*

Even if someone is on the donor register, their relatives are still asked if their organs can be used, and may refuse to allow it. A recent report suggested that this happens in 14% of cases where the dying person wanted their organs used, with 1,200 people missing out on a life saving operation over five years. Talking about death can save lives.

When I asked Hannah if patients in hospices talked about their forthcoming death, she replied,

'I think it's quite unusual. We're talking about a culture where we're in denial of death. In my experience, it is a common approach to the dying process. That's not always the case, some are fully prepared, happy to talk about it… it's never too soon to prepare, whether that's writing a will, an advanced directive, talking to family members, or organ donations, all those things…

'One of the practices nowadays, which wasn't available when I was working in palliative care, is the use of anaesthetic drugs at the end of life; this is now relatively common practice, to ease the transition. Sometimes this course of action is taken without full consultation with the relatives and/or the dying person. I think appropriate use of drugs is a wonderful blessing, but it needs to be in collaboration with the individual and the family. I've seen relatives who've not realised their relative is dying, and this drug has been administered and their relative may become unconscious before they have had the chance to say good-bye properly. I'm not saying don't use drugs as and when appropriate, but it must be with everyone's consent and prior knowledge. Communication is all, as it always is, in-depth conversation is all that needs to happen.'

Iain, the patient at the Scottish hospice, told me he was happy to talk about death, but it was not easy for him, many people, including good friends of his, have died since he started coming to the hospice; this could be quite hard to deal with

'Because you become friendly with many people, they are all different age groups. Most of the time you associate death with

old age but not at a hospice. It also hits home that life is precious and is definitely for living as we're all going to die at some point.'

E thought that such conversations could lead to people having 'a better death.' She told me of meeting the relatives of a patient of the Welcome Hospice whom she was visiting in his home. They lived a long way away and said they didn't know what he wanted to happen after his death.

'I said, "let's ask him." He said he wanted cremation, and said where his ashes should be scattered, and "as for the rest, I couldn't give a monkey's. I won't be there. You can fight it out amongst yourselves." Then they were happy, and did what he wanted. It's so easy once the conversation has been started.'

However the GP, who has many such conversations, said it is by no means easy to start them.

'I think one of the things that is very important is that we do have conversations about that, but it's not always easy to find the right time: either to have enough time to do it properly, or the right time in that they are in a place where they want to talk about it. Sometimes we feel that there is an imperative to talk about it, because we can see that it's coming soon, and they may not have accepted or be in that place yet... it feels very uncomfortable. It feels like I am trying to hasten their death in some way, but it's not really about that. It's about having a conversation about how to make what's left as good as possible, and ideally to make the end to be everything it can be. If you haven't thought about it then someone will dial 999 and that's not what you wanted. But if you haven't thought about it, then people have to do that.'

For the GP it is not only individuals and families who need to have conversations about the end of lives, as a society we need to be more open to asking difficult questions about resources and priorities; we are all involved in deciding on such priorities.

'It is not just the medical profession that is involved. We all need to think about such priorities. The resources of the NHS are finite. It shouldn't be about being ageist, but very carefully considering individual cases, not having blanket decisions but we should be asking more: is this the right thing for this person to go into hospital, or for this person to have a very expensive operation, weighing up all the pros and cons.'

Sarah said,

'The money that is spent on keeping people alive unnecessarily, and often in great distress, could turn the whole NHS around in a day.'

I am not sure how accurate Sarah's calculation is, but it is clear that we cannot afford, or are unwilling to afford, what we currently try to afford through the NHS. We need to consider these questions, but it is hard as so many of us refuse to think or to talk about death and dying, and the result is that half of us die in hospital, which is not what we want, and the NHS is in dire financial straights.

Some people and organisations are working to change this. The Conversation Project works to make conversations about our end of life wishes easier to have. Their website offers a 'starter kit' on how to start such a conversations, including 'ice breakers', such as 'I need your help with something', followed by suggestions as to what to talk about and how to keep going.

From October 2015 to March 2016 there was an exhibition entitled 'Death, the Human Experience' at the Bristol Museum and Art Gallery. As well as showing artefacts related to death from around the world and over time, including 'mementos mori', the exhibition invited visitors to think about death, including how they would like to die. There were exhibits inviting the public to think about such matters as suicide and assisted dying. Some sensitive items were behind closed doors, which visitors had to open, so that they would not be seen by those who preferred not to look. From January to March there was another exhibition in the same gallery, looking at assisted dying, with a replica of the room in which those who go to Dignitas in Switzerland will die.

In her book *H is for Hawk*, Helen Macdonald writes of how she took up hawking for her grief at the death of her father. She tells of how she was offered black forest gateau on a black plate by a waiter in a restaurant, to whom, when he asked her what was wrong, she told him of her father's death. The waiter did not know what to say, but felt he should show his sympathy in some way. A black plate must have seemed appropriate; perhaps words, if he could have found the right ones, might have been more so. But these words do not seem to come easily.

So there are important practical reasons for talking about death: it could reduce fear, it could save lives. Moving to the more emotional and spiritual reasons for talking about death, Paul, a regular death café participant, said,

> *'Various influences on my life have chimed with the death café and reinforced my appreciation of the value of stepping back and looking at myself and what's happening; looking at the world and my place in it and trying to work out how best to engage with it, and also with that I think an appreciation of the value of kindness as part of that picture.'*

I was slightly surprised at his mention of kindness; I said it seemed to me a leap from contemplating death. Paul replied,

> *'When I look at the world and the suffering in the world, and the harm that people do to people – kind people don't try to harm people. So to that extent kindness can be prized as a value, it*

helps to diminish suffering, and reduce harm so when I look at
my life and other peoples lives and how I would like us to be, I
think kindness is a kind of pointer in that direction.'

This gave me a new thought: could the refusal to discuss death be linked in any way to the lack of kindness in society? Something to think about, but no other contributor mentioned kindness. Kindness is another expression of the truth that ultimately we all share the same life, but our individual lives are finite. I suspect this is part of what the Quaker advice means when it suggests that contemplating death frees us to live more fully; I shall return to this in the final chapter.

E, said, 'I think people want to talk about death more than we think. We do encourage it.' I asked how she might encourage such conversations.

'By being open with them. I have the benefit of time, which other
professionals don't. We're able to build up relationships, so con-
versations about death can be easier. A lot comes from our own
feelings, people are often protective of others. I'm not bothered by
it, and this comes across so people feel more able to talk about it;
they talk about fears, fear of the unknown.'

I asked Anne if she ever discussed death in her letters to her death row pen friend. She replied,

'No. I didn't feel comfortable going into that territory, because I
actually wrestled with that when I was writing to him at the time.
He was a convert to Islam (he was a Baptist I think) he converted
in prison. He was a devout Muslim, he practised Ramadan,
he was very strict about it, and with his diet: if he was given
something he didn't think was right for his diet, he would reject it.
He knew I was a Catholic but he'd never showed any interest in
discussing religion. In a letter I wrote about Eid, after Ramadan,

and the big party of Eid held every year in Trafalgar Square. He wrote back touchingly, but he never went into any detail. I felt it would be intrusive at that late stage, and I didn't think it was my role.'

I was slightly surprised by her answer as she had told me of talking to dying patients about their deaths. She explained that a letter is very different from a face to face conversation.

'When talking to someone, when I have to say something unpleasant to someone, I'm watching their body language all the time; I can't do that in a letter. Once I had a letter from my present pen pal and he was obviously in a very dark place, so I responded to what I read, actually I was writing to him when his letter arrived, so I continued in the vein of his letter – I changed tack, I said "you're obviously in a very dark place," talking around that and about his personality and his strength, and how he should use those.

'I suppose indirectly I wrote about death, and I did say to him "you have grown so much – there is more life in you than in many people who are free, outside." So indirectly I did talk about death, but I didn't talk about the life hereafter, if that's what you mean by death.'

At a small meeting of letter writers for Lifelines, which organises the writing of letters to death row inmates, I asked if others discussed death in their letters. All said they would not unless their pen friend introduced the topic, which most did not.

My death row pen friend wrote to me, when he knew of his execution date, that he was a bit worried that those who talk about hell might be right. I replied immediately that I was convinced that they were wrong. For me, I said, God is love. My pen friend had become a very evangelical Christian in his many years in prison. I wrote:

'As for going to hell, I am convinced in my own mind that there is no such place. God is love. I think the idea was promulgated by those who wanted to keep others in line.'

In his farewell letter to me he did not sound either frightened or angry. He said he was 'doing fine and ready for what may come.'

In my final letter to him to actually reach him I wrote:

'Some time ago you said that you were worried that perhaps there might actually be a hell. I said I couldn't believe in such a place – it is a human invention. In your last letter there is no talk of such a fear, and I am glad as I am sure you are going to a place of love, forgiveness and peace. God is beyond our powers of comprehension, and is within us all.'

Could it be because we are so unwilling to discuss death, even our friends and relations now find themselves unable to listen to our griefs, that there are now very many professional and voluntary bodies that the bereaved can talk to? When there is a disaster and multiple deaths, for example a school shooting, the news frequently reports that trained counsellors have been drafted in. Do we feel more comfortable talking to professionals, to strangers, rather than our loved ones? J, whose son killed himself, tried several organisations and found they could not help her, before eventually finding a psychotherapist who helped her to reconnect with life. Similarly Ellen had unhappy experiences before finding a counsellor who she felt was on the same wavelength. She said also, 'the child death helpline at Alderhay hospital, that was a lifeline to me.'

E told me of HOPE,

'A local organisation for teenagers who have parents who have a life shortening illness; they support them pre- and post-bereavement. It's very user led, child friendly – a lot of the support they do is generated by the kids themselves.'

She said there are also online organisations, for example RIP RAP a support service for children and teenagers who have been bereaved. Teenagers turn naturally to computers for support.

Talking about the time immediately after a bereavement, R said,

'Your judgement is not particularly good at that time and to be clear and concise about things you need to get out of that period, when really the world is going on around you, and you are not really part of it...I think your reactions at that time are probably not sufficiently mature to be able to have useful counselling sessions.'

He used the phrase, 'come to terms with it.'

M talked about the different stages of shock,

'The first stage is numbness, and that protects them; sometimes people say they can't cry and that's their body protecting them. Then some people do cry a lot, but they're still in shock, they've got to come to terms with the fact that that person is not there any more. It's some time later before they're able to work out what they need help with, a lot of the time people need a listener, someone who can be there and give them the time that other people can't, rather than a counsellor. There's a big difference, not someone to try and get them to move on, because they're not ready, they can't move on, they have to live in that limbo, and stop for a while before a bereavement counsellor can help them to move on to the next stage; you've got to wait for them to be ready.'

R volunteers with Cruse, and Sam with the Samaritans. Both told me of the professional training given to volunteers in their charities. Both charities take good care of their volunteers with careful de-briefing, or supervision, so that those working for them have somewhere to deposit the misery they have been listening to. R, a very recent recruit to Cruse, felt this was excessive. He thought he spent more time on this than with clients and called Cruse

'An inward looking organisation. Very much the focus is on the bereavement volunteer, and supporting that person, because they are concerned about the pressure on those individuals in dealing with those people. You might argue that is a very good thing, but all the work I've done in industry is very much more outward facing. That's where I come from, and to me the client is king... you put all of your effort into supporting the client, not into supporting your own internal structure.'

However, R, when I talked with him, had only had two clients, and I suspect will find the support more important as time goes on. Those who grieve need someone to share that grief. Those who share their grief need, in turn, to share it. Certainly Sam, who has been with the Samaritans for six years, was very appreciative of the support provided, which happens before the volunteer leaves at the end of their shift, even during the shift if necessary. Sam said,

'Without off-loading, people would burn out quite quickly; we try and keep our volunteers healthy. We support our volunteers... I think the people who do this kind of volunteering are quite caring, so that contributes: we look after each other well.'

Both Nicola and R agreed however, that counselling is not for the very recently bereaved. Nicola said,

'When someone dies close to you, the first stage almost without doubt, generalising, is shock, they're shocked, confused maybe – the whole body is closed. I experienced this with my dad – you're unable to take it in; there's a whole lot of processing going on, so going to see someone too soon ... I don't want to make any rules either, if someone's really upset then they may need to start

sooner, but it's difficult to talk about something you haven't yet come down from. It's a very important stage, I think, the shock stage, there's so much adjusting, the body's adjusting, the psyche's adjusting. It's a sort of freeze it's kind of neurological, like I think animals do. The body needs to adjust.'

M said,

'Those who've been recently been bereaved need someone to talk to, someone who can be there and give them the time that other people can't. Because it takes time before you can get bereavement counselling. At that stage they need a listener rather than a counsellor. Listening can help them come to terms with it.'

M listens.

Pammy said, 'I think that is a basic need for all of us, to listen and be listened to on the subject of death.' Julie said,

'I go out and do the daffodil appeals, tin rattling, it's nice because people want to stop and talk – even if it's not Marie Curie they've got a story they want to share. Once somebody's passed away, those stories never get told, it's just "we don't talk about that" , but people want to talk about it, and they know we're there to listen and to show empathy.'

When I thanked Phoebe for talking to me, only about a year after her father's death, she said,

'It's something I feel comfortable about; it's quite cathartic as well, I quite like talking about it sometimes. It feels a positive thing to say it out loud. I say different things every time I talk to someone about it, it's helpful to me to be able to say it, to sort my thoughts out.'

How might we make it easier for the bereaved to to talk about their grief? Caroline wrote for a Quaker journal an article entitled 'Grieving', in which she said we need education for grief. When we met we discussed this, and I wondered if this could be part of the school curriculum, though teachers would not welcome yet another topic added to that. Caroline said,

'Any grief education would have to take account of the fact that people are so different; but the key thing is: grief affects – it has a powerful effect on people whether or not it is apparent, and it might not show itself for years and years to come...The degree to which it would be talked about would depend on the degree that the person teaching it was OK with the subject... Furthermore, the value of any grief education would depend on how able the teacher was to talk about it: had they experienced loss? How had they coped?'

We agreed that grief education could probably not become part of school education, however Dying Matters publish lesson plans for schools on their website.

Several contributors said that children are far more open about death than adults. Phoebe told me of taking her five-year-old twins to see a child in their class who had died.

'It was the first time I'd seen someone who was dead. We all went and it was definitely the right thing to do, and we all went up and saw him. His sister was there, and the way the family did the whole thing was just so amazing. His sister was stroking him and kissing him and it helped. And it was definitely right. When we came downstairs my son was playing with the other boys playing with the dead child's toys. We all cried together when we had been to see the school friend – I think it's OK for children to see grief. What struck me was how matter of fact they were. They all *wrote about the child in school and the things that were written were so touching. Quite matter of fact.'*

Similarly E said,

'Children have less of an issue with this, adults have much more baggage. Children are more able to deal with those kind of issues, death is a normal thing for them.'

The Welcome Hospice frequently involves children in its caring activities. It has a labyrinth made by local Brownies. Children sing carols at their annual evening to commemorate those from the hospice who have died in the previous year. The hospice organised a competition for local children to paint pictures for a fund raising calendar on the theme of 'Who Cares', linked to the Caring Communities project. Gill, a volunteer at that hospice, wondered if things might be different when these children grow up. But others suggested that when children become teenagers this may change.

Some might question the wisdom of taking children to view someone who has died, or involving them in ceremonies to commemorate the dead. But those who have done these things are sure that is the right thing to do.

I asked Sister Ally if the patients at the Hospice of the Community of the Many Names of God often wanted to talk about death. She said,

'The hospice is such a safe place, such a lovely warm environment, people are more able to ask those questions or broach those subjects. Although they may not want to.'

She said the hospice tried to provide what the patients want. For one young man of only 26, dying of muscular dystrophy, that was to cut the grass. So they fixed a lawn mower to his wheelchair. He said he wanted his ashes scattered where he had mown, and was ready to talk about his death, 'but his mother, who brought him, realised that it was quite real, and quite scary so she stopped it.'

It seems it may be the relatives, not the dying themselves, who are unwilling to talk about death. Sister Ally told me of another patent at that hospice, who fought for a long time against accepting that she was dying; but

'Once she accepted it, she was completely different, she talked about the coffin, her plan of action. She was going down to a hospice near Bournemouth to be near her sons, when she wasn't able to come here any longer. She had a sort of bucket list, which included spending time with and being close to an elephant. We enabled her to fulfil this dream by letting her spend a large chunk of time with our elephant Valli, about two weeks before she died: this made her and her husband extremely happy... she managed to die where she said she would die, and she really fulfilled that – that was very amazing.'

(Fortuitously the Community has the only temple elephant in Europe).

The two hospices I visited both offer safe spaces, where those who want can talk about their deaths. The Welcome Hospice offers 'diversional therapy' which might suggest that the subject of death is being avoided, but perhaps such therapy can enable the dying to accept the reality of their deaths, and be free to move on to making the most of what remains of life. Those involved in the Welcome Hospice did not agree about how much patients wanted to talk about grief. E thought they did, but not to relatives, because they did not want to upset them, so the hospice provided the space they needed. However, when I asked, Chris, the only man I spoke to volunteering at the Welcome Hospice, if patients often wanted to talk about death he replied, 'One or two have over four years, but not to any great depth. They tend to keep up their defences.' Similarly Jenny, another of that hospice's volunteers, said, 'If they do come in and feel they need to talk to somebody, there is a chaplain we can call in and a quiet place they can go. But in the art room it's entirely different, there's a lot of laughter.'

Death cafés also offer safe spaces to talk about death, for those who are not necessarily facing it in the immediate future. I met several of my contributors through the local death café, where talk about death is expected. All said how helpful they found it. Pammy stressed the importance of listening as well as talking, and always says something about this in her introduction. At the end all participants say how they have found the experience. I have never heard anything negative said at this point. Once someone said that we never disagree with other participants, and I suspect this is because we are all actively listening, as well as talking. There is a sharing of thoughts at a very deep level.

Pammy said,

'Not everybody has to come to the death café! I had one woman who said, "Well I might come to it if it wasn't called the death café, why is it called the death café?" And I said, "Well it's called the death café because we talk about death!" I would say that for most of us Death Café goers, we're sort of exploring the mystery of it. People take totally different things from the Death Café. Some people come and want a high level of discussion about all sorts of things, death related obviously, some come to help them face their fears, they're very frightened. I get people to contact me before they come to their first Death Café, so that I can tell them what it is and what it isn't. For instance, I make it very clear that we can't offer counselling, it's not therapeutic in that way, but I think everybody who comes says it has a therapeutic effect. Some clearly want to tell the story of their own near death or the story of somebody's death that they've been affected by.

'The discussions we have had at the Death Café do go to very difficult places indeed, and it depends totally on who comes and what they talk about. Anyone can say anything. Sometimes people

*say things that are very light-hearted, and sometimes people will
tell a very moving story of people who maybe have just died and
they want to recount the death. Sometimes we do have a laugh,
that's very important; I'm sure sometimes we're laughing because
it's funny, and sometimes we laugh because it's a way of letting
the emotions out.'*

Hanna is one who finds the death café helpful. A retired nurse
who has cared for the dying, she said one reason she goes is to share
her knowledge of the facts of death which are not well known, which
adds to the fear and uncertainty. She said she always felt 'enlivened'
after a death café session, 'because it puts everything in perspective
in a way that's quite rare.' She sees death cafés as,

*'Contributing towards a culture where death has more of a
common currency and people can feel easy talking about it.'*

Paul said,

*'The death café looks at death from all angles, the practical, the
medical, emotional, psychological, ethical and spiritual. I think
anything to do with death is welcome in the death café.'*

Martin S said,

*'One of the things I like about the death café is meeting with
death in a sort of practical and pragmatic way.'*

He wanted to go even further than talking about death. He not
only wanted to weave his own casket for when he dies, but to involve
others in making theirs at the same time. With the help of a basket
maker, he planned a weekend workshop where people could learn to
weave their own caskets.

*'My interest was in the process around how, if we have opportu-
nities to talk about it, in what ever way, we do some processing*

and meet with our own mortality in that way. I've found over the years that often people will talk while they are doing something in a way they won't face to face. So I wanted to support that process by having an opening session on the evening before it started and a closing session at the end of each day – just to see how people were doing.'

This is something he has been wanting to do for 20 years, when a young friend of his died. She knew she was dying, and she knew she didn't want a cardboard coffin. Her mother asked Martin S if he could make a woven casket. Martin knew of a coppice worker and hurdle maker who would be able to help with the making. He said,

'The significant part for me was that she came to visit her casket not too long before she died, and she wove a couple of ribbons into it. I don't know exactly what it was, but I just remember the power of the experience of meeting with your own casket.'

Unfortunately, not enough people signed up for the workshop, and it was not viable. Eventually Martin S ran a much smaller workshop for just three people, and now has his own casket created by himself. I asked him how it felt now that he had created his casket. After a laugh he said,

'A good question. It's not as clear as I thought it would be. I sort of imagined that I would have a strong sense of an end of something; and to some extent it is the end of a journey of 20 years. So that's undoubtedly true, but I think I imagined that it would feel like I'd made my own casket, and it didn't actually feel like that, which was a bit of a surprise. I know that's the case, because during the weekend we were making caskets, a friend rang me to say his sister had died,(I knew she was dying) and would I be interested in selling the casket he knew I was making. I didn't bat an eyelid, I just said "OK if that's what you want."

I then rang a funeral director, to find what it was worth, and thought about the logistics of getting it there. But then the friend rang to say the partner of the woman who had died said he just wanted something very simple, a cardboard plain coffin. But it left me with an idea that this is going to get used for somebody... In answer to your question it feels like a completion, but I don't feel any strong attachment to it for myself, it's just a thing to be used.'

He thinks one of his parents might use it, but storage is a problem:

'It is massive, it feels massive, and takes up an huge amount of space.'

I asked if the conversations while they were making the caskets were as meaningful as I thought he had been hoping. 'There was a lot of gallows humour, but not really – there was a lot of hard physical work, and it required a lot of focus... It was a busy, busy couple of days.' He went on to tell me of a funeral recently of someone who had a thing about rainbow coloured jumpers.

'He wanted to be buried in his collection of jumpers. So someone sewed these together to make a wool shroud. It was fantastic. I'd really encourage anybody to give it a bit of thought and visualise it. I think it's a very interesting way to approach the subject. Anything that helps to demystify or reconcile us to the idea has got to be a good thing.'

This chapter has looked at reasons why we seem so reluctant to talk about death, and why this needs to change. I suggest that hospices and death cafés are places where is is safe and acceptable to talk about death, and perhaps to help death to emerge from obscurity to be a normal topic of conversation. Perhaps the most important reason for talking is that our reluctance to talk about death seems to extend to an inability to talk to the bereaved, who say this is what they need above all else. This is so important that grief needs a chapter of its own, and will be the subject of chapter three.

*   *   *

There is an elephant in the corner

There is an elephant in the corner.
It's amazing that such a presence
can remain unseen, unfelt,
until you ask "How many children do you have?"
then I reply, "I had five, but one died last year."
Then, if you gently ask, "How?"
I will tell you.

Benny was a beautiful boy
Twelve years old, full of life.
The middle child of five.
Intelligent, inquisitive, quirky, loving.
A fiddler.
Yes, a great fiddler. He died through his fiddling.
A stupid accident, no-one was to blame.

Then maybe you will tell me about your elephant,
A bond will be forged,
Or maybe just by acknowledging mine
It will be transformed into the spirit
Of a twelve year old boy.
With sadness, yes, but also with joy.

But if all you say is "I'm sorry"

Then change the subject , awkwardly,
the elephant will remain,
a large and uncomfortable presence
too difficult to bear
So we will move away
and you will never know
how the elephant could have changed
into the spirit of a boy.

(by Lilli May, 22.2. 2008 -not one of the contributors,
   the daughter of a friend)

3 Someone to grief with

The Grieving Ground

What torture this is
This grieving ground that
Relentlessly carves into my being
A moment of ease, blessed anaesthesia
before, labour-like
The next wave of pain
Swamps me in its intensity
The ravage of sheer loss
Ages me by years in days
Life-blood sucked out by morning
That will have its way with me
Regardless of my will.
(Caroline)

'I think the loss of a child is probably the worst thing you can go through. (Ellen)

I am sure Ellen is right; she has gone through it. Her son died just before his ninth birthday. The Child Bereavement Charity published *Farewell my Child*, where bereaved parents write movingly about the children they have lost. Sometimes one parent writes, sometimes both. In the case of Benny, whose mother wrote the poem at the end of the last chapter, his four siblings also added their thoughts on his life and death. His 14-year-old brother says he will never recover from it, which is what contributors told me. Peter Stanford edited *The Death of a Child*, in which a dozen bereaved parents and siblings describe what they went through. In an 'afterword', the psychotherapist Dorothy Rowe writes that when someone one loves dies, a sense of their absence becomes part of one. The contributors to this book would agree with this. As they would with her calling 'platitudinous lies' the idea that 'time heals', or that they should 'seek closure'. They hide their grief because, according to Dorothy Rowe, it is ugly and disturbing. They know that, someone lost can never be replaced; their grief will last forever.

J used the phrase 'someone to grief with' when she re-wrote my account of our conversation about her son's suicide. I found this a powerful phrase. Grief is not in the dictionary as a verb, but making it one seems to make the concept of grief more profound. Those who have not experienced such a loss may find it hard to understand just how deep grief can be. I hope that what these contributors told me may help our understanding. This is perhaps the most important reason for talking about death. For grief is not a 'condition', something for which one needs some form of 'treatment', as can be implied, rather it is part of the human condition; in denying it, we deny a part of our humanity. Ellen told me that a psychiatrist said of her, after her son died, 'she's not mentally ill, she's grieving'.

For Ellen, someone to grief with had to be someone who had also lost a child. When her son died, she was so desperate for someone to grief with that she sought out strangers, some through the local newspaper, who had lost a child. Only those who had had this experience could understand her pain, and adequately grief with her. She said, 'I was thinking "you can't imagine, my pain's worse than yours", because that's the way you feel.' She eventually started a group for bereaved parents, Caring Friends, which is still running after 12 years. She said,

> *I will never forget someone I met on the Alderhay hospital child death help line, she said "you're in a boat that nobody wants to be in". I will always remember those words, because you always*

think this is something that happens to other people, you never imagine it's going to knock on your own door.'

J, on the other hand, did not want to go to The Compassionate Friends, a group for those who have lost children, recommended to her by a friend who had lost a son in a sporting accident.

'I wasn't keen to talk to other bereaved. That friend said she'd attended the Compassionate Friends conference, but felt overwhelmed with sorrow by all their stories. I thought I might have more in common with someone who hadn't necessarily had that experience, but who was just good at conversing with me.'

Bereavement and grieving with are different for each individual. The pain is different, the emotions different.

Nicola, the counsellor, said,

'You just have to really be there with someone who's lost a child, be there for them, be with their feelings, their longings it's so important, that area… you can't imagine what that must be like, we have no idea: it's terrible, terrible, but again it's just deep listening, just being really there. I think with all counselling it's following the person, not bringing too much of your ideas of what they should be feeling – you just keep trusting the process.'

Many of the bereaved contributors I talked with told me how hard it was that no one wanted to hear about their loss. Gill, a volunteer at the Welcome Hospice, said,

'They don't want to talk to loved ones, don't want to hurt or upset them; maybe don't realise that they share the same fears, feelings or understandings… a friend in the village said that I was the only person who had said how sorry I was to hear about her husband. People used to cross the street. I've heard of that before.'

I fear others have had that experience; one of my friends said it had happened to her when her daughter died tragically.

In this chapter I will report what a few bereaved people told me of the physical and emotional pains of bereavement, the loneliness, what helped and what didn't. This will not be comfortable to read; writing it was hard, but I felt I needed to give voice to the deep pain and anguish I was told of. Some said they could not share their thoughts at the time, not because they could not put their grief into words, but because they felt no one wanted to hear them. They had no one to grief with, or even anyone prepared to listen to them. While we may not be able to 'grief with' the bereaved, we can at least listen to what they need to tell us and try to empathise. Denying them that can only add to their misery. R, the bereavement volunteer, wanted above all when he lost his wife to be listened to, not to be taken to the pub for a drink, 'what you really want is the complete reverse of that – you want someone who's going to listen.' Once again I need to point out that these contributors are few in number and cannot be seen to be typical of grieving people. But that does not mean that we should not listen to what they have to say: their voices deserve to be heard.

Gill said,

'People don't approach you, because they think you need time, but sometimes all you need is someone to come and have a cup of tea and talk. It's difficult to deal with.'

Sam, the Samaritan, spoke of the need to be 'on the same wavelength' as her callers. Perhaps being on the same wavelength is not quite the same as finding someone to grief with, but even if we are unable to grief with someone bereaved, we could try to find their wavelength, or just find a simple act of kindness, show that we are there, that we care; even if we cannot fully understand, nevertheless we share a common humanity.

Sister Ally, the young nun at the Community of the Many Names of God, cared for a 97-year-old fellow sister as she was dying, and spoke of her gratitude to the older nun, for teaching her to grieve. This sister had taught her all she knew about work in the hospice, and now her death taught her of grief.

> *'Being with Sister L was one of the most moving experiences of my life, and also what came afterwards. I didn't realise that I would grieve, and I did; so now I can empathise more with somebody who's lost somebody. Even though it was a perfect death, she was 97, she wanted to go, we wanted her to go, it was perfect... I hadn't experienced grief before; I'm very grateful for that experience, and I can now go to somebody knowing that. You can't know what someone is feeling if you haven't ever been through it and now I have.'*

Sister Ally is now more able to grief with others.

Some contributors had experienced their pain quite recently, for some it was many years ago. What impressed me was that the way in which they spoke of it was very similar however long ago it happened. Ellen's account of how her nearly nine-year-old son collapsed and died at the bottom of the stairs 12 years ago, sounded as if she was describing an event in the previous week.

No two contributors had experienced the same grief; grief is totally unique to the relationship between the person who died, and the person grieving. R said, 'The point about grief and about bereavement is it's very, very individual.' He must know, having lost his mother when a teenager and his wife three years before we spoke. Ellen echoed this, saying of the deaths of her husband and her son, 'They were completely different bereavements.'

J compared her grief for her mother with that for her son (T).

Caroline, who also lost a grown up son, said,

'With my son and my mother that's been very different, both relationships were different in important ways. I think grief is very, very much determined by the nature of relationship with the person who has died. And every Cruse counsellor will tell you that every grief is different, and you needn't think that because you've weathered your way through a massive one, you will be protected from subsequent ones because that's not been my experience.'

Many contributors wanted to tell of the unexpected physicality of the pain of grief. Christine, the artist whose brother died of leukaemia 20 years ago, said,

'When my brother died the grief was physical, and I didn't expect that at all. I expected to be able to deal with death in a mental way: he had died and had gone somewhere, and that was it; people do die. That's fine. But the grief was physical, you couldn't get away from it, you couldn't... I hadn't understood the physicalness of grief – emotional grief. I now understand why people self-harm, because I started to scratch myself and that took away the pain that I couldn't do anything with, this made it possible, perhaps distracted it. I thought I'm in the process of self-harming, and I must stop that. The pain of grief is just overwhelming and that has gone. It was physical, and the physical could distract it. I could put it somewhere else.'

J said,

'I lived alone. I could cry as much as I liked. I found myself crying a lot, sobbing. I found it eventually physically hurt me in the diaphragm.'

Ellen said,

'I used to wake up, like in a nightmare and you think it's not true, and you want to wake up and find it hasn't happened, it's all been a horrible dream. I used to have a shower, and I thought the tears were more than the water coming out of the shower. It went on for a long, long time. The pain in here used to be sort of like indigestion, it was absolutely horrible: it was physical. I can remember sitting in the bedroom window and wanting to jump out, because I couldn't physically cope with the pain... I thought my pain was so deep, I really didn't want to be here any more. I can understand why people take their lives, because, the pain is just so deep.'

Caroline said,

'On the day of his funeral I can remember one part of me going through the motions of what I had to do to actually function, to get to the funeral and what I had to do at the funeral. But I was kind of numbed, just going like a robot while I was doing that, and feeling at the same time like I had a dagger in my heart just being twisted. It's a completely different world that world of pain. That was something else I hadn't been prepared for, just how physically intense grief is.'

She went on to say that when her mother and two aunts died more recently, just when she lost funding for some work she loved, and moved house, it brought back all the pain from the death of her son 14 years earlier. 'Everything was going on at the same time, it was death written large really.' Then she had a fall.

'I think the fall was symbolic. It was the final straw on the back which was ready to go; I'm very aware of how the body speaks. The body will speak if you can't speak, or you are truncating the

amount of emotional and mental exploration. The body will shout, "I'm hurting".'

She saw a specialist who reassured her that the pain was not muscular-skeletal.

'I was worried that I had nerve damage from the fall, because I was getting all sorts of weird sensations in my legs, it felt as if my body was here, but my legs were somewhere else. Lots of pins and needles, and numbness, but she assured me that there was absolutely no nerve damage. So I said "If it's not that, what is it?" And she said, "Your body is simply saying "I hurt".'

Caroline's grief when her mother died brought up all the emotions of her son's death. She said,

'I think what has been happening is that subsequent deaths have impacted back onto that one, which I think is inevitable... that's been my experience; I'm much more vulnerable to other blows, and other griefs.'

Tom echoed this, saying his daughter's stillbirth, brought back all the pain of his wife's stillbirths 30 years before. His other daughter's miscarriage brought back his wife's many miscarriages. The pain of grief for death before birth is more common than one might suppose: in 2013 one in every 216 births was a still birth, while one in every 360 babies born dies before the age of four weeks. Tom told me of the organisation SANDS: the stillbirth and neonatal death charity, which he found helpful, and which he now supports.

Tom told of two lives ended before birth, and of several long before. These deaths bring a particular sorrow. But even these have lessons to teach us about love, about care and belonging. Tom used the moving phrase 'childless mother' to describe his daughter's position. He also told me of his feelings of guilt, in the 1980s.

'Nobody was dealing with what you were going through emotionally, what your mental feelings were, the psychological effect it
was having on you. I used to feel dirty when I walked into the
ward. As a man I felt unclean because I wasn't physically affected
by this thing, and there was my wife in the bed, bleeding, and
watching a life run away from her.'

He went on to compare the support his daughter had after her
stillbirth, with the almost total lack of support 35 years ago. His
daughter's family had been able to spend a weekend in a special unit
with the baby, until they felt able to say goodbye. He had not even
seen his own stillborn child 35 years before. He told me 'I never deny
that that granddaughter was my first granddaughter, although she
never took a breath of fresh air, never took a breath of air outside of
the womb.' The unit that supported his daughter was provided by the
NHS, but all the equipment there came through SANDS.

M, who supports the newly bereaved, mentioned a website for
childless couples where they can write about the experience of being
childless.

'One dad put "today our 7th child died". His wife had had seven
miscarriages, but so often we don't think of the men and how
difficult it is for them. The wife goes through this physical and
emotional pain... It is only in the last 30 years that you can have
a funeral for a miscarriage, before that in law it wasn't a baby.
Now it is recognised as a bereavement.'

She spoke of a beautiful service in a local cathedral for parents
who've had children who died before birth.

Probably deeper than the physical pain of grief is the emotional
pain. So many emotions are stirred up by death: anger, guilt, fear.
The Tibetan Book of Living and Dying says that grieving is like
going through a kind of death for the one who is grieving, who needs
reassurance that what they experience is natural, normal. Sogyal

Rinpoche quotes someone he calls Caroline, who told him that the most important thing for her, after her husband's death, was the people who kept calling.

About a week after my father died I was rung up by a district nurse, whom I had never met. She said that, before he died, my father had asked her to ring me and make sure I was 'all right'. He had said, 'Mary tends to get emotional.' This was obviously a criticism of me. I assured the nurse that I was all right, that I was at that moment talking to a friend, 'about death in general, and my father's death in particular.' I remember the words, though it was very many years ago. I was all right; I had a friend who listened.

The suggestion that there is something wrong with expressing our emotions seems closely linked with our reluctance to discuss death, and, again, seems to be something of a masculine trait, if by no means confined to men. Caroline said,

> *'I feel the stiff upper lip, British thing, is very much a kind of – "lets go out and have some fun," or "there, there, it'll be better soon", that kind of minimisation of the intensity of what somebody is living through… It has to be validated, it must be validated. And if it isn't validated they will hang onto it for however many years they need to, until it is validated.'*

She told me that the nurse who had told her that her son had died hideously had said, 'don't cry.' Later she partially excused that nurse saying,

> *'The hospital had been dealing with him and trying to save him, and couldn't, and presumably she was protecting herself by saying "don't cry".'*

R said that death heightens deep-rooted emotions in a family.

'What happens, much more than people realise, is that all the issues you had within in the family before the death, all the concerns, all deep-rooted feelings you might have are expanded like you wouldn't believe at the time of the death... All those years and years of pent up anger, concerns, issues whatever it might be, will become more acute, will become critical at the time of death.'

One of the emotions most frequently evoked by death is probably fear: we are reminded that we we too, will die. In the middle ages, when death was inescapable, mementos mori were everywhere: artwork designed to remind the viewer of their mortality, and of the shortness and fragility of human life. Very largely, I suspect, as a warning of hell for those who did not obey the rules. We have lost these reminders, but not the fear they were intended to evoke, even though the fear may now be less about hell, more about extinction.

Hanna, the retired nurse said, 'For some people [death] will be a subject that is largely unfamiliar and unknown and therefore it is dreaded or feared... The death that most of us fear is the ending of what's familiar.' Nicola, talking about counselling, agreed,

'It's also about bringing up their own fear of death – the fear of death, fear of life, that can be really explored. I'm not saying that happens with everybody, but it can be taken and used in a constructive way, but you're still taken into that area of what do you want to do with your precious life?'

Julian Barnes in his book *Nothing to be Frightened of* quotes Aries who said that in societies where death is not discussed, it is more greatly feared, which supports what many contributors told me: if you have experienced the death of someone close, or cared for a dying person, your fear of death goes, or becomes less.

I wondered if one of the consequences of the fear of death is the ageism of our society. This is the only inequality at which it seems acceptable still to laugh. Adding age to the equality legislation came last, and is still not complete. The old often feel lonely and excluded in many ways: is this because they are a reminder to the not yet old that death is coming for them, and that we will all come to it in the end? They are living mementos mori. Corinna, the end of life doula, spoke of a similar denial of ageism as of death.

'You get the same thing with anything that has to do with ageing "I won't lose this," again we are living in denial, we don't want it, it's not me, and I'd do anything to not have this in my life.'

Anne, a retired nurse, similarly saw a link with how society treats older people:

'People reject elderly people; they don't want to see old age because they are frightened of it, and the elderly have no value as they no longer contribute financially – they are considered a burden.'

I think it could also be because we know that old people will die, and we don't want to think about that.

While emotions are normal in bereavement and need to be acknowledged, they are not without dangers, according to Swami S, of the Community of the Many Names of God. He said,

'Being a vehicle of the manifestation of the divine love of God enables the carer to totally give, and be a channel for that manifestation of love. When there is attachment, when there is confused emotion involved from the carer, that brings that down; it doesn't mean that love is not expressed, but that love can very often get diluted or confused by that emotional attachment.'

Sam said of talking to someone in despair,

'I think to do that, you need a lot of self-awareness, to be aware of your own experiences and your own emotions at that time – and put them on one side. You try to adjust to wherever they are.'

I asked if it was difficult to put your own emotions to one side:

'Yes, sometimes you can and sometimes you are half way through the phone call and you have to put them down again, and sometimes you finish the call and then everything will hit. I think for me the most successful calls, if you can call them that, is when that process has happened; and I know that caller has felt I've been on the same wavelength as them, whatever the outcome.'

Julie, the Marie Curie nursing assistant, said that when her partner was admitted to hospital she was able to be his partner again:

'Once he was in the neurological centre, then I could be his partner again, not just his full time carer. I always washed and showered him, shaved him – he never had that done by a nurse, always something we did together.'

Death necessarily involves grief. Grief, and the pain of grief, are part of the price we pay for love. If we do not love someone, then our grief at their death will obviously be less. When strangers die, we try to empathise, we may express our sorrow, but we do not experience the intense emotions described by these contributors. In what appears to be an attempt to isolate ourselves from the pain of others, we may be denying ourselves some of the experience of being fully human. A death that does not leave someone sorrowing is not a good death. We need to mourn and to be mourned.

Corinna said,

'I think we are selfish, so we don't want someone to go because we don't want the feeling of loss, because it hurts. They are saying, "You have to stay, because I can't bear it, I can't deal with my emotions. I can't bear difficult emotions, that's why you have to stay." We say, "Oh mother I love you, and because I love you I want you to stay."'

Julie, on the other hand, said,

'Often people who are dying are extremely selfish, extremely. All they can think of is, "Well I'm the one that's dying, you've got the rest of your life." You're over, when you die, they've got several years left to try to adapt.'

Is it possible to love unselfishly? Perhaps, if we were more able to listen to, to accept, the pain of bereavement we might be more able accept death, acknowledging rather than trying to deny the pain.

Father P, told me that for a Catholic death is not the end, but said,

'It doesn't mean the grief is wiped away, the grieving has to take its natural course… it's an end, it's a loss, but it's also saying it's not the end.'

Phoebe said her grief at the loss of her father was no less because he had wanted her to take him to Switzerland to die.

'It felt very much like he was being released; it felt like a positive release because it was what he wanted. It doesn't make the grief any the less.'

The pain, the fear, the isolation of grief were seen by some as stirring up, or heightening, other emotions. Christine said,

'You get what you call post traumatic stress, and if you are a visual person you see things you don't want to see. The other senses are heightened and I found with grief that the boundaries weren't there – I would read the papers and sob at the stories. There was one on hedgehogs, and my husband wrenched the paper away and said "stop reading the papers". But I just couldn't stop reading the stories. The grief of the stories added to my own grief. Other people wanted to tell me their grief stories, and I wasn't able to say I didn't want to hear their stories.'

J said her tastes in music and books changed.

'My senses were so heightened for sound and I suppose the other senses. I couldn't stand loud voices, and birdsong sounded like a creak of rusty wire. That was hard. Music: I can only say grief heightens it – any tune that comes in is kind of stirred, and you are already stirred… When you listen to music you should be stirred and if it's good we are.. I couldn't bear that, it was very, very hard. Sometimes friends would offer music, thinking it might soothe. Music didn't soothe, it caused an uncomfortable emotional response.'

Caroline said,

'I can remember only hours after the news of his death, I'd gone out very early in the morning and I was walking past a white-washed cottage that had dark red roses against it. I remember thinking that they were the most exquisite roses that I'd ever seen in my life before. It was like everything was intensified. The level of grief burst me open both to the intensity of pain, but also to the intensity of beauty. I remember my other son saying to me some years after his brother died, that it seems that the lower you've been the higher you can go. It carves spaces. I certainly remember the vividness of things, and the extraordinary mix of intense pain *and yet numbness simultaneously, very strange... there can be beauty in grief if you're prepared to go in it enough, but there is no beauty if you can't go in it. I think that in a way is what we cheat ourselves of by keeping superficial. I think that the result of contemplating our own death and the death of others, is what brings us back to the starting point – of death giving life meaning, or value, or whatever.'*

She went on to quote *The Prophet*:

'"The deeper that sorrow carves into your being, the more joy you can contain." ... he talks about love, you can choose not to go into the threshing room, but you will only laugh half your laughter and cry half your tears. I think if we can't go to the depths of it we're not going to get it.'

Corinna also spoke of the heightened sensitivity of the dying to all the emotions going on around them. '... all these dramas and these wonderful processes that are going on.'

Not only are all bereavements different, individual, but bereavement changes over time. Elizabeth Kübler-Ross, in her widely acclaimed book *On Death and Dying*, has suggested that the bereaved go through five stages of grief: denial, anger, bargaining, depression and finally acceptance. I wondered how this related to the griefs reported here, and how M, R and Nicola, who all listen to the bereaved, found this applied. Nicola said,

'There are definitely stages, not necessarily those or in that order. There's not enough acknowledgement for how angry people can feel. We don't know how to deal with anger very well in our society.'

I asked her if she thought it was possible to 'get over', or 'move on' from the death of someone close. She said,

'We're not supposed to want to totally get over it, but there can be acceptance... I have had people who find it very hard, to move on – they get stuck, but I would never give up. There probably are some people who, for whatever reasons, find it easier than other people to move forward... When it's a young person you may think about them every day, but there can be a way of moving forward... I seem to have accepted the death of this friend of mine, I have acceptance that that was meant to be – somehow he's gone on, maybe to something else.'

She tries to provide a safe place, where even men could cry.

'It's a bit like the anger, we've been raised not to feel tears, not to cry; so I will give a lot of reassurance that it's fine to get upset, great to let it out, so I'll be very gentle. I must be careful, not saying you must cry, really just encouraging the tears – being held and witnessed in their grief is very powerful.'

Nicola used the phrase 'moving on' several times. Her function as a counsellor is to help people to move on.

M said,

'You don't get over the death of a loved one. You become more accustomed to them not being there. You can move on but it takes a long time, for some longer than others.'

There is an important difference between the two phrases, 'move on' and 'get over'. The first suggests adaptation, acceptance that life will never be the same, but it may be life, the second suggests that things might return to what they were before the death.

R said,

'You're never going to make them better, but one of the things you will do, I think, is help them to come to terms with it... coming to terms with it, in your own way.'

Dad, in Max Porter's novel *Grief is the Thing with Feathers*, says, when 'moving on' is suggested to him early on in his bereavement, that this is a concept for stupid people. Those who shared their experiences with me would agree with this: the rest of their lives were changed irrevocably. Corinna said society expects one to move on after a bereavement, but spoke of how hard this can be.

Sarah, whose daughter attempted suicide, but was 'saved', and survived severely brain damaged, has lost the daughter she had. Her grief was as intense as the grief of bereavement. She said,

'A year after Imogen's brain injury, I wrote to her consultant to tell him what he'd left us with and how badly our lives were being affected, living with a daughter with a severe head injury. Our son would have this burden for the rest of his life, and was deeply affected by the violent mood swings and rage which our brain injured daughter frequently displayed; and we were tied to Imogen who we had, in effect, lost. Her mind and personality permanently altered for the worse, but left in the body we still recognised, a mere shell of her former self. We would also never have closure. We watched, helplessly, as one by one, all her friends stopped contacting her and her boyfriend left too. We were left with an Imogen who was nothing like Imogen we'd lost, who veered between extreme aggression, when she violently attacked people, to being very placid on occasion and often extremely sad, crying for days on end without knowing why... Her friends gradually disappeared and fell by the wayside as they couldn't have a conversation with her, there's nothing left of the Imogen we loved apart from the physical shell. She has been left without either empathy or sympathy and is often cruel and vicious to other people. The daughter we once had was kind, sensitive and caring and all those attributes have gone for ever ...

'We have been through unimaginable hell over the years. It has put immense pressure on the rest of our family. I have friends

whose son committed suicide years ago, a tragic death, but at least they have closure now and can get on with the rest of their lives, something we can never do.'

Sarah was the only contributor to use the word 'closure'. J would not agree with her: for J, losing a son is not something one can 'get over' or 'move on' from. Some of the most hurtful things that were said to J at the time included, 'you need to move on', and, within a few months, 'I didn't know you would still be going on about this'. A friend she'd known for many years, but with whom she had little recent contact, rang up just after he died, and said,

"'I'm so sorry; they say, you'll need 40 days of grief". I simply moved the phone away so her voice was not too loud – I was very sensitive to sound – but it was the words which did not resonate with me, in fact I found them abhorrent. The length of grieving time was of no consequence to me. I was simply in the middle of it.'

J continued,

'One does not move on. Nor should one. I thought that to say these things to me was inappropriate.'

She quoted Julian Barnes, the writer who lost his wife, and went on,

'You don't move on and leave something/someone behind, you wouldn't want to do that anyway. You will always be making your way round this awful event, finding ways to reconnect and live with the person. T had to become part of me in a new way. Any idea of moving on presents an image of detaching from the lost one; one already feels detached and reeling from this. With T it was as if he had disappeared entirely, his death being so unexpected and sudden, so much so that I couldn't any more

properly imagine him, he felt so utterly gone. To myself I used the word 'gone-ness'. I felt isolated from a normal current of life, life had indeed stopped... Moving on, forgetting, putting it (T, his death) behind me, was unthinkable, frightening... It was only in psychotherapy that I began to "see" T again, to see him in colour, see him moving. But no one would have guessed this.'

Ellen also lost a son, and said this is a loss some never get over, 'but you can learn to live with it, particularly if you have the support of others in the same situation.' That is what her Caring Friends group can offer.

Those who had lost someone close told me both of what had helped them at the time as well as what had not. Caroline spoke of a couple who were able to help her when her son died, because they, too, had lost a son, so were able to grief with her.

'The degree to which a person can be with somebody else's grief is the degree to which they have been able to ride through their own grief. They were absolutely fantastic, because they had lost a son about ten years before in a car accident, and I went and stayed with them. I didn't know them well beforehand, they weren't personal friends, and they really showed me the best way to deal with somebody in grief. What they did was give me ample space to be as emotional as I needed to be, and encouraged me to be so, and validated it and shared in it, and shared their own experience in it, without shirking any of it. Then they would wait until that particular wave had passed, and then took me to something beautiful – like we'd go for a lovely meal, or go to a gorgeous place, it was like they were saying to me, "this is hideous, this is ghastly, we know where you are, AND life goes on." To share with someone that they feel has the experience sufficiently to be able to communicate to them – not necessarily in words, but with their

being: "I know where you are, and I've gone beyond it." That's the greatest gift anyone can give to someone in any situation.'

I think this is what J meant by 'someone to grief with.' Caroline appreciated Quakers, Friends, who gave her the opportunity to talk or not, giving her the choice.

'I was very blessed, in that Quakers were excellent, they gave me that listening space in a way that I think I wouldn't have got outside that fold. I never had the experience with Quakers of anyone doing the equivalent of crossing the road so as not to speak to me. They didn't change the subject, they did honour how hideous it was... Some of my friends helped hugely: they just left messages on my answer phone saying, "we're thinking of you, if there is anything we can do please get in contact. Don't think you have to reply. Call when you're ready." That was so important, because the pressure I could have felt with all these messages, I might have thought I had to get back to them. They let me off the hook of that. But they were telling me they were here for me, but were waiting. Then there were other friends who would turn up on the doorstep with a cake and say, "we can come in if you like. But we can equally just go away." They were putting it in my court, but making their presence felt.'

However, this did not extend to listening to her when her mother died.

'That was old hat, mothers were dying all over the place, everyone's lost a mother. What's the matter? Even in Quakers, there was quite a bit of joking: "you've joined the orphan clan." ... and yet my mother had been my mother for 60 years, and a very, very strong character; very dominant and very much someone I turned to in the course of my life. So to suddenly, at the age of 60, to have her not there, was horrendous. I'd have to readjust *my whole sense of what life was about: in some ways I've lost my identity. I think probably because I've been very much struggling with the loss of my mother and my aunt who was like a second mother, especially in the last years when my mother had a bit of dementia and wasn't the same person she had been, so her sister had taken her place. So for them to go out of my life… because they had been there when my son went.'*

Men, some men, seem to find talking about, and listening to, grief more difficult: Ellen said, 'talking was my medication', while her husband was unable to talk about their son's death and turned to alcohol, eventually dying of 'alcohol related, disseminated fungal disease.'

Tom felt men are less able to hear about grief. When he told a group of workmates, with whom he was enjoying a 'Blokes day out' that he had received a text telling him of his daughter's still birth, their first thought was to put him in a taxi.

'I was with mates from work, it was supposed to be a celebration day. Everyone just saw the life drain out of me, it was such an experience. And when you turn round and tell the group of 'blokes', as we called ourselves, on a 'blokes day out', it just killed the whole atmosphere. They said, "well – that's terrible, what can we do? Lets just get you in a taxi and get you to wherever you need to be."'

I asked if they thought of a taxi because they did not want to be involved in his pain. Tom replied,

'Yes, yes, very much so. They saw this bloke they'd never seen in that state before, and that sort of frightened them. I think they did identify but didn't want to. That was the feeling I got from it. But then later, privately, I got the messages one by one.'

Obviously a blokes day out is not a safe place for grief, or for listening.

Tom told me that 30 years ago he believed that he should not show his emotion, when his wife suffered her miscarriages. He said that as a child he had been horrified to see his father and uncles crying at his grandmother's funeral.

'That really scared me because I'd never seen men show emotion: they were the people who could pick you up on one hand, big strong men and to see them cry really affected me, that stayed with me. So this "men don't cry" thing, I had to fight it off, and my chin used to be quivering, but I fought it off because it frightened me so much seeing that funeral. That stuck on me. My daughters understand, and my ex-wife. I've apologised to her for not being able to show my true emotions back then, and explained why. It's a horrible experience seeing grown men cry, these big strong people...I have great respect for both my daughters and my wife – the steely determination they showed, I feel I'm like a blubbering ball of jelly, often I have to wait till I'm alone to do that. I've often felt very inadequate in face of the strength people can show.'

Similarly R talked of men friends inviting him to the pub, to forget, when what he wanted was to talk about it.

J used the phrase 'safe place', when telling me of the psychothera-pist who was finally able to help her. M spoke of a 'safe space' which she tries to create for the newly bereaved where even men can cry if they wish. This phrase was also used by Sam when telling me of her work with those in despair. E talked of the Welcome Hospice being 'A safe space to talk about fears and experiences.'

However, safe places, or safe spaces, seem rare. I heard more unhelpful things that had been said to the contributors, and again this varied. James, the funeral director, did not appreciate being told, 'He's in a better place' at his father's funeral, although Kalsoom, the

Muslim, found great comfort in this phrase. As well as being told she could 'get over' her loss, and 'move on', J also objected to a counsellor saying, 'I hope you're not blaming yourself.'

> 'It felt like I couldn't say what I needed to say, regardless of whether it was 'true' or not... I remember struggling to get round it, just to get it out, saying, "Well I'm acknowledging things." She interpreted that as self blame and wouldn't allow me that luxury even for a moment... she could have gently tried to discuss it, but no. Yet I needed to talk and blame myself for not seeing that T was unwell. Preventing me from doing so felt hugely frustrating.'

This is echoed by Denise Taylor interviewed in the *Guardian* newspaper in 2014, in an article entitled 'Can a parent get over the death of a child?' in which she gives the answer yes, but says that there seems to be an understanding among professionals who have to deal with them, that a grieving parent should behave in a particular way. She said they lose sympathy if the bereaved do not behave as expected, and withdraw their support. Wanting to blame oneself is obviously not expected behaviour.

A bereavement counsellor had said to J, 'It will feel like losing a limb'.

> 'I didn't think the pain of limb loss could equate with the loss of a loved one. I wasn't asked what bereavement felt like. I wrote a poem about imagining my limbs floating away, with the lines "it doesn't correlate with the marks you make, the space you leave." I tried imagining being without a limb, and because of the physical and emotional pain I was in at that time, I couldn't imagine that the pain would be similar. T's absence was much bigger than his presence had been. After many years, now I think they may have meant that without a limb one would have to negotiate any move, the absence would always be there, there was the risk of imbalance. This way of looking at it makes sense now, but was

quite inappropriate at the beginning, there being no explanation or discussion.'

Similarly Christine told me of a friend who asked her why she had not seen her recently; Christine replied that her brother had just died. The friend said, 'Yes, but you knew he was dying.'

Ellen told of a bereavement counsellor attached to the local health centre.

'One of the first things she asked me to do was to describe my son in his coffin. What an absurd thing, why describe him in his coffin? I want to remember him running out of school towards me happily. She said, "I was just trying to get you to open up." I said, "If I was suicidal when I came in, I'm far worse hearing you now".'

Later Ellen found two more helpful counsellors. 'I think I was very lucky, because the bank I worked for paid for back-to-work counselling, and the fortunate thing was the lady who was my counsellor there, her daughter had died, knocked over by a taxi. I don't know if it was coincidence or fate, but she helped me through it.' She was able to grief with Ellen.

J also told me how hard it was to answer the question, 'Do you have children?' In a remarkable way this was eased for her by a baby, belonging to a new neighbour.

'I was offered the baby to hold and she was beautiful, gazing at me and cooing. At this point, the mother said, "Have you got children?" It was as if the baby, who continued to "talk" and coo, was helping me with the answer, and the baby's mother was very gentle and understanding and we have since become good friendly neighbours. Mostly, if I have been asked the "have you got children" question, people have been very supportive. But I

am always aware that, for them, it is not easy and, of course, unexpected.'

What J really wanted, she said, was for someone to ask her, 'How are you?' A simple normal greeting. But no one did, she suspects, because they were afraid she might tell them, and they didn't really want to know. Grief, in modern society, alienates when it should, naturally, evoke empathy and solidarity as it seems to have done in the past. Because we seem unable to grief with one another, to share one another's grief, bereavement leads to loneliness. Jean said, 'I think when I let go of my mother I turned to the world. But I had to turn and face an awful sense of loneliness and grief.' Sam spoke of the 'loneliness in death'.

Grief for those who die, but are not close, can be different. Anne told me of the death row prisoner she had been writing to for five years, and who was finally, after many appeals, executed. A pen friend can be rather less than a friend or possibly more. I asked her how she had felt.

'It was total inevitability – M wasn't innocent and America has the death penalty for crimes such as his. He initially had a terrible lawyer. I knew the probability was he would be executed, and I reconciled myself to that as he had. I was very sad, very, very sad, especially as I was on holiday at the time... When I knew all appeals had failed and that he was going to die, I wrote to him every day; I sent it express mail to the States, which cost a fortune, but I wanted to be sure he got it. He was transferred to another prison to die; it's called "Bonne Terre", a dreadful name... Eventually I actually burnt all my letters from him; I ritualised it, and buried them and planted a shrub over the top. When he actually died I felt very sad that day, but realised I had to carry on, it was part of my life's journey.'

I, too, wrote to a death row prisoner who was executed in Bonne Terre. In my case I had only been writing to him for less than a year, and there had been a gap in our correspondence when letters were not getting through. I knew he would die when I took him on as a pen friend, but I was not prepared for the depth of the sadness I felt when I knew he had died. Unlike Anne, I still have not destroyed his letters, I have all these, and a card I sent, after my final 'farewell letter'. I was not sure if it would get there in time, and it did not, as I did not use express mail. It came back labelled, 'Return to sender. Refused. Unable to forward.' I have not felt able to open it. In my case there is also some guilt: I had promised my pen friend that I would be thinking of him at the time of his death, which was one minute after six am. (UK time). I had written that, in the Quaker phrase, I would 'hold him in the Light' at that time. I always wake around 5 am, but on this day I slept until 6.15. I was horrified. At the last I had failed him.

Anne, however, had told her pen friend 'I will be with you spiritually at the time of your death.' She said,

'I woke up at 5.30 and I just put myself into a meditative state. I hoped that he would know that I was with him, another presence, if you like. I can't explain the spiritual connection, but I had a strange experience the next night – I know he came to me. I get very emotional. I was in the bedroom that evening, and a peace came over me it was like a soft glow; I had a knowledge that M was there and was OK, he was at peace. He'd had his life's journey; he's now continuing his journey.'

Anne was moved to tears here. In both these cases our sadness was probably tinged with anger against the death penalty. I suspect that this anger is part of the reason that people want to write to those on death row. However, it was not anger I felt at my pen friend's death, just sadness.

Many writers have written incredibly moving accounts of bereavement. One of the best known is Joan Didion's *The Year of Magical Thinking*, which was adapted as a play for the National Theatre. Didion tells of the sudden and unexpected death of her husband. She gave away his clothes, but could not dispose of his shoes for a year, because he might need them. That was the 'magical thinking'. Joyce Carol Oates, in a similar account of her husband's death, *A Widow's Story*, tells of giving away her own clothes, but not his. Neither could she get rid of his coffee in the fridge, although she does not drink coffee, nor move his books. Jill Bialosky in *History of a Suicide: My Sister's Unfinished Life* quotes Joan Didion, but says that for survivors of suicide the magical thinking is that one can change the past. Similarly, Stephen Levine in *Meetings at the Edge* said a bereaved mother had told him how hard it was to give way her son's clothes. She had to tell herself that if he came back she could buy new ones.

Julian Barnes has written two books on death: in *Levels of Life* he shares his grief at the death of his wife. In *Nothing to be Frightened of* he tells of his lifelong fear of death. Libby Purves chose to write a novel, *Shadow Child*, about a young man's death in a tragic accident, soon after the suicide of her own son, Nicholas Heiney. Decca Aitkenhead wrote a powerful account of the death of her partner, who drowned while saving the life of their son, *All at Sea*, saying that if she did not write about it, she might forget. More such books are listed in the bibliography.

All these accounts of grief are very different, and different from those I heard from contributors. We each need to be able to grieve in our own way.

Caroline talked of therapeutic writing.

'That's been my working life – therapeutic writing – I think that people can write that which they wouldn't feel safe to say. They also find in the writing that it writes itself, in a way that it doesn't necessarily when you are conversing. So I think writing is hugely

important; but there are an awful lot of people who are grieving who are not writers, so they can't benefit from that. I know that people said to me about my poems, "Your poems put words to what I felt but couldn't say".'

J, too, found comfort in writing poetry after the death of her son. The poem she wrote when she was told her son's death would feel like losing a limb is below.

Out of the depths of the pain reported in this chapter, contributors seem to have found ways to continue to exist. Life after bereavement is inevitably, and permanently, changed. But, although this seems cruel at the time, life goes on. Nicola said,

'Death can be like an energy – if you suppress it, it's like anger, but if you put it into something, it can be creative. Any death can be a creative potential, the receiving end of the grieving process.'

How the lives of some contributors may have been changed in such ways by their tragedies is examined in the next chapter: life after death. Perhaps what they have found is some renewed and deepened connection to the human race.

*   *   *

Limb

Purple Hairstreaks have left the Oak. Sacred groves and ailing vaults let in the wind and the leaves are thin. It doesn't, yet, fall or lean but bleeds and rain gets in. Stiff stems of rusted dock like tracery, ring its foot, screen its broken limb, and high on the bark, a brand carved by the break – a heart.

When they say,
it will feel like losing a limb, I imagine mine float away,
benign: it seems so small a thing as burns burrow through
all my rings, skin stitched with stings. It doesn't
correlate with the space he still fills, the mark he leaves,
as I negotiate how to breathe, stand, balance.

(J)

4 Life after death

'As the months turn into years, it's important to hang on to the notion that there is life after death. After the first few months in survival mode, you do begin to feel like living again. For some people it takes a year or less. For others it can take ten years before they feel any sense of happiness. The pain of bereavement is always there – like a dull ache, but many WAY members have turned their lives around in surprising ways after their partner has died.'

(WAY website: www.widowedandyoung.org.uk/
bereavement-support/life-after-death)

R, a bereavement volunteer, told me of an organisation he had contacted when his wife died three years ago: the WAY foundation. Widowed And Young is a self help group for those who are bereaved under the age of 51. I went to WAY's website (www.widowedandyoung.org.uk) and was quite surprised to find 'Life after Death' under 'Bereavement Support'. I hadn't thought it was a religious organisation. It is not. This section of their web is about how to get through the first year of widowhood. It acknowledges the fact that life will never be the same again.

Elizabeth Kübler-Ross, in her book *On Grief and Grieving*, says that one does not 'get over' the loss of a loved one; you learn to live with it. Life, will not and should not be the same.

This seems to be the case for the contributors to this book. Ellen used the same words, talking about the loss of her son,

'You can learn to live with it, particularly if you have the support of others in the same situation... There's no point in being bitter,

*you just have to accept what happened and move on... I try to
think you have to get a positive from a negative.'*

In the previous chapter there seemed general agreement that you
will never 'recover' from a bereavement, however much friends and
acquaintances think it is time for you to 'get over it' or 'move on';
yet contributors also reported on how they had learned to live with
their loss, perhaps as a different kind of person. Talking of his work
with bereaved people, R said that you can never make them better,
but he thought you could 'Help them to come to terms with it.' He
explained,

> *'What you are acutely aware of, as somebody who has been
> bereaved, is your place in this world, and the fact that everything
> you know, and everything you rely on can go just like that. So
> you don't have that complacency that other people have that they
> will go on for ever, and that everything in the garden is going
> to be rosy; you have a far greater capacity to do the "what if?"
> conversation.'*

Ian Clayton wrote in his book *Our Billie* about the death of his
daughter in a tragic canoeing accident. He writes of imagining
her as a mermaid, swimming in a fairy grotto, not trapped under
the water. He says it helps him to try and let go without letting go.
This is an interesting idea, which can perhaps, resolve some of the
apparent contradictions of the contributors. Whether or not you call
it 'moving on' or 'getting over', I was impressed by how many of those
I talked with had, indeed, found a new life after a death. I was moved
by what some told me of ways they had come to terms with their
bereavements, letting go without letting go. Finding a new life. Two
had made career moves.

James told me that he had become a funeral director, having been
a carpenter,

'Which I later discovered is a traditional career path. We were called Clever Decks, doing outdoor carpentry work all over Southern England for ten years.'

He told me that he made the change because the funeral for his father had been so dreadful.

'We sat in silent disappointment at the end of this wretched duty minister's twelve minutes of talking about our "dearly beloved brother... gone to a better place ... well loved in his community ... blah blah blah blah." My dad was a rascal: he was really interesting, he was a brigadier in the Gurkha's in the war, he liked his Guinness, and he played the squeeze box, singing rude songs that he made up on the spot ... he called his horse Business, so he could be "out on business". There was a lot that we could have done and said that would have made it a proper kind of "farewell dad, warts and all."'

His family got together to do something better for his mother. He described her funeral as a 'really uplifting and authentic funeral.' These two experiences made him decide to become a funeral director with a difference. He calls his business Family Tree Funerals and helps families to be involved in creating meaningful funerals.

'The title came as an idea, and influenced what we do and how we do it – especially in our collaboration with the family. I related it to my mother really, because it felt as if she was a big old tree and she'd fallen in the forest and we were all gathered round the stump and the branches and we remembered. We told stories about how we'd scraped our shins on her bark, and been amused and even exhilarated too; and we realised that there was a huge hole in the forest canopy, and that's what we were standing underneath, with us as the saplings on our way up to fill the hole, and in our time we would fall. So Family Tree was that. As well *as she was now an ancestor and she stood on the shoulders of her mother, and, and, and, and back into for ever. So that felt like an important thing to remember: ancestry and the experience of saying good bye to something, which is, after all, natural.'*

Julie became a Marie Curie health care assistant after the death of her partner; a job she says she is 'passionate' about, describing it as,

'To help them to live until the point when it finishes and they no longer live... I had no care experience until my partner died and I obviously nursed him. Then I thought I've got to get back into work. I'd had my own business up to that point which I had to give up... I saw an advert for a palliative care nurse with an agency, and I thought I could do that. I've done it. I don't have written experience but I do have physical experience so that's fine. And then a job with Marie Curie nurses came up... I absolutely love it, I love the charity. People say it's a depressing job, but it's not.'

Others did not go so far as changing jobs. It was his experience of bereavement that led R to become a Cruse bereavement volunteer.

'I lost my mother as a child, and three years ago my wife died leaving me to bring up the kids [he is now the single parent of four teenagers]. I think those experiences of death made me want to put something back. Because it seems to me a great pity to waste what knowledge you have acquired going through those fairly grim circumstances, if you just kept that to yourself.'

He went on to tell me about the bureaucracy that follows death, which he now understands, and is able to share with others. He continued, 'So I trained as a bereavement volunteer and I now go out and talk to people who have suffered a significant loss in their life.' This must be a powerful motive. I am sure he is better able to grief with others as a result of his experiences.

Caroline had been involved with therapeutic writing before the death of her son. When I came to read the conversations and found this theme of life after death, I emailed her to ask if life had changed in any way after her bereavement. She emailed back:

'*It wasn't something new for me, but a deepening and widening. For a while, I became a voice-piece for the disabled in articles I wrote for* Big Issue, Community Care *and various other things, about disability and the attraction of alcohol for those who already feel marginalised. It felt like the last thing I could do in honour of R's life, and our family struggles with him and his condition (and, of course, it was part of my own healing process to do it.) My therapeutic writing work (with other people) developed in that I had much greater empathy for those who were going through the hell of intense grief, and it enabled me to be unafraid of intense feelings in others – because I had been there myself. And, perhaps most important of all, it intensified my spiritual search and practices because I knew how much I needed that help.*'

Once again she seems to be writing of the increased ability to 'grief with'.

Like very many bereaved people, Tom, Phoebe and Sarah now work to support charities relevant to their particular bereavements. Tom's experience of still births took him to SANDS (the stillbirth and neonatal charity); Phoebe supports campaigns to make assisted death legal in this country, so that others will not need to go to Switzerland as her father did; Sarah supports Papyrus, which was set up to try and prevent young suicides. Sarah said,

'*Imogen* [her daughter] *used websites to tell her how to kill herself. We learned, to our horror, that there are people, "trolls", who encourage young people to kill themselves. That's why PAPYRUS was started. The parents who started it found that their son had been groomed by an internet consultant in his early 40s, and encouraged to hang himself when he was severely depressed. They took him to court, but the judge ruled it out of court as inadmissible evidence because it wasn't face to face grooming. As the law stands at the moment in the UK it's legal to groom young people to kill themselves, but it's not legal to groom them for sex. We still haven't succeeded, despite endless campaigning, to persuade the government to force the internet providers to police their websites, and eradicate the websites which encourage suicide... The law is a mess, and the decision not to police these websites will continue to have disastrous consequences.'*

Sarah also does a lot of campaigning around improving conditions for people with acquired brain injury.

When describing the death of her brother, Christine said,

'The grief was physical, you couldn't get away from it, you couldn't. You had to let time do it I suppose.'

When I asked her if time had done it, she said yes, but she had done a lot of work around it also.

'We come from a Christian family, and I found that my Christian faith was completely useless. So I then thought this is what happened when my brother died, and I wasn't that close to him, so what would happen if my husband died? I would never recover. I needed to have something that would help me to cope with this, so time yes, but time as distance. It's distanced me from the grief, but it's also time to be a stronger person about death. If he hadn't died I don't think I'd have done any of the spiritual work I've done or the reading; it gave me a drive to do something about living better, and, I suppose, dying better.'

She has returned to being what she calls an 'odd' Christian, who believes in reincarnation. This belief she says, has helped her to understand the dying process.

Both Ellen and J lost sons: J said this was something she could not get over, nor even move on from. She told me that initially she felt she needed 'distractions' to her grief.

'I had a lot of anxiety, always needing to distract myself reading science, knitting, map reading/walk planning... I needed the knitting to help with anxiety, not depression. With depression I would be too lethargic to knit, but it helped with anxiety. If you have to follow a pattern, it can helpfully occupy part of your mind. If I did nothing, there was just too much to process in my mind. If I could knit something, feel the lovely wool and have a small finished product, it was helpful. Handling beautiful wool was a need. It helped when so much of me was hurting.'

Later she joined a particularly supportive choir, with a very sympathetic leader in a town about 30 miles away, and sang with them for four years,

'Staying overnight with various friends, which was therapeutic in itself. The choir leader knew of my loss, as did a few of my friends there, but I didn't otherwise share it – it wasn't the right time to do so. That worked for me. I loved that choir. It became a kind of drug for me, and therapy... very much so. Right at the end lights were put down and we would sing, "all shall be well" in harmony. The leader was a caring person, she had been a counsellor with Winston's Wish [the charity for bereaved children]. For years I took two buses and walked up a hill to stay with friends. You just hear those harmonies, that helps, you are doing something, you are using your voice.'

Later still, J found a psychotherapist who was able to help her, and then she started writing poetry.

'I had told the psychotherapist I couldn't "go home without my sorrow", words from a Leonard Cohen song. The therapist quietly said, "you can leave it here, can't you?" At first I thought that impossible. I thought leaving it there would choke him. But I figured it could seep out of the walls and windows. So gradually I began leaving my sorrow there. I wrote a poem about it.'

Going home
(After Leonard Cohen's 'Going home without my sorrow' from *Old Ideas*)

You can leave it here.
You can leave it here, can't you?

So I can leave
what's adhered at the heart?

I take it home again.
It puckers my skin.

Sleep comes, though,
on a new breeze.

I worry it'll stifle,
hang around here as cloud,
not go,

but there are windows,
a roof-light,
a filtering Willow.

It snags on grasses, metal,
unravels as I shuttle.

What'll be left? Cowls
of cloud loosen, fall away.

Wood breathes, doesn't it?

Walls inhale.

I let go of the moon,
forget its distances,

its speed as it spins,
see it simply shining in;

I abandon the space station,
and let in waiting children

whose names mean mine
and sorrows, their faces

drawing me into the daylight,
back to the clay.

You can leave it here.

It doesn't stay,
relieved to be gone across the valley on the air.

J said she, like Caroline, started writing poetry to honour her son;
now some of her work has been published in poetry journals, and

she runs a small writing group. She also goes into a local Day Centre twice a month, to share the reading of some poems.

> 'They tell me they never hear their own voices, otherwise. I've also encouraged them to write – I write down what they say – using the framework of two poems 'Open the Door' by Miroslav Holub and 'The Table' by Edip Cansever, we end up with poems they can call their own… I had never intended to work with the elderly – but when thinking about what I might do in the community (with no car) I came up with the idea of poetry at the Centre.'

The Door, inspired by Miroslav Holub

Go and open the door.
Maybe there's nothing,
or some flowers in the garden,
and bees buzzing in the flowers.

Go and open the door.
Maybe the next door neighbour's there
with his little daughter, Mary.
Maybe it's only the rain, pouring,
or just the cat, clawing,
to come in out of the rain,
or for food.

Go and open the door.
If you heard the milkman,
there'll be milk on the door-step
for the cat.

Go and open the door.
Even if it's only the postman,

there may be a letter
from mum or dad,
the Inland Revenue,
the Football Pools.

Even if
nothing
is there

Go and open the door.
At least there might be
a bird, tapping,
or some sunshine.

(by Elizabeth, Mick and Jack)

Ellen feels that she has moved on.

'I'm bound to be a changed person – anyone who goes through a bereavement is a changed person. I've also made a lot of very close friends, because we're all in that boat. It's been quite a long road, and having children has given me a new focus, and I'm really more alive than before... You can learn to live with it.'

Of her group for bereaved parents, Caring Friends, she said,

'I think I actually get certain satisfaction, a reward, out of it – helping somebody, that to me is a positive. You only have one life, and sometimes I get a bit frustrated and think people must make the most of it. If you've done something while you're on this planet, you've just got to strive for what you think is important. You've got to get out there and live your life. There's no point in worrying about things you've no control over, we none of us

know when we're going to die do we? You can spend so much time
worrying about things – you could have used that time.'

She told me of other positives that have come from the death of her
son, and of the good friends she has made through the group Caring
Friends. She also has two younger children, whom she thinks they
might not have had, if the child they lost had not died. She told me
how the life of a cousin of hers, whose husband had left and who was
utterly desolate, had been changed by her son's funeral.

'She sat in the funeral and realised she was wasting her life, so
that is a positive that came from it: her turning point – she's since
remarried.'

After our conversation, Kalsoom, the Muslim, suffered two
bereavements and said she wanted to add something to what she had
told me. She wrote:

'I have recently lost two people in my life who were my age, one
had children my age and died of cancer. Death at any age or
circumstance is tragic but someone who dies young, with their
whole life ahead of them, is even more so…

'As a Muslim these deaths have served to remind me to be
grateful for each and every thing I have in my life and to continue
to strive to be the best possible Muslim and to show other people
that Islam is a religion of peace and love. It has put my own life
into perspective and this is what Allah wants from us, to reflect
on death all the time. This does not mean we cannot pursue a life
of happiness, we must strive to fulfil our duties and responsibil-
ities to our children, our parents, our families, our neighbours
and friends and have fun but within the framework of Islam.
Fulfilling our duties in this way is in itself worshipping Allah and
will increase our good deeds.

'I strive to stay humble and grateful for what I have and for the people I have in my life. I strive to uphold and maintain the relationships in my life, not only my family but with my neighbours and friends and people who I may not know that I can possibly help... I strive to fulfil my duties as a Muslim on a daily basis. I hope I can continue to do so, so that I can gain the pleasure of my Creator as the return is to Him. I also strive to instil these values in my children as I was taught by my parents.'

Bereavement is life changing. But life goes on; for some it seems that the new life can be more fulfilling, more rewarding, and more linked with the community.

Nicola told me that in her experience as a counsellor she finds that sometimes, after a bereavement, someone finds a 'new lease of life'. She said,

'What shocks me, if they've lived with someone for 60 years, I cannot imagine what that must be like to be suddenly on your own after all that time: all the dependencies that can build up, the attachments. I can't work out if it's a character type but they can be really sad, and miss their departed ones, and they move on. They almost get a better life, a good life, they do suddenly things they might not have done. In long term relationships I think it's difficult not to get your identity tied up with your partner, and it's as though they've lost part of themselves to the person. It's hard to explain what or how, maybe you give up things, all sorts of entanglements go on once your partner's gone – it's really sad, but suddenly there's a part of you you can really discover, it may have been crushed or forgotten.'

M, who supports the newly bereaved, said something similar had happened to her ex-mother-in-law after death of her ex-father-in-law, whom she described as not 'a very nice person.'

'I think his wife had probably been preparing for some time, he was about 85 and been ill for some time and she'd looked after him. She's had a completely different life after he died. She's joined different church groups that care for older people and goes on outings, and goes out to lunch once a week, she has friends. She's got a proper life now which she didn't have before, because she looked after him, and he didn't like her leaving him for long. She'd had a very restricted life.'

Perhaps M's ex-mother-in -law was 'freed to live more fully.'

Corinna, the end of life doula, on the contrary, told me of how hard the husband of the woman she had accompanied to her death was finding his life now.

'They didn't have a social life, they never entertained, they had each other. Just the two of us – what happens when that breaks and the other is only half of the unit? That is very challenging, what I do now is to help him to kind of redefine himself, if he is not 50% of a couple any more, so what is he? He has to relaunch himself as a person... I still have a really wonderful relationship with the husband, there's no official definition of this, it's not part of my role: just being a human being. I go to him each week for half a day, and we go through his wife's clothes.'

Jenny talked about the work she does in the Welcome Hospice bereavement group.

'That can be very sad, but by the end of the group they've found friendships, and they can talk about the death, and It's a joy to watch.'

Brushes with death, whether a near death experience (NDE), or surviving when we did not expect to, or losing someone we love all seem to bring life changing consequences. This is the theme of

SA's two near death experiences. I asked him how his life had been affected by these. I did not ask other contributors if, or how, a death had changed their lives, and only asked SA this question because I had read that this is a common feature of NDEs, and because the theme of life after death was by then apparent from what other contributors seemed to want to tell me about. He said,

'It changed my outlook on life: life's too short. If you don't like the situation you are in you don't have to stay in it; change it. Do what you want to do. Live for today. Don't worry about tomorrow... there was a rebirth like being born again. You don't know what's round the corner, live for the now, don't be afraid of death, don't be afraid of dying.'

Like R, J and Ellen, SA also used the phrase 'put something back'.

'I felt that a lot of people helped me, and I felt I wanted to give something back to humanity. Help people, alleviate suffering, help people to live healthily. So after that I didn't drink, smoke or take drugs, got into yoga and meditation, a much cleaner more spiritual life.'

His first NDE came after eating magic mushrooms. I wondered if it was just the effect of that, but he was sure it had been a NDE.

'I felt it was an NDE – because I felt I had the choice, and because I've had a lot of psychedelic experiences, and this was totally different.'

His second came after open heart surgery, and here he wondered if it was more of an out of body experience than near death.

'But I've had times when I've had astral projections, through my explorations of the occult when I was younger... but when I was in recovery in hospital it wasn't that.'

Both SA's experiences are very similar to published accounts of NDEs. Peter and Elizabeth Fenwick tell of many in their book *The Art of Dying*, as does Patricia Pearson in *Opening Heaven's Door*. The publisher Hay House lists over 300 books on the subject. NDEs seem comforting: do we turn to their accounts perhaps to ease the fear of death? In SA's case some common features of NDEs came in the first and some in the second. In the second he did not experience the light, which features in most accounts of NDEs. This came in the first, where he felt himself drifting lower and lower into a spiral, at the end of which was an 'amazing brilliant white light which was all encompassing and all inviting; I wanted to go.' This light was absent from SA's second experience. But in both he felt that he wanted to go further, to leave life, but on both occasions he felt himself being called back to life, by friends and family. He did not meet relatives who had died, which is a feature of many recorded NDEs, but he thought they were genuine NDES because, 'I was given a choice, I had the invitation. And the light was very enticing.'

After this first experience SA said he wanted to rush out to the pub and tell everyone not to be afraid of death. He did not actually do this at the time, as he felt very weak after the experience, and not well enough. His second experience had a much deeper effect on him, and changed his life dramatically. From working in a large logistics transport firm with a stressful job, working shifts in a management position, with a wife, a son, and a mortgage, he joined a class doing creative visualisation, life enrichment, and meditation. He took up yoga and found an interest in alternative medicine, eventually qualifying as a homoeopath. He found his previous life unsatisfying, and was eventually grateful to his wife for wanting a divorce. His NDEs convinced him that death was nothing to be afraid of but something to embrace when the time came, but that for him that time was not yet.

Tom told me of very deep life changes he had experienced, which were partly because of redundancy but also a result of his experiences around stillbirths and miscarriages. Rather like SA, he moved from working in the oil industry to being the warden of a Quaker meeting house. He said,

'I was really glad I was in a position to take the job. A lot of people I used to work with thought I was mad, but I'm really happy to have let go of the high earning job that was taking so much out of me, physically and mentally.'

He is happier now, and more able to express and share feelings. He said that as a result of his experiences of stillbirths, and the reaction of the 'blokes' to this,

'It took me a while, and made me look at men's feelings a lot since. I've been able come closer to men and I've been able to do chaplaincy work, both with the Buddhist organisation in prisons, and university chaplaincy work, also counselling courses. Because the one area I'm interested in is men's conditions: that we can't share our depressions, our anxieties, our feelings. Often we can't share with our partners, or our families, and the one big lesson this has taught me is to share when it's appropriate with others.'

While some of these changes might have happened without his experiences, when I emailed him later, he told me of the tragic and unexpected death of his ex-wife and good friend, he emailed that he felt he had a place in this chapter.

'My life had already changed and those changes were influenced by my experiences of death and bereavement but this, I feel sure, will have the biggest impact and in many ways.'

Perhaps Tom is better able now to embrace his feminine side, which, according to Jung, we all, men and women, have within us.

Father P thought the funeral could play a part in this change of life.

> *'If the funeral has been celebrated as it should have been, for the mourners it's been a rite of passage; when they emerge they are not in the same place as when they went in.'*

All these contributors are living more fully. All these life changing experiences seem to involve the individual becoming more a part of the life force that unites humanity. There will be more on this in the final chapter. What contributors told me fits with things I have seen in friends and acquaintances, and have read in the media and elsewhere about the life changing effects of bereavement. Many organisations and much charity work comes about through someone's grief. Local newspapers are full of stories of what individuals have done in memory of a loved one.

Sometimes, on the other hand, the media seem to support lifelong bitterness: refusal to move on or to forgive by relatives of a murder victim, for example. The media are in the business of telling us stories, but so often the story is one of harm, of vengeance, of blame. So we read the headline, 'I can never forgive.'

Yet, in her book *If You Sit Very Still*, Marian Partington tells how she was affected by learning that her sister Lucy, who had disappeared 21 years before, had been one of the victims of the notorious Fred and Rosemary West murderers. After much deep distress and heart searching, Marian found she was able to forgive the Wests, and now works with the Forgiveness Project and goes into prisons talking to lifers about their crimes. She, too, has been freed to live more fully. This does not seem to be a story the media have much interest in sharing. In her book Marian Partington shares some words of wisdom from the mother of another murder victim: forgiving involves giving up hope of a better past. This is something the bereaved, too, have somehow to manage. Perhaps the processes involved in forgiveness and in coping with bereavement are similar.

Denise Fergus, mother of James Bulger the two year old who was murdered in 1993, has published an account of this 25 years later, *I Let Him Go*. In an interview for the *Guardian* about the book she admits that her life might have been easier had she been able to forgive, but she feels that to forgive her son's murderers would be to betray him. She cannot let go of a better past, still blaming herself for what happened, when she let go of her son's hand. She admits that talking to her ghost writer about the murder had been therapeutic for her. She had found someone to talk to, if not to grief with. Had she found this 20 years ago, could her life have been better? Would the media have allowed her to forgive?

In *H is for Hawk*, Helen Macdonald tells how training a goshawk enabled her to come to terms with her father's death. He had been a hawker, and she became so involved in training her goshawk, Mabel, that she almost became a hawk. This sounds like one of J's 'distractions', rather than a life changing experience, for at her father's memorial service she realised that she had been wrong to turn to the wild in her grief; she realised that she should use her hands to hold other human beings, not as a perch for hawks.

In all these examples individuals can be seen to find themselves 'freed to live more fully', in the words of the Quaker advice. For them, this has not come through 'contemplating' death, rather from having death thrust onto them. Those who go to the death café say they find talking about death, contemplating it, while perhaps not life changing, yet rewarding. Rosa, the Jew, used the words, 'Really enriching'; Hannah, retired nurse, feels 'Enlivened' by the death café; Jean, a carer, said, of death café conversations, 'It's life affirming to talk about death.'

I have not yet mentioned what contributors said about death itself, what actually happens when someone dies, the dying process.

One thing that those quoted in this chapter seem to agree on is that witnessing, or contemplating, death has taken away any fear of it they might have had. What I learned from contributors, particularly those who have worked in hospitals and hospices, about the dying process is the subject of the next chapter. In the following chapter, 'Dissolving into Love', I will look at what was said about the possibility of 'a good death'.

*   *   *

Smoothing Me

Like a river smoothing stones
This loss, this grief
Is smoothing me
Into something
I was into once
But am becoming.

(Caroline)

5 'When death comes'

'It seems to me most strange that men should fear;
Seeing that death, a necessary end,
Will come when it will come. '
(Caesar in Julius Caesar, Act 2, Scene 2)

Although I am now in my 80s, I have only seen one person die, and did not even see a dead body until I was in my sixties, when my 90-year-old father died. My mother had died over 40 years before my father, and my brother nearly 50 years before. Both of them died far from my home: my brother in hospital, at a time when my own babies and small children prevented me from even visiting him. My mother was on holiday with a friend in Sicily, and it was many weeks before her body could be flown home for a funeral. My father was quite angry when I asked to see her body, to say goodbye. For him death was final, and it had to be for me. He was a doctor, and I am quite sure that for him death meant failure; I do not think he had actually seen many people die.

Had I lived 100 years ago, it would be remarkable that his was the first death I had seen, but today I believe this is not uncommon. After the death of my brother, my father, like Ellen's husband after the death of their son, hardly mentioned him. I suggested to Julie, the Marie Curie nursing assistant, that doctors don't often see people dying, that is left to nurses, and people like her, so doctors might see death as failure. She agreed:

'An organised, a well planned death is anything but. That final leg of your journey is something to be proud of, not to feel that

you've failed. You've got to agree at some point that it is not going to get any better, this is a path that you can't come back from.'

Anne, a retired nurse, also said it seemed that the consultant who ignored a dying patient, felt that 'the patient had failed him because he was dying rather than recovering.'

Now that we have banished death from the home we fear it more, because it is unknown, final. Yet those who have witnessed death at close quarters report that it is nothing to be afraid of.

In his poem 'The journey of the Magi', TS Eliot writes of the similarity of birth and death, which he had thought were different, but Jesus' birth was like death.

Eliot also wrote, in his *Four Quartets*, about his beginning being his end and later, his end being his beginning. More than one contributor noted the similarity between death and birth. Hannah, who cared for the dying as a nurse, said that in a natural death, not sudden or traumatic,

'There is a labour in both; dying is akin to a woman going into labour, there is a natural rhythm... somehow the person is being carried away in a natural rhythm; death will do itself, if it is allowed to happen and the person is comfortable enough. When I say comfortable enough, most medical people are referring to physical comfort. In my experience it's the mental, emotional and spiritual angst or anguish that could also block the flow of a natural demise. For most Westerners, particularly in a culture where the self and the individual are valued so highly, it's very difficult to let go and accept that actually time's up.'

Julie, similarly said, 'I believe it takes a lot of energy to go.'

Jean, the carer, speaking of her mother's death, said, 'I thought this is amazing, it's like a birth.'

Today most pregnant women have a birth plan, deciding where they would like their baby to be born, whether they want drugs, what music they would like to support them in their labour. Most husbands now expect to be with their wives and see their children born. In the past childbirth was hidden from men, who were kept busy boiling water, or just smoking in a hospital waiting room until it was all over. My own children (now in their 50s) perhaps belong to the first generation born with their fathers present at their births. It was found that men do not, after all, faint at the sight of blood, and could be of great support to their wives. Perhaps we now need to move on, or perhaps back, to seeing death as another natural event, from which relatives and friends should not be excluded, and where viewing the body is normal practice, and we talk freely about the death. The Natural Death Centre campaigns for this. Much of the physical pain of death, as of birth, can now be alleviated by drugs. However, most of us do not have death plans similar to birth plans, although the NHS is trying to promote Advanced Directives, which are similar. The Dying Matters poll found that found that only 6% of us have an advanced directive and only 21% have even discussed their end of life wishes. Of course, as with a birth plan, an advanced directive may have to be ignored for practical reasons, as when a woman who had planned a peaceful water birth finds herself having an emergency caesarean section.

If it is true that we fear what we do not understand, then the more we know of the facts of death, the less our fear should be. I am sure that knowing more about what happens at death would have made my father's death less traumatic for me, and so possibly also for him. In this chapter I hope to share what these conversations taught me of the facts of death, to make them more widely understood, always bearing in mind that I talked only to a few people who are by no means typical. While some of the contributors work, or have worked, with the dying, none of them would consider themselves to be an expert on the subject. There seem to be two important, closely linked but different, aspects to death: the physical and the spiritual, perhaps the body and the soul. I shall report first on what I was told about the physical side of death and then go on to the spiritual.

Like birth, death is mysterious. We feel we need to understand it, but I suspect we never will, until we get there ourselves. It remains the Undiscovered Country. Nevertheless, from these conversations, I saw that both birth and death are part of life, both are sacred, as is the time between them. In the past women in labour, and those ending their lives, would be attended by the local doula, a woman who might assist at both times. Today the midwife has taken over the role of the doula at birth, and some are re-learning the role of the end of life doula. Corinna is a doula: when I spoke to her she was just completing the training course run by 'Living Well, Dying Well' for end of life doulas. Hannah had thought of becoming a doula, she told me, but said this is what she does already for her friends. Corinna felt that those dying need a doula to accompany them as much as those giving birth need a midwife.

'Doula means a female helper, female server; they come at the beginning and at the end. To facilitate, to be there, to help, to give advice; there are many roles that are very important to help people to face it.'

She described the role of the doula as very different from that of the hospital or hospice nurse, and felt she would not be welcomed at a hospice.

'It's a new profession, if you work in a hospice people see you as competition, you come in and step on their toes. What else can you offer? You're not a nurse, not a volunteer, we don't need you. You have very little to contribute. You mostly go to private situations not in hospices, that territory has already been taken.'

I asked what was the difference between the palliative care nurse and the doula.

*'A palliative nurse is very different from a doula, it's very simple:
the doula is more the being and the nurse is the doing... There is
someone who combs your hair, who washes you, and moves your
body so you don't get any bed sores, and makes you comfortable;
but there is also someone who just spends time with you, and
maybe just shares the peace, just to be. In Western society we
are so into doing: running and performing and achieving, but in
Eastern society it's all about meditation and being.'*

Nicola, a counsellor, also stressed the importance of just being in
her work. 'Being held and witnessed in their grief is very powerful.'
Sister Ally said that in the hospice run by the Community of the
Many Names of God, the dying

*'Can just be... just sit in silence... you just sit with them, and let
them know you are there, and that you know they are still there.
Just be with them, doing something as simple as massaging their
hands, or painting their nails.'*

Like others who had work in palliative care, she thought one could
do and be simultaneously. There is no doubt that those working in
hospices have more time to devote to the dying than hospital nurses,
a doula has even more.

Gill, of the Welcome Hospice, also explained the difference
between palliative care and end of life care; I had not been clear
about this before.

*'Palliative care is where we try to improve the quality of the life
you have left. About helping people to get a better life. End of life,
is when you might be in last few days, or few hours, when you are
nursed by specialist nurses.'*

She felt the term 'palliative care' was confusing, as people think
they have come to the hospice to die, but with a day hospice, like the

Welcome Hospice, they come for different lengths of time. They come when diagnosed with a 'life limiting illness', which may mean death quite soon, but no one can say how soon, and they may live with the condition for years, as Iain has at the Scottish hospice. 'Some recover and are discharged,' said Gill.

Those of the contributors who had witnessed the death of another, often spoke of it as a privilege. Julie, said that to be with someone at their death is as much a privilege as being a midwife at the beginning,

'Because to be let in to something so private, and be trusted by all these people is just incredible. I use the word "buzz". It does sound terrible … but it is what keeps us going, it's what makes death bearable, because you're making that as good an experience as you possibly can and you know that's going to help in the long run. It's going to help the person who's dying, and its going to help the people who are left.'

Nicola used the word privilege several times in our conversation, including the privilege of being with someone who is dying, and the privilege she had listening to grief as part of her work as a counsellor. Similarly Annabel, a retired nurse, used the same word, 'It is a privilege to be around that sort of mystery.' M, who has also been a nurse, said, 'It's a great privilege to ensure that someone is as comfortable as they can be, clean, their hair brushed, shaved if it's a man, with make up for a woman. So that the family see the person they were as far as possible, not this very drawn person.'

Hannah said,

'I have always seen it as a great privilege, because it's a very intimate, personal, private time, a bit like having a baby.'

Those involved in both hospices spoke in very similar terms of their work, and used the word 'privilege' to describe it. Isabel talked of the privilege of working at the Welcome Hospice.

'We just find it a privilege to be alongside people at such an important time of their lives. There is joy. It sounds strange, but there is joy.'

E, also working at that Hospice, used the same word, as did the hospice's chaplain, who said,

'It's a huge, huge privilege: you are allowed into people's most intimate thoughts at a time of great distress for some, a time of great uncertainty and a time of fear.'

Swami S, of the Hospice of the Community of the Many Names of God, used the same word:

'The privilege of being involved in palliative care.' Tom said of staying at the unit with his daughter and stillborn granddaughter, 'I was privileged in that my daughter and her partner could share that with us as well.'

I did not feel it a privilege to be present at the death of my father: it was very distressing, as he appeared to be in great pain. I had never been close to my father as an adult, and all I could be aware of at his death was that pain. I am sure I would have found it less distressing, and been better able to support him, had I known something of the facts of death. He had a syringe driver, something I had never seen before, and could give himself morphine, but he seemed to be moaning and groaning even when unconscious and unable to press the button to release the drug. The doctor said I could press it for him, which I did. I sat by him for hours, wanting to relieve his pain, quoting the words of Julian of Norwich, 'all shall be well.' But I was very aware that this would not be before his death. Eventually I just had to leave the room and go to the toilet. When I came back, as quickly as I could, the Marie Curie nurse who had been with us all the time, said, 'I think he's gone.' But a few moments later he drew that last rasping breath, what I think is known as the 'death rattle', or cheyne-stoking. At that point his little dog, who had been under the bed all day unnoticed, jumped up onto the bed, and sat on his chest, staying there until the undertaker arrived several hours later.

My father, a retired doctor, used to tell a story about a cat in a hospital he worked in many years ago, who would sit underneath the beds of dying patients. One day she was sitting under a particular bed, and the staff said, 'She's got it wrong this time. He's not dying.' The patient died that night. My father said they drowned the cat the next day. I have heard similar stories at death café conversations.

Being with my father as he died made me wonder if there is a stage when a person is neither alive nor dead. I asked Julie if there was some specific boundary between life and death, one perhaps that only animals can recognise. She did not seem to think there was.

'I try and explain to people you can't say it's as long as a piece of string, because lots ask "how long is it going to be?" The family want to know are we talking days or weeks. I've known people go on a long time, I've seen people who've been a lot more mobile and passed away overnight. It's when the body has decided it's had enough. And the people round the bed, when they do the cheyne-stoking, and when they stop, the people look at you and say "he's gone," and I have to say "let's just wait," and generally even when they go, you've still got all this electrical activity and twitching so you can't say. You generally can't take a pulse, because it's so weak and it can go very slow, and then it races on and it's difficult; if there's somebody sitting there with their hand on a pulse, I think that's not dignified.'

Buddhists believe there is an intermediary stage of the bardo, between life and death, or between death and rebirth.

While my father's death is the only one I have personally witnessed, I have seen three other people the day before they died. One was a cousin whom I had not seen for years, and who had lived in a nursing home a long way away, suffering from dementia in his final years. I happened to be staying with my son, who lived quite near, when my cousin was dying. I asked his sister if she thought I should visit. She said not, he would not recognise me. The last few times she had seen him he had just been lying there 'with his mouth open and his eyes closed.' The nursing home told me that I could visit, but it would be for my sake, not his. My son had also known my cousin, and we decided we wanted to say good-bye. When we went into his room he was, as his sister predicted, lying there with his mouth open and his eyes closed. I went up to his bed, took his hand, and told him who I was. He opened his eyes, and a soft sound came from his mouth. He was obviously trying to communicate. After we left my son remembered that he had left his sunglasses behind. When he went back for them, he said my cousin was again lying with his eyes closed and his mouth open. I cannot say if he was aware of our visit, or if it had upset or comforted him. But I believe, as Julie said, that he was alive up until the time he was no longer living. For both me and my son it seemed the right thing to have done. Goodbyes are important. Perhaps for the living more than the dying?

The second person I saw the day before he died was a prisoner, in the days when I was a Quaker prison chaplain. He died in hospital, watched by two prison officers; I will call him Eric. Eric taught me a great deal about death. He was a gentle man; though he would say he wasn't religious in any way, he was deeply spiritual. He came regularly to our monthly silent meetings for vulnerable prisoners. Several of this particular group, including Eric, were scientists or very interested in science. After the silence, we frequently discussed the relationship between science and religion, how both are based on doubt and uncertainty, not at loggerheads, as some popular scientists seem to believe.

For a few months Eric was missing from our meetings, and I assumed he'd got out. Then his friend Bill told me that he'd developed secondary cancer and was too weak to reach the chapel.

I visited Eric in his cell for some weeks, then I saw him in the health-care centre of the prison. Finally I heard he'd been transferred to the oncology ward of the local hospital. When first I saw him there, he seemed much better. He was still very weak and attached to various drips, with oxygen to help him breathe, yet he was being guarded by two prison officers. When I remarked on this he said, 'my daughters persuaded them to take the handcuffs off.'

We talked about what might happen after death. I quoted the song 'The Joy of Living', written by Ewan McColl when he realised he had not much longer to live. It includes the words, 'So that I may be part of all you see.' (The song is printed at the start of the final chapter of this book.)

'I think I'll be going back to where I was before the Big Bang,' said Eric.

Next week I was shocked to find him near death in a side ward. He decided there was no point in delaying his end, and asked for all treatment to be stopped. He was very weak, hardly able to speak. I heard little of what he said, but managed to make out: 'funny old world… funny way to go.' Then he was obviously trying to say something important, and after I had asked him to repeat it twice, one of the prison officers said, 'he said, "don't look so solemn, Mary."' I smiled at him, and he smiled back. He died next day, and obviously lived until he died.

The third was a 90-year-old Quaker, who was living in a care home. For the past many months she had suffered from Alzheimer's which made her very distressed: she could only say, 'what shall I do? I don't know what to do,' which she repeated over and over again. This day, in the care home, she seemed at peace. I was able to have a conversation with her, though she didn't say much. I asked her how the care home was, it was the first time I had seen her there. She replied, 'good.' She had a portrait of her late husband on the wall, and we talked about him. She was very weak, but I felt that she had discovered what to do: she would die. She had found peace, and died the next day.

I felt guilty for some time for not staying by my father until his final breath, but I learned later that this is common. It seems that many people want to die alone, and wait for visitors to go before dying. Andrew Motion wrote a beautiful poem about when this happened at his father's death – 'Passing On' (in 'The Cinder Path') . A nurse had told him and his brother that, nothing would change for a while. So they went to a pub nearby, and the call came to say their father had died just as they were ordering. Eve, a follower of Rudolf Steiner, told me of the death of the father of a friend of hers, who had a large crowd of relatives around him when he died.

'Then they all went downstairs to make a cup of tea; only one daughter stayed with her father and said, "it's all right if you want to go, Dad." And he did; he was sort of being kept there by all those people wanting him to stay, which I think is a great mistake, particularly after someone is dead… When somebody is dead they need to be free to move on; it's a great mistake to wish them back again: love them for what they were and how we knew them, and send them on with good wishes for their happiness.'

It sounded almost as if people need permission to die. Julie suggested that some needed a priest to give this.

'Often they've just wanted the priest or vicar to come in and give them permission to go. They're just looking for permission to go.'

Julie told me of an example from when she was working at a hospice. She said,

'Sometimes they don't want somebody to be there, they don't want the perceived grief for that person. One lady, she should have passed away three or four days before, and there was always family there. It was quiet, but there was always somebody there. It got to about the third night and the family were exhausted and the nurses said, "look, she's still as stable as she was. You need to get some sleep". They hadn't left the grounds of the hospice before she passed away.'

Annabel said,

'There are many situations where it seems that people at the bedside who have strong attachments to the dying person can make it difficult for them to leave, and they often choose to die when those people leave the room just for a minute or two. This is very common. I have also witnessed people holding back their deaths so that important people can say goodbye. Against all odds somebody will stay an extra few hours such as if someone's coming from abroad. That's very striking.'

Some people choose to die before the medical staff think they will, some live far longer than is predicted. M gave me an example of a man she was caring for when she was working as a nurse.

'I was working an early shift and when I went off duty I said, "I'll see you tomorrow". He said "No you won't, but thank you so much for your care." I said, "Yes I will, I'll see you tomorrow morning". He said, "You may be here, but I won't." I remember thinking "That's a bit daft." The man died at 4 am the next morning. The only reason we could think was that his son was over from Australia and he knew his son would look after his wife, deal with the funeral arrangements, and everything else. It was the most convenient time for him to die, so he decided to die that night, and he did. And because his death was not expected,

well it was, but not that quick, they had a post mortem; they half
wondered if he had kept some tablets, but he hadn't. He just knew
that was the time for him to die, and sometimes the will is that
strong, for people to decide when to die.'

Paul, a death café regular, told me of the remarkable death
of a friend, who said the day before she died, 'I think I might die
tomorrow.' Paul said,

'I was amazed because, I'm not a medical person, but I thought
she would be around for a while. That while she was getting frail,
I thought her decline would take days if not weeks.'

He also said,

'One of the things I've learned, not just with this friend I was
talking about, other people have been close to their deaths and
being able to say "it's OK to go when you're ready. You don't need
to hang on." It's very common I think.'

When an elderly Quaker died recently, we were told of her relief
on being told that she would be offered palliative care, no more
treatment just to keep her alive. An email went round local Quakers,
which said 'Thank you all for all the love and affection, comradeship
and patience and understanding and so much else you have given me
over the last 30 years or so. I hope there may be at least a week or two
left which will give me time to get in touch with many of you, but I
will need time to myself as well.'

Two weeks later another message went round, saying this Friend
had 'asked to let us know that she knows that she is loved. Two weeks
on from her message, she has reached a place where our phone calls,
cards, photographs and visits are having the effect of preventing
her from feeling able to let go. She asks us now to hear her need for
stillness.' She died a few days later.

Hannah said, 'What determines the timing of death is way beyond our ken.' It seems to be part of the mystery of death that, even when very frail and weak, the dying seem to have some control over the moment to go. We all die somewhere and sometime, and we may have some choice about the time and place. I will now share what I was told of what happens to the body in the last few days or hours of life, before moving on to the more spiritual, the most mysterious, aspect of death.

Julie said,

'My job is to help them to live until the point when it finishes and they no longer live. To that point they are still very much alive, very much a spiritual being, they're a person.'

How the time leading up to death can be a time when the individual is very much alive, will be discussed in chapter seven. Yet final moments, the very end of life can be distressing. Both Hannah and Julie, who care for the dying, told me they try to reassure relatives that the possibly alarming process of death is quite natural. Julie said,

'We also support families. Often we support them more than the patient, because they've got lots of unanswered questions they haven't thought of yet, like they can cheyne-stoke, when the breathing changes, and I say to the family "it's very normal, it doesn't mean necessarily that they're at the very end, it's just part of the process." Because nothing frightens them more than seeing their loved ones stop breathing, and they think "he's passed", given him a cuddle, and then he goes, "AHHH". I think that would be so traumatic, so we forewarn them, explain to them that this will happen and I say, "if you find it upsetting, count the breaths, count the gaps and you'll find it's nearly always the same all the way through"... that last breath, the very last one seems to go on almost indefinitely, because it just seems to get quieter, and

quieter and quieter, but I don't know if people really understand (and I don't) whether that's the final bit of the air leaving the body, or if it is the final breath – it's difficult to pinpoint.'

Father P, said that when a monk died at his monastery the other monks sit by him from the time he died until the funeral.

'There's rota, we have two on at night. It's quite interesting to be in a dark church with someone who has died, it can be quite spooky. What can happen is that gasses build up in the body and sometimes there is what sounds like a deep sigh, but that's OK.'

Hannah said,

'If the relatives don't realise that the end of life is near, I have also seen it as part of my role to let them know this fact in a way that is as kind as possible... I do think that one of the primary functions of someone who is relatively familiar with the dying process, is to support the primary care giver, and any close relatives or friends who are part of the person's social situation. The person who is in labour – in the throes of dying – provided they are not in physical pain, that's all taken care of. But if it's the first time you've watched, or been alongside someone who is dying I think it can be alarming for the onlooker, who may be anxious about what to expect. In my experience it is often the close family who are under the most strain and pressure in the situation.'

She told me of the death of a farm worker.

'Those who are close to death sometimes get very agitated, as if they have superhuman strength, having been very weak and lying in bed. This man had strength, he was used to using his body, and he said he wanted to go outside, in the middle of the night. With the help of his wife I got him into a wheelchair and we got him outside into the air. It was a very rural area, the moon was out. I

was following my gut intuition that he felt an urge to be close to land: a primal urge in him, so we did our best to go along with it. But unfortunately when we got back he was still very agitated. So I had to call the GP as we couldn't contain him safely and he needed medication. They'd had him at home for last six months but the last few days he spent in the local cottage hospital. This often happens, people lose their nerve at the end if they don't have the support of the right kind. You hear it time again, people spend their last few days in hospital, but with adequate support the relatives could have managed the loved one at home.

'... If you work with people who are dying, you know the signs. But if you've never seen somebody dying before, you don't necessarily realise that this person may only have a couple of days to live.'

I asked what were the signs that death was near:

'You develop a kind of sixth sense... you can see the life-force dwindling, the extremities might get cold, there might be breathing change, first slowing down, then it can become erratic. This is often accompanied by a gentle losing of ordinary consciousness which may mean there is very little engagement with the external world apparent in the final stages.'

The restlessness Hannah described sounds like Swami S's account of the death of his father:

'He kept saying "Let me go, let me go, let me go". He was very, very distressed. He said, "Put your hand on my head, say a prayer and let me go." So I did that, put my hand on his head, said a prayer, talked quietly. Then the district nurse came and gave him a bit of sedation, he was on morphine on a syringe driver. A Marie Curie nurse came in (a big Ethiopian man – not your

archetypal nurse, but a lovely human being). He was so gentle, so caring, so sensitive to my father. I said, "Do you mind if I pray, and chant?" and he said, "All right", and he joined in with some of the Christian prayers. My father seemed to be stabilised, so I left at 2 am to have a couple of hours sleep. At 6 am the nurse said he'd been fine in the night. My three sisters started arriving and he got agitated. There was nothing we could do to make him comfortable, he was too hot, he was too cold, the bed needed to go up, needed to come down – everything was jarring. Everything was a drama and he couldn't express himself properly. It was quite a distressing situation, but most of the distress I think was because three of his children were there, and he couldn't express himself; he was in discomfort and he just felt pressurised.'

Swami S's father finally died remarkably peacefully, in an atmosphere the Swami described as one of 'beautiful harmony, unity and oneness'. I will describe this in the next chapter, which reports what contributors understood by a 'good death', which the Swami's father eventually, undoubtedly had, as he moved to the final unity that is death.

Annabel said,

'I've seen many dead bodies when working in the hospice. The face looks completely different after death, the face changes, the light goes out of the eyes, the whole texture of the skin changes, the body stiffens. I always felt a deep respect that this was a person who had lived and had many connections.'

M, who saw many deaths when she was nursing, told me of the process of death:

'They may seem to see something and be clutching something they can't reach, or perhaps fiddling with the sheets. It's all part of the dying process. When someone's body is dying their brain is

getting less oxygen than it was, and some people will get hallucinations and they may grasp at something they can't quite reach – they can see something, but not tell you what it is, but it's all part of the process. Sometimes people see someone who's died, someone they've loved who's died. It may be God calling them home. Sometimes they have long conversations with someone. Sometimes they can see themselves on the operating table, the heart has stopped and they see the doctors operating on them and see themselves from above their body and talking to someone who's died. And that person says, "Go back it's not your time." And they feel themselves going back into their body. And when they talk to the doctor afterwards the doctor will say, "That's when we were working on you. Your heart stopped and we got it back". It happens more than you might think, and scientifically I can't explain it, nobody can, but sometimes people do last a lot longer than they thought they would, or than the doctor expected, and that has to be something to do with the mind – something to do with their faith. Sometimes it's just the mind saying "No, I still have things to do, I want to carry on." Very often people will die after Christmas or the new year. They hang on for that.'

Some of this sounds very similar to what SA told me about his NDEs. Like many such NDEs, it seems to suggest that death is not to be feared. It can a positive experience, can be welcomed, 'nothing to be frightened of'. Julian Barnes, however, in his book with that title, where he wriates of his abiding fear of death, not lessened by the death of his wife, does not seem to agree. Yet, of those I spoke with, most said that witnessing death has led to the end of any fear of their own deaths they might have had.

Jean said of her mother's death,

'It was very hard to see my mother wasting away and only being able to breathe, there was not really any other movement apart

from breathing, and the slightest of facial expressions. She didn't appear to be in any pain at all. At times her breathing got a bit rattly in her throat, it was a bit distressing for all of us. I think this was just a bit of moisture in her throat.'

Her mother died in a care home, under the Liverpool Care Pathway (LCP). Jean told me about this.

'The LCP, which is no longer in existence as it came under criticism, was a document which formalised good practice in the care of people according to their individual wishes, to promote their dignity and wellbeing during episodes of medical care, which might be end of life, but not necessarily. It definitely was end of life care with my mother... We were all given a helpful sheet which explained the LCP: it didn't seem complicated at all, it all seemed very obvious – there was an understanding that there wouldn't be any medical intervention, as that's what had been requested and it was not appropriate. "We are here to help your mother to be comfortable, and to retain her dignity, and to live as she wishes, and die as she wishes. And we're here for you too, to offer you any support you need. You can have food or drink at any time of the day or night, just ask." It was explained that in my mother's condition her body wouldn't be able to cope with food or drink. Her metabolism was going to be very different from how it was before. Her body was winding down and food or drink would make her stomach bloat and cause pain and more problems... she had agreed that she wanted a peaceful death. She had told me when I was a child that in the past pneumonia was known as the "old man's friend" and she felt that people should be allowed to die when it was timely. So that was what we went by and what they did.

'I know from my job as a carer about end of life care, and they explained that they would come in to provide regular care,

mouth care and turning and make sure that she was comfortable, and they did that regularly. When they came to do that we left the room, to give my mother that space, and they were very quick and efficient and when they came out they always had this calm feeling with them, and I think they didn't put on any miserable airs, they were smiling and I think that we were probably different as well.'

We discussed the LCP and Jean said, 'I would just say in our situation it was just a way of enabling our mother to have a good death, or as good a death as possible.'

The media criticised the LCP some time ago, when relatives complained that their loved one had been denied nourishment.Anne, who had also nursed people at the end of life, explained this to me.

'[It was] ended, rightly ended, it should never have been put into hospitals. It was designed by Marie Curie nurses in Liverpool for Marie Curie nurses working in the community, and district nurses working in the community. If they found a patient was not eating, they would ask, why? If they were not taking their drugs – why? Is it because they have difficulty in swallowing? Why? Have they got thrush in their throat – which is very common – do they need help with fluid in their lungs? Do they need subcutaneous fluid? I've worked on wards and I know nurses don't have time for all that, it's not that they don't care, they do care, but they don't have time. So, happily, it's being removed.'

Anne is now working on a local end of life committee for something to replace the LCP in her city.

Why did the media decide to make such a big thing of the LCP? Death makes a good story, but particularly if, in our culture of blame, we can point the finger at someone. I have yet to read of an outcry against the futile and sometimes brutal resuscitation of someone who did not want to be resuscitated; that is not a story, unlike relatives seeing a 'do not resuscitate' notice which they had not sanctioned. When did a newspaper run a story of an old person having a peaceful death at home, because this is what they had chosen? Or even, a story of someone who died, despite the medical profession's having 'done everything' and how they suffered in that? Like Marian Partington forgiving the Wests, this is not a story.

B, the Buddhist, said that the Buddhists see death as,

'The gradual disintegration of the body and its connection with the mind. The mind gradually becomes free.'

While what the body goes through, in terms of changes in appearance, breath or strange activity, may alarm those with a dying person, death is far more than the end of the body. Both GKP, the Hindu, and Swami S described the body as a 'vehicle'. GKP said,

'There is no death. The body, the vehicle, dies; but the essence of who we are is eternal. It lives on for ever, its aim is to return to Brahma. We are part of Brahma.'

The Swami said,

'Our view of spirituality is that the body is a vehicle, you are not the body... when the person realises that I am not the body, I am the spirit, and there may be pain, discomfort but that vibration of love enables that person to transcend those things at the end of their life.'

Jennifer Worth, who wrote the best selling book, subsequently adapted for television, *Call the Midwife*, went on to write about the deaths she had witnessed in her work as a nurse: *In the Midst of Life*. She writes of a change in the vibrations of the body, mind and soul producing a different sound; she describes this as intangible, and it happens just before death.

Many of those who had witnessed it agreed that death is more than just the end of the life of a body, it is something spiritual. The moment of death was frequently described as 'beautiful',or 'peaceful.'

Annabel said she really enjoyed working with the dying, and when I asked her why replied,

> *'I think that it affirmed the spiritual dimension of life... when they have died, the quality of the atmosphere in the room is often very strong, it can feel like there's a spirit in the room, like the person who's died is somewhere in the room... At this time you come face to face very strongly with the deep meaning of life.'*

Jean said,

> *'The quality of the atmosphere changes when someone dies. When a client died, I thought everything seemed different.'* She said that when her father died she thought *'That clock's far too noisy, I wish that clock would stop ticking, you don't need a clock ticking now. I thought, something's happened. He's died.'*

Corinna, when I asked her why she decided to train as a doula, said that she had not been sure why when she started the training, but,

> *'Now I think at a very, very deep inner level I have a very strong longing to somehow be in touch with something, let us call it the spirit. A very strong longing to somehow connect with that, and the closest way I can find to do it is to accompany someone who is much closer to the spirit, compared with those who are doing their normal life stuff.'*

I loved Julie's description of her work, quoted above. 'My job is to help them to live until the point when it finishes and they no longer live. To that point they are still very much alive, very much a spiritual being they're a person.' Yet Julie described herself as 'not religious', and felt that was useful in her work. She said she was happy to listen to whatever her patients and their families believed, without judging or comparing.

Even Jean, who described herself as 'A diehard sceptic and non-believer' said,

'Something spiritual happens when someone dies... We are so tuned in to each other, but not conscious of it. There are all sorts of ways we can perceive things more than we realise. I think that there is a very profound change in the environment when someone stops breathing. And there's that kind of exceptional stillness, in an animal way. It's going to have an impact on us because we are very tuned in and perceptive – that would be my explanation. We humans have aspects to ourselves that we underestimate.'

Christine, the artist, said of the death of her mother,

'Something left her, something spiritual, and it went up to the corner. I didn't know about reincarnation then, but it definitely left her and went up to the corner. I didn't get that when my father-in-law died, I wasn't as close to him. But there was a spirit with mother. I've done some work with the anthroposophical community with something called "observing the life forces", I know that I've perceived sensing the life force. I just had a sense of that, a movement up, as if something completely unseen came out of her head up to that corner. Life force.'

I once met a journalist who told me that she visited the Dignitas clinic in Switzerland to make a TV programme. There she met a patient, an unbeliever, on the way to her death. This patient asked the journalist to accompany her to her end. In the last few minutes of her life, before she drank the draft that would kill her, the patient asked the journalist to open the window: 'so that if I have a soul it can fly out.' I asked the journalist if she had been aware of the soul flying out, but she told me that she had left the room before the patient's death, feeling filming that would be prurient. But she said she was sure it did. Even now, years later,

> 'I think of her whenever I see a butterfly or a moth trapped in a window, I always open the window and let it out, in case it's her.'

I asked Jean about the people she had cared for many years ago who were diagnosed with HIV/AIDS.

> 'I remember one client who lived in a very positive way, his funeral was very different, quite unorthodox actually: he was very proud, not ashamed of his lifestyle, and he didn't seem to regret anything. He had a great sense of humour. There was this spiritual light or depth that I felt he had, so he could travel that path in a positive way.'

Hannah said,

> 'Things are very delicate, tender, open around the time of death, flexible, because there's a sort of opening out, almost an altered state of consciousness in the dying person. If you are open to it, it's available to all. After someone's died that protective cocoon or bubble also envelopes those nearest and dearest. It's something that must happen when the life spirit is moving on. Ideally the people around someone who's dying need to have a great sensitivity and the ability to be quiet and listen.'

Hanna's first experience of death was when she was only seventeen. She was helping to care for a friend of her mother's, who was suffering from a condition where her airways were congested and she needed oxygen. The oxygen cylinder was not working, and Hanna went to get a new one; when she returned her mother's friend was really struggling with her breath; she died soon after in Hanna's arms. Hanna said she felt an absolute peace,

'That was a presence in the room. I can remember the quality of that presence now, but I can't remember the details of the story.'

I asked if she had experienced that peace when working in a hospice. Hannah paused before saying, 'It varies, as much as individuals vary.' Anne, also, didn't remember this from her time in hospices. Yet peace seems to be a common factor that runs through all these accounts of death. Death is a mystery, but a peaceful, not a fearful one.

Annabel told me that the spirit of the person who has died stays in the room for a while. The Anthroposophists say for three days, for the Buddhist it takes longer. Jews sit Shiva for seven days. Anne said, 'I don't believe the Spirit goes at once.' She was unable to be present when her father died, but the next morning,

'He was still present in the room, I do believe that – it's my own view, nothing theological. As a Catholic I believe very strongly in the fundamentals of my religion, and I believe that the Requiem Mass has a lot to do with it, the Consecration at the Requiem, that's when we are released to go.'

SA, the homoeopath, told me of a friend of his whose father died recently, and who was with him when he died. 'They could almost see or feel his spirit leave his body when he died. They said his spirit filled the room and they could smell something and see it and smell it, and then he left.' He ended with a question, 'What was that?'

Sometimes there are strange experiences after death. Violet, a Quaker attender, told of how, immediately after the death of her mother, she was asked to say something. Those with her mother included her Buddhist brother, her spiritualist father (her mother had also been a spiritualist) and herself. Violet felt that this was much to ask, as she had not slept for several days, and the beliefs of those present were so various. But she felt she had to try:

'My belief was, and is, that life continues after death (or the leaving behind of the body) and I felt that my mother was probably present in the room with us still. So I stood up and quietly collected myself, and I must have received inspiration from a higher source on that occasion which, I presume, was God. I heard the words that were to be spoken, maybe you could call it clair-audiently, but certainly the words came into my mind from another mind, they hadn't come from my own mind, which was barely functioning properly. It was almost like a dictation, in short phrases, with no stop to it, it was completely fluent and, as I heard, I spoke. Whilst I was speaking from the dictated words given, I could hear simultaneously, the next words that were to be spoken, and it came phrase after phrase, and they were beautiful, poignant words. I felt the words came from God himself. The opening words, so far as I can remember, were something like "Heavenly Father, You have welcomed your Angel into Your arms this morning..." Then it went on. I recall the words spoke to the varied religious beliefs gathered – Christian, Spiritualist, Buddhist and I recall, in particular, the use of the phrase "...and in Your great compassion..." and I understood, at the time, that this spoke to the heart of the Buddhist present.'

Eve, who accepts Rudolf Steiner's views on reincarnation, reads to her deceased husband every day. She read to him when he was dying and going blind, and promised him she would continue to do so, and has done for more than eight years. She said she is sure he is aware that she is doing this, even if he does not hear the words.

Annabel said of the death of a close friend,

'I wasn't able to be there when she actually died (I saw her the evening before) but early in the morning I had a clear sense of a visitation from her. When she actually died she came to me and I felt it very strongly; I felt that my whole body opened up *to something completely other. It was love really and I knew that it was her. It was very memorable and touched me very deeply. A couple of other powerful memories are connected with this friend. A year or two before she died I had the intuition that I was going to accompany her in her death. I also recall the powerful dream she had over the Easter weekend which was one week before she died and it was about large pillars connecting the earth with heaven, and somewhere in the dream was a reference to the Second Coming of Christ. She was a woman of strong spiritual connection but she was not specifically Christian.'*

Ellen, who said she lost her Christian faith after the death of her son, told of a strange experience her mother had at his funeral. 'My mother said during the funeral service she could see my son sitting on the bench with my father, who died some time ago from motor neurone disease, and my uncle. All sitting on the bench, as happy as anything.' Later, her mother had a stroke, which she survived, although she was not expected to.

'My mum said that when she was in hospital and they were trying to revive her, T was at the end of the bed saying, "it's not time to come, Grandma, not time to come". My Mum is not somebody that makes up stories like this. On occasions when she's in the town she says he's there, holding her hand as he did when he was tiny and she took him to nursery.'

Christine told of a strange experience when her brother was dying. She had a friend who was a medium, she rang her to ask for comfort. This friend did not know Christine's brother was dying, but when she heard,

'Her reply was "ah, you're the one who this message is for." She'd had a message the night before and she didn't know who it was for… The message was that "Now is the time for the pain to end…

pain of body mind and heart, holding your hand as you come to us, you will find love such as you never knew before." And a whole lot more. "Do not fear to leave those you love, for they will still have love in heart. Do not be afraid, my boy, for I am with you and will hold your hand." Beautiful isn't it?'

It is.

Sister Ally told me that when the 90-year-old nun was dying, one of the sisters would spend the night sleeping on the floor beside her.

'The sister who was there said it was as if someone poked her and said "She's gone. Get up, she's gone." And she woke up and sure enough she had gone.'

Patricia Pearson gives many examples of similar occurrences in *Opening Heaven's Door.* All such accounts seem to fit with the idea that there is a spirit, which may not leave the body immediately on death, but is present for those who were particularly close to the person who has died.

I have personally never had quite such an experience, although friends have told me of very real presences of someone who has died, perhaps a child, or a husband. I have no idea what this spirit might be; some of the contributors were sure they knew what it is, others, like me, were more doubtful. I do know that after the death of both my parents, and, long before these, that of my younger brother, I felt that I could sense their presence. I still can to a certain extent, particularly with my mother to whom I was always closest. I can't see them, hear them, smell them. It is just as if something of them is with me, and always will be. I wonder if such experiences were what the disciples wrote about after the death of Jesus?

To me, these accounts of the final few moments of a person's life suggest that human beings are more than just their bodies; something mysterious becomes evident at the time of death. Even Jean, the 'die-hard sceptic and non-believer', felt this. Several mentioned the beauty and peace of the final moments. It would seem almost crass to say they were reporting 'good deaths'. But this is a common phrase, and one that several contributors used, so the next chapter will look at what, if anything, contributors thought this phrase means, and whether it could help us in talking about death.

* * *

Death, be not proud, though some have called thee
Mighty and dreadful, for thou are not so;
For those whom thou think'st thou dost overthrow
Die not, poor Death, nor yet canst thou kill me.
From rest and sleep, which but thy pictures be,
Much pleasure; then from thee much more must flow,
And soonest our best men with thee do go,
Rest of their bones, and soul's delivery.
Thou'art slave to fate, chance, kings, and desperate men,
And dost with poison, war, and sickness dwell,
And poppy or charms can make us sleep as well
And better than thy stroke; why swell'st thou then?
One short sleep past, we wake eternally,
And death shall be no more; Death, thou shalt die.

(John Donne, Holy Sonnet 10)

6 'Dissolving into love'

'He got letter after letter, visit after visit from people – just an outpouring of love for him. I had this almost tangible sense of him being carried along on this sea of love'
(Phoebe, on her father's death in Switzerland.)

'Dissolving into love', which is how Phoebe described the death of her father at the Dignitas clinic in Switzerland, sounds like a wonderful way to die. Julie, the Marie Curie nursing assistant, used the phrase 'a good death' in one of the early conversations. In this chapter I will look at what contributors, as well as others, including respondents to the Dying Matters poll, understand by the term 'a good death', and will share their accounts of such deaths. This will be followed by accounts of deaths that could not be described as 'good', before finally considering how far it might be possible to prepare to have a good death, and concluding, yet again, that how we live our lives is the most important factor.

We often assume that death must be traumatic, the worst thing that could happen; it can be, frequently is. But several contributors told me that death can be a beautiful, even a spiritual, experience. Julie had been telling me how, when her partner was diagnosed with a brain tumour, the district nurse was visiting.

'We were all chatting about it, because there's never been a taboo on talking about death in this house, never. And the district nurse said, "Well you want a good death for both of you". And I thought what a strange thing to say, "a good death".'

Later, the hospital asked her what she thought about treating an infection her dying partner was suffering from.

'They asked me what did I want, asking me how I feel. They could rush him into intensive care and try and get him over the septicaemia, or they could just let nature take its course. He was losing his eyesight which frightened him more than dying. I said why put him through his last moments of life in intensive care, where he doesn't want to be, so that he could possibly have the kind of death he doesn't want to have, where he's going to go blind in between, because we knew that was on the cards, which scared him. I'd never seen him scared. I would think he would, I would, rather he was allowed to die, quietly, with dignity with the room he'd fought so hard to keep, with his music playing and how he wanted it... For him it was good. He wasn't scared, because he didn't know it was coming, he just went into a state of unconsciousness, wasn't ill, wasn't sick, wasn't in pain, and for me it was a good death, because if I look at all the i's and all the t's they were all dotted, all crossed. The music he chose for his funeral was playing on the ipod as he was dying– 'Desperado', by the Eagles – and it was relaxed, with people who knew him.'

Later on in our conversation, she defined a good death in her work as,

'One where they just go to sleep, and everything just shuts down slowly, and they're not gurgling or struggling for breath or anything... no pain, no anxiety, or as little as possible, and falling asleep.'

Many contributors saw a good death as falling asleep. Corinna, the doula, said, 'For a lot of people a good death is to just fall asleep, have no pain.' Sister Ally said of the death of the 90-year-old nun, 'She just slipped away in her sleep.'

The Dying Matters poll, mentioned in chapter two, found that when asked what was the most important factor in a good death, being pain-free came first, chosen by a third of people (33%); followed by being with family and friends (17%); retaining your dignity (13%); being cared for and able to die in the place of your choice (6%); being involved in decisions about your care, or if you are not able, to for family and friends to be involved (6%); and having your religious/ spiritual needs met (5%). Respondents were asked to put these five factors in order of importance. I wonder what the answers would have been if the question had been the one I asked the contributors to this book, 'What do you understand by a good death'? Probably not so neatly quantifiable.

Dying Matters respondents were further asked about how concerned would they be about various matters when thinking about their own death. Adding the 'very concerned' to the 'concerned' 49% were concerned about not making adequate financial arrangements; 32% were concerned about family disagreements over money or belongings; 28% about funeral arrangements not being followed; 54% about lack of capacity to make their end of life wishes known; 43% about not having their end of life wishes met. Again the alternatives were given by the researchers, respondents were not asked, 'What would concern you?' Here I invite you to listen to those who have been free to say what is important to them, even though their words cannot be transformed into statistics and percentages. These conversations suggest that we might worry less about these concerns if we had had conversations about death earlier. I make no apology for saying yet again, we need to talk about death, including our own deaths.

Jennifer Worth has a chapter entitled 'A Good Death' in her book *In the Midst of Life*. She tells of a friend whose husband died peacefully at home, after refusing treatment in hospital that might have kept him alive a little longer. The friend told her that it was a beautiful experience. In the same book Jennifer Worth tells of a dying Jew who says that from ancient times Jews have described death as 'God's kiss.'

Caitlin Doughty, in her story of her life as a mortician, *Smoke Gets in your Eyes*, says that for her a good death involves accepting that death is inevitable, not fighting against it.

Virginia Ironside, in her book *You'll Get Over it: The Rage of Bereavement*, says that the idea of a good death is a pernicious fantasy. For her, death is always bad.

Death is so unique, it is unlikely that any two people will have the same wishes, the same worries, or the same definition of a 'good death'. Phoebe's definition was rather more than any of the Dying Matters' categories, when she described the death of her father with Dignitas in Switzerland.

Later I asked her about the ages of the grandchildren, they were all adults. I asked what she understood by the phrase 'a good death' and she said,

> *'It may sound a bit silly, but just thinking now, off the top of my head, it's a bit like dissolving into love. He was surrounded by love in the lead up and at the time of his death … dissolving into love.'*

For a time I asked the people I was having conversations with what the phrase 'a good death' meant to them. I asked Jean, the carer, if she thought her mother's death, in the nursing home under the LCP, surrounded by flowers, scent and music, had been a 'good' one.

> *'I think so. I think my sisters absolutely agreed with me that she wanted to go… the care home manager said that the staff said it was the most peaceful death they had experienced. It wasn't easy. Those last days were hard work, but we each had time alone with our mother from time to time… The Liverpool Care Pathway was not very intrusive, it just meant that we could all be together in*

the way we wanted to be to support my mother, and the care was in place for her. We didn't have to worry about what to do, we could focus on being together and saying goodbye and whatever we wanted to do.'

M5, a member of the Quaker Fellowship of Afterlife Studies, replied to the question,

'I suppose something that is gentle. When my first husband died it was gentle.'

Eve said,

'Being prepared for it, not being sudden, or an accident. Perhaps having the family around, but because I'm a loner, I always have been, I don't think it would upset me if I was alone when I died. My mother was; she seemed to be happy enough.'

Julie said,

'I suppose it's the actual process people fear, most people are very accepting, they say they're not scared of dying; "I've had a good life," they say, but it is a subject most people don't want to talk about.'

Annabel, retired nurse, told me of patients in the anthroposophical nursing home not wanting pain killing drugs because they wanted to be fully aware of the dying process. She has worked in hospices, and thought that they were very good at controlling pain, but said that in the anthroposophical nursing home,

'Several people I nursed said they didn't want pain killers, because they wanted to be as conscious as possible of their dying, even when this meant experiencing high levels of discomfort such as pain. It is good to witness people having control in this way even if uncomfortable to witness their challenging and

distressing symptoms, because they are dying in the way that they are choosing.'

Corinna, the doula, said,

'...I think what would be important for me, and what I try to facilitate for people, is to bring as much consciousness, alertness (if one can be alert) and awakeness to the process. That sounds completely paradoxical: can I inwardly be alert, can I meet it, can I walk into that process while I'm awake, consciously, mentally, not necessarily physically, can I meet it with my consciousness? I think that would be a good death for me, what I want to facilitate. It's like anything in life, what really creates life's quality? I think you'll find that you must be able to experience it, meet it, to breathe into it fully, then that will be for me a worthwhile experience, within the limitations of being bed-bound etc. But can I be as conscious as possible, can I as much as possible walk into it: that for me would be a good death.'

She had given this reply a great deal of thought before responding to my question, but said, 'I've no time to give you a real answer that's not superficial.' She was clear that the above would not be everyone's description of a good death, 'for a lot of people a good death is to just fall asleep, have no pain.'

When I asked Paul, a death café regular, what the phrase meant to him, he told me of the death of his friend of his.

'She was remarkable in demonstrating to me, and teaching me, how to approach death in an aware and joyful way. She was very matter of fact, very accepting, very organised.'

He went on to tell me of how she'd made a will, was sorting out her possessions and deciding who should have them. She'd even visited crematoria to choose the one she wanted for her funeral.

'By this stage she was very weak, but very cogent, very clear thinking, cheerful isn't the right word, but she said, "no one tells you you can be happy when you're dying." She was having her pain managed reasonably well. As a result of the bowel cancer operation she had a stoma bag, and the thing for collecting urine, and by this time she had a hospital bed downstairs so she could look out into the garden and see the birds and the trees. And it was for her, in many ways, as good as it could be.'

Swami S, of the Community of the many Names of God, said, 'When a person is dying in that consciousness of love – that is what we would call a good death. A good death can be a beautiful experience, amazingly powerful.' It sounded to me as if he would describe Phoebe's father's death as 'good.' However, the Swami is totally opposed to assisted dying, and said,

'I would never judge another human being. I would just say that when she said the end would be very grim, we can never be sure what the end will be. That experience with my father bore that out, and even at the last moment something can be transformed. I never expected that manifestation of that intensity of grace that came twenty seconds before he took his last breath. So I would say it is our duty to give love unconditionally, and to support a person and give them the opportunity to experience love right through to the end of their life.'

The Swami's account of his father's death, a few days after his distressed, 'let me go' sounded like a good death.

'Initially I began chanting in my mind, and then this chanting to a specific aspect of God seemed to change, and I had this amazing meditative oneness: there was no difference between me, and my father, the floor, the room, the bed, my sister, everything was just one beautiful harmony, unity and oneness. There was this

beautiful, subtle vibration in the room, my sister felt it too, and we just sat there for hours. Part of it was a bit comical, because every so often this little Irish nun, about 80 and bent over, came in and she said, "you're still with us, John? Still with us?" and poke him. But it wasn't jarring, because she was doing it with a lot of love. And then it was very clear that his breathing was changing, there were long gaps between each breath, and then that changed again, and his breathing became very, very soft and this feeling of oneness was growing more and more tangible in the room. My sister went out, and asked the staff if they could not disturb us, and they were very good.

'*We were sitting there and as I was looking at him I could almost see, like the web from a spider, an incredibly fine web, a fine line, a fine thread of spider's web getting thinner and thinner and thinner, until you could almost see it would break. And that was the connection linking the body with the spirit, and I was able to see that getting thinner and thinner, perceive it, and feel it. With that came the absolute knowledge that that line could not be broken prematurely, it had to be a process that was natural. By the grace of God that would break when it was meant to break, and if it was broken prematurely then that would mean that the grace the soul was able to receive, that soul would not be able to receive.*'

Sister Ally, of the same community, told me of the death of the 97-year-old nun, which in many ways was similar to Swami S's description above, but also very different.

'*For some time she didn't speak much any more, she was bed-bound, or chair-bound, she couldn't do much for herself – she could interact with you, but not talk. She was a very, very special woman, you could see she was ready, she was 97, she was really ready, and we were really ready.*

'Her passing away was a very beautiful experience... We were with her through that whole process... It was so beautiful and there was such a beautiful presence in her room – she always had a beautiful presence around her, because she was a nun and a kind, loving person. Even though she couldn't talk, she radiated that divine love, and that just increased... That divine love grew and grew until on the Saturday it was absolutely unbelievable in her bedroom. You'd walk in, and what you'd experienced in the temples, that immense peace and stillness and freedom and love, that is what was present in her room; not fear, not terror, not anxiety, just bliss. You walked into her room and you went "Aah", and you could sit down beside her and close your eyes, and just smile because it was so beautiful. The room had been kept beautifully, there was the smell of rosewater that had been sprayed, and beautiful music playing and flowers, and it was so beautiful – there was an absolute torrent of grace flowing into her room. I felt it was her giving in to it, finally coming out and leaving the body and merging with that totality of God – energy, whatever you want to call it – it was freedom. Her innate divinity or soul was separating from that small body, and was now everywhere, absolutely beautiful.

'It carried on, through the services and the pujas (worship), and the whole community as they were all thinking of her. The pujas were amazing because it was about that. Then it started dissipating (it was still beautiful) bit by bit. The last few days, there was just a little body, that was all: it was just pumping, the lungs were going and the breathing was very rhythmic – her eyes weren't open. There was nothing any more, just breathing. We would go in and kiss her and tell her that she was doing well and thank her and then on Monday morning she just slipped away in her sleep.'

I was interested that with this nun, for the last couple of days the beautiful atmosphere dissipated, which accords well with what other contributors told me, whereas with Swami S's father the grace came only at the very end. Swami S mentioned 'meditative oneness' rather than 'dissolving into love' in his account of his father's death, but it sounded very similar to me, as did Sister Ally's account of the death of the 97-year-old nun, 'That immense peace and stillness and freedom and love, that is what was present in her room'.

Jean described most beautifully the death of her mother which had happened in a nursing home. She told me, 'My mother's death was really quite incredible, and I need to talk about it.' She described the last five days of her mother's life with great poignancy and in detail. Telling how she and her sisters brought music, perfume and poetry to the dying woman, making her death a very special experience for all her senses.

'We felt that those last days were a celebration – we're here! It was awful, it was profound and moving, but there was the feeling that it was the right thing. Perhaps it was a bit too late, with all the suffering, but she didn't want to carry on, she'd seen our father go to his dementia and death that was awful, so painful.'

I said that what she described sounded beautiful.

'Yes, there was a lot beauty in it. When I arrived I saw a dramatic change from the last time I'd seen her, and the next day it seemed that she was getting younger. There was a photo on the wall of her and my father on their wedding day, and I kept looking at my mother's face and I thought she looked like she did on her wedding day. I think my mother's face changed, it was getting younger. It was as if all the cares and all the lines were relaxing, all the care evaporating. I spoke to my sisters about it, and they said "yes, it's amazing: she looks so like her wedding photo". And the transformation kept happening ... we'd opened the window

so that she could feel the air on her cheek and the sunlight. We were trying to provide quite a lot of sensory stuff, for us as well, and I'd taken a CD of harp music and birdsong. She always used to smile when she heard harp music, and it was really beautiful, so we played that and it evoked a lovely peaceful feeling with the window open and the breeze coming in. The other thing was eau de cologne, the care staff used it for her personal care when they went to freshen her up. As much to calm me and my sisters, I stroked her forehead and said it was OK.'

This sounded so much like Sister Ally's description of the death of the 97-year-old sister and Swami S's account of the death of his father. Both stressed the spiritual aspects, and this is echoed in what others told me.

Father P, the Catholic priest's, definition of a good death was similar to Swami S's.

'Because the purpose of our life is both to prepare for and move into eternal life, a good death is when someone has reached the point when they are both ready for the transition, looking forward to being with the Lord, and a death where there were blessed moments, a peace, and whole sense of it "Yes, the time has come." And they make the transition, where there is not just an atmosphere, but a whole sense of rightness, of yes, with people who can almost echo the words of Jesus on the cross – "It is done." Finished. He's going on to the Lord, so that's the whole context of a good death.'

The chaplain from the Welcome Hospice said that the 'hospice at home' service is, 'Wonderful, it's as near as we can get to a good death; they want to be at home, and the family want them there.' When I asked how she would define a good death she gave me one of the most moving definitions I heard.

'One where the person is prepared, where the person is accepting, where the family are prepared to let go, and one that is free of pain, as peaceful and beautiful as it can be. It is particularly poignant when there is not a huge outpouring of grief at that moment of passing but almost a silence and stillness. Then the grief starts, but if it's been prepared, then some of the grieving has already taken place.'

Corinna said,

'It's very interesting that Elizabeth Kübler-Ross talks about the many little deaths we are dying all the time, it's not just the big death, our biological death. That is one death and then you have little death experiences on a daily basis: disappointment, not bereavement but loss of hope or illusion. Something little dies and if you learn to appreciate that and work with that death filters through your life, rather than the huge division: here is life, and there is death. I think that's what doulas can do: bring dying into your day to day life and not have this dichotomy of the two. Living well, dying well. How can you die well if you haven't lived well?'

Anne, a retired nurse, said a good death is, 'a catch-all phrase, almost a sort of cliché term.' While E of the Welcome Hospice said, 'Good death is a phrase people bandy around. A lot of it is cultural: we live in society where we don't do death.' Then she continued to talk about the need for conversations.

However, Anne went on to say what she thought the phrase meant.

'For the person who's died, I suppose it's someone who dies at peace, ready to move on, out of pain. To have all her family round, and be spiritually supported, if they have a religion, by a pastor or representative, and knowing that the family have come to terms and accepted the death. For me that would be the most

important, because it wouldn't be difficult for me, it would be my daughter, more than my son who would just have regrets, but my daughter would feel it more acutely. I can only speak for myself, but that would be my good death I'd want some warning that I'm dying. I'd certainly not want a heart attack! I'd want to be told, "There is nothing we can do for you". OK I'll be shocked. I could come to terms with that. I've already got my funeral service planned; it's next to my will.'

The phrase is also vague in that what is a good death for the dying person might not be for those around them, as several people, including Anne, pointed out. Those around a dying person seem to want so much to delay the death, that the dying person has to wait until they leave the room to be able to die. For many of those being forced to say good bye, a good death might mean no death. Could it be partly because we so fear bereavement and the isolation it seems to bring, that we are reluctant to let our loved ones go, even if that seems to be what they want? As some contributors pointed out, it is ourselves we are concerned about, rather than the one who is dying.

Helen, who had been given six months to live, expected to die in her sleep:

'Every morning I'd think, "still here", it's so intense you can think of nothing really.'

Had she not woken each morning, would that have been a 'good death', dissolving into love? I think it would, but I did not ask her; she was surrounded by the love, care and concern of all the others in the co-housing, and as she added, also the surrounding community and her family.

I was not going to ask Sam, the Samaritan, what she thought the phrase 'good death' meant. I assumed that any suicide is bad: Samaritans exist to prevent such deaths. However, what Sam told me made me revise my views, as contributors so often did. While the aim of the Samaritans is to reduce the number of people who die by suicide, in the last resort, a Samaritan will respect a person's determination to die, even to the point of staying on the phone to be with them while they die. I didn't expect to hear the same words that others who had accompanied people to their deaths had used, but Sam spoke of this in terms remarkably similar. She said it was a 'privilege' and an 'honour'.

She said,

'I have had occasions where it is someone's final moments and sometimes they will say things they've not told anyone else before, which is quite an honour. You are the last person they've spoken to, the last human being, there's privilege that goes with that. Death is a very personal thing. Sharing such a personal experience with someone is an honour. But it is also horrific – you get both. In those moments everything gets laid bare, you give everything up – you give up life, and that act brings with it huge vulnerability. Actually experiencing that alongside someone is a powerful thing.'

I was quite surprised at this. I had thought suicide might be seen as failure for a Samaritan, but as Sam described it, it sounded rather as if she were helping someone to make an important decision.

'I think there is that, but for me there's always sadness that that had to happen with a complete stranger. But in the circumstances people would intervene rather than let someone take that decision, and you can completely understand that. Anyone dying prematurely is a sad thing, even when it's their choice. For me that will always be a very sad thing, but there are some unique (positive is the wrong word) qualities to it as well.'

After a while I stopped asking about a good death, and returned to less structured conversations, where contributors set the whole agenda, rather than me. However, others brought up the phrase without my asking. What seemed to emerge was the idea that a good death follows a good life. Phoebe, who gave me the phrase 'dissolving into love', quoted the definition of a good death from SOARS (the Society for Old Age Rational Suicide). 'A completed life, I think that's it. I've thought about that a lot and Dad clearly thought his life was complete, he'd led a very full and active and fulfilling life.' She did worry, however, as it seemed to imply that those who had had hard lives, which could not be described as fulfilling, could not have a good death.

B, the Buddhist, talking of how Buddhists help other Buddhists to die, said,

'We help by using our connection, our meditation, our prayer, and being inspirational and encouraging people. If people get worried that they haven't done all that they should, or feel guilty about things, helping them to let go of that, saying, "You've had a good life, now is the time to move on"'.

Annabel thought

'A good death might be when someone is able to die in their own home or that you've had a good life, not just fulfilment at the end.'

Death, and the concept of a 'good death', are individual and immensely variable. Later on in our conversation, after telling me about the district nurse saying they would want a "good death" Julie said, 'if you can have a good death, there's got to be a flip side. If you don't have a good death what do you have? A mediocre death?' I said that she had mentioned an OK death.

'An OK death would be when it's been going on for a long time and they just want to go, and they're getting pressure sores and breaking down we can get the district nurses out and pain relief. '

Although Julie said she thought most of the deaths she had witnessed had been 'good,' not all deaths are even 'OK'. She told me of the worst she had experienced, which she described as horrendous. 'One particular gentleman was in so much pain. He had no family, two girls who lived opposite were looking after him to allow him to come home.' She knew these girls would not be able to cope with the end, so had given them her personal phone number, although this was against the rules.

'But then I've never followed the rules. I had a call at five o'clock in the morning from one of the girls to say "he's in agony, he's jumping off the bed, we can't find the district nurse's notes, we don't know what to do". A man who was so private, he was sitting on the edge of the bed calling out "I want my mum", but he wanted nothing to do with his family... He sat on the edge of the bed and I was cuddling him... We got the district nurses out who gave him pain relief. But he's still in agony. I called them back half an hour later and they gave him more pain relief, and he's still in agony. Eventually by nine o'clock we managed to call a doctor out: the emergency doctor came out and said he's going to wop his morphine up so high there is a risk of respiratory arrest, but to be honest that's the least of his worries at the moment, and he finally settled down. So when he passed he was at peace, his body just slowed right down, but that last six hours was horrendous.'

James, the undertaker, told me that his father's death had been anything but good.

'For my dad his good death would have been falling off his horse while out hunting and breaking his neck. In stead of which he

had Hodgkin's lymphoma, all his hair fell out, he was bald, his balls shrank to the size of peas. And he lingered and lingered and lingered, and shrunk and withered and eventually died. That in my book is not a good death, nor is it in his book. I suppose I'm not sure I'd want anyone with me. I'd rather turn my face to the wall and be left in peace. I don't want someone making conversation, or chanting, or lighting scented candles, "buzz off, leave me alone, I'm going to die now. I hope." I don't think I want lots of people around, because they don't know what to do, don't what to say. "What d'you have for lunch ?" and all that.'

Christine, the artist whose brother died, defined a good death as,

'When you're ready... perhaps where the person dying has entirely accepted and embraced the leaving of life... I don't think my brother's was a good death, because he was so isolated. Nobody wanted to talk about it, which is perhaps why I want to talk about it now. I think we got to the point where the family, if we talked about death or dying it was as if we'd given up. He had leukaemia... everybody was very positive, so to talk of death would have taken the hope and "we believe he's going to survive it" away. And so he had to face it on his own. That was a bad death.'

My own father's death was anything but good. When I said that I was not close to him, that was an understatement. I don't think that I ever loved my father after childhood. I was the only member of his close family still alive to be able to be there, but my being there did not make it a good death for either of us. There was no love for him to dissolve into.

Sarah wanted a good death for her daughter Imogen, who attempted suicide. Instead Imogen has been condemned by the medical profession, according to Sarah, to the torture of a horrendous living death, while the real Imogen died years ago. 'Imogen would constantly have tubes forced down her throat to draw out the saliva, because she couldn't swallow. She would be like a landed fish, thrashing about, obviously in huge distress every time they carried out this process. It was horrendous to watch.'

We would all like to die a good death. From the above it would seem that the best preparation would be living a good life, however one might define that. Rosie and Paul both told me of courses they had attended on preparing for death. Rosie told me of a course with William Bloom.

'He had a refrain about going into the clear light; whether you're sitting with somebody, or if it's yourself, he talked about how important it was go into the clear light… We had to think about our own good death, how would we like it to be, then we had to take a deep breath and imagine a death we really, really didn't want to have, and he helped us to see how the death we really didn't want to have could still be a vision of the clear light… my personal preparation is the meditation which I do every day on getting up for 40 minutes to an hour each morning. I suppose it's a linking in with saying goodbye – each day, each moment, is as complete as it can be.'

Rosie went on to talk about the different stages of life, Hindu belief holds that there are four: first 'Brahmacharya' or the Student Stage, then 'Grihastha' or the Householder Stage, third 'Vanaprastha' or the Hermit Stage and finally 'Sannyasa' or the Wandering Ascetic Stage. In the last stage the person becomes a wandering recluse, who has no home or worldly attachments, dependent on others for food, dedicated to a spiritual life. He is preparing for his death, hoping for release from the cycle of birth and death. Rosie said one of the tasks of ageing is to leave a legacy, and she is writing a journal for her granddaughter. She is also trying to reduce her possessions, as well as daily meditation. She said it was important to say good bye, and (not totally seriously) thinks each day when she says good bye to her husband 'this may be the last time'.

Rosie said she had read 'a lot about Jung.' Jung, too, thought and wrote a great deal about death, and how to die 'well'. He said we all need a myth about death. His concept of myth was not an untrue story, but an archetype, a primordial image or idea, from the collective unconscious. Jung said we all have not just an unconscious mind, but share a collective unconscious, filled with archetypes from the past. We all need a positive image of what death is: we need to see it as not an end, but a goal, the destination of the second half of our lives. He offered guidelines for preparing for a good death: to be more conscious by paying attention to our dreams and acting on their guidance, becoming more self directed, or what Jung called 'individuation' whereby we become more truly ourselves. This sounds very similar to what I heard from contributors: a good death comes from a good life, or a life well lived, where we are true to ourselves. Jung wrote, 'What happens at death is so unspeakably glorious that our imagination and our feelings do not suffice to form even an approximation of it.'

Rosie also mentioned *The Tibetan Book of Living and Dying*, which Sogyal Rinpoche wrote to update the 'Tibetan Book of the Dead'. This seems to have as much to say about how we should live, in particular how we should meditate, as about how we die. He says he wrote the book because he wanted no one to be afraid of death, and to change the way we live.

Rosie also recommended the book *Life Lessons* by Elizabeth Kübler-Ross and David Kessler, saying it was,

'Very good preparation for death because it was asking, "What am I here for? What are my life lessons? What are my tasks left still to do? What can I manage to squeeze in before I depart?"'

Elizabeth Kübler-Ross, who had written many books about death and dying, and after nearly dying herself of a stroke, felt the need to write one more, on living. This she wrote with David Kessler. The lessons of the book, which come from those whom the two had cared for as they were dying, are about such things as love, relationships, loss, power, guilt, forgiveness and happiness. They say, that loss shows us what is precious, while love teaches us who we are. The most important lesson is to live every day to its fullest.

Eckhart Tolle's books *The Power of Now* and *Stillness Speaks* offer similar advice for living fully, as does Bronnie Ware's *The Top Five Regrets of the Dying*. Bronnie Ware's book is based on conversations she had with dying patients in the course of her work as a carer. The top regrets she found were: wishing they had had the courage to live a life true to themselves, not the life others expected; wishing they had not worked so hard; that they had had the courage to express their feelings; not staying in touch with friends; and wishing they had let themselves be happier. This last is so sad: happiness is something hospices seem to understand, and facilitate.

Paul told me of workshops he had attended on Stephen Levine's work.

'He was doing lots of work on death, dying and bereavement …
It's another way of preparing for death – by trying to live as best
we can.'

It was Paul who said that preparing for death could increase the kindness in the world. Stephen Levine's book *Living this Year as if it were Your Last* offers similar lessons to those of Elizabeth Kübler-Ross. He gives a month by month account of how one might live, as he had done, as if this was the last year of one's life. He writes that at the end of the year he found a new joy in life: living more fully, after a year of contemplating of death.

Christine said,

'I feel I have come to terms with my death, and I am ready to go whenever, and that would be a good death.' When I asked how she got ready she said, 'I think it's very individual, and my process was spiritual. In my case it wouldn't be any different not being in the physical world. I don't have a problem with the actual death, but I don't want to die horribly. The way we're treating older people – that's not a good way to go.'

Many of those I spoke with agreed that a good death necessitates a good life. In SA's words, 'Life's too short... don't be afraid of dying.' Once more, conversations about death, and a good death, seem to be about life: a good life.

While definitions of what makes for a good death varied widely from not wanting to be aware of it to wanting to savour the experience, even the pain, nevertheless there were commonalities: it is peaceful, for most it should be pain free, the dying person is ready, has accepted that they are dying, has dignity, and knows that they are loved, and love. Surrounded by, or 'dissolving into', love. A good death is the end of a good life.

However, no good life, or training for death, can ensure that we will not die prematurely in a horrendous manner in a dreadful accident, or from one of the more terrible degenerative diseases. Only James and Julie mentioned these. Julie said, in her experience, such deaths were uncommon. Sarah spoke passionately in favour of being permitted to choose to die. This will be considered in chapter eight. Unusually, I think, Julie was offered this option for her partner.

In the last chapter contributors told me of some kind of presence, or spirit, around the deaths of loved ones. Perhaps the dying person becomes aware of this in the time between knowing that they are going to die, and their death. Many of those I spoke with told me of a variety of ways in which the last few weeks, or days, or even hours of a person's life became mysteriously enhanced, and they seem to live more fully. This will be explored in the next chapter. The conclusion to this chapter seems to be that what is a 'good death' is as individual as the person dying, and remains a mystery. Whether a death is 'dissolving into love', or dying alone, in pain and frightened, or whether one is completely unaware at the end, is another mystery. Death is part of life, integrated with it, and only explicable in terms of the life which is coming to an end.

*　　*　　*

Epitaph on a Friend

An honest man here lies at rest.
The friend of man, the friend of truth,
The friend of age, and guide of youth:
Few hearts like his, with virtue warm'd,
Few heads with knowledge so inform'd;
If there's another world, he lives in bliss;
If there is none, he made the best of this.
(Robert Burns, in Poems for funerals).

7 The blossomest blossom

'I love that quote, 'The blossomest blossom'. My dad was a bit like that, I remember when he was in hospital for just one day, the day when he got the diagnosis. He gathered all the family and he said this is what is going to happen and I'm ready for it, and I'm going to have a good last month. That's what he did.'

(Pammy on the death of her father)

Pammy, the death café organiser, said of the death of her father,

'He had a diagnosis of pancreatic cancer; so he was very fit and well, a bit ill, then had this diagnosis, knew he was going to die in about a month... It was a difficult, poignant and wonderful time. He embraced life really in that last month, had a wonderful month seeing all his friends.'

I said that sounded a bit like the amazing televised interview that Melvyn Bragg had with Dennis Potter, so soon before his death that he had to pause from time to time for a sip of morphine. This is published as *Seeing the Blossom*, by Dennis Potter with an introduction by Melvin Bragg. He speaks there of a nowness, and of a different way of seeing things, the blossom was not just 'nice' but the 'blossomest blossom'.

Pammy said her father,

'Went round the village saying good bye to everyone, and they were all stunned, they thought he was joking. He went round the village saying – "I won't be seeing you again". He had not long started sailing, so he very poignantly went for his last sail, and had his last drink and everything. Every evening he would sit

with Mum, going over their long and happy life together, and mulling over how she would be; of course it was very difficult for Mum, but overall the lead up to his death was as good as it could be with that diagnosis.'

Several contributors told stories of similar heightened awareness and a unique quality to life shortly before the death of a loved one. In this chapter I shall report some of these, and some other cases, most of which were followed by what might be called a 'good death', before considering whether it could be possible to experience the blossomest blossom when not confronted with the fairly immediate prospect of death. However, it is important to note that this chapter will not be considering sudden or horrific death, where experiencing the blossom is unlikely or impossible. Suicide, for example, will be discussed in the next chapter.

Jean, the carer, whose mother had suffered from dementia in the last years of her life, said that in the few days before she died she seemed to be more present:

'I had a strange feeling that she was more present than she had been for a long time... she had become incredibly calm.'

Like Jean's mother, the 90-year-old Quaker who died the day after I last saw her seemed more 'present' than I had seen her for some time. Jean and her sisters had spent five days around their dying mother, bringing flowers, music, poetry, and perfume to the room. She agreed that 'there was a lot of beauty in it.'

Phoebe, whose description of her father's death with Dignitas was 'dissolving into love,' spoke of a 'precious time'.

'The nearer he got to going to Switzerland, the more he felt sure it was going to happen, the more relaxed he became. About two or three weeks before we left we told a few close friends and family, and it was, for me the whole summer for me was, a wonderful

time. It was a really precious time, we knew it was limited, all our time together was. Sometimes when you are with people you're not quite with them, but our time together was so, so beautiful. Everything I could ever have wanted to say to him I did; it was not just me, he got letter after letter, visit after visit from people – just an outpouring of love for him. I had this almost tangible sense of him being carried along on this sea of love from all these people... the whole summer for me was a wonderful time: a really precious time.'

I said this sounded like Dennis Potter seeing the blossom. She replied,

'Absolutely it did: I don't know exactly what he was experiencing, but there was a deep calmness and peace that came over him that was completely unperturbed. He was unaffected by tensions and worries in other people. It felt like he had dropped into this place where all the stuff that we think is important, doesn't matter any more... it was filled with love. There was an outpouring of love towards him, and he just revelled in it. It was just beautiful, yes, it's sort of bizarre but it was beautiful.'

I asked Paul, a death café regular, who gave such a moving description of his friend's death if perhaps she had experienced Dennis Potter's blossom. After a pause he said,

'I think she was really appreciating the intensity of life as she approached its end.'

However, James, the undertaker, told me that from time to time he was asked to visit the dying before they died, which he described as 'a wonderful part of my work'. I asked him whether he had witnessed the blossom in any of these clients. He suggested that in Dennis Potter's case, it could be the morphine, 'Well why not? It's a very dreamy drug.' But, I think, in many cases the blossom comes before the morphine. Neither Anne not Hannah, retired nurses who had both worked in hospices, were able to describe this among their patients. Hannah paused before saying, 'It varies, as much as individuals vary.'

In contrast to many other contributors, Helen, who was given six months to live, did not experience blossoming in her eight months of chemotherapy; quite the reverse, her life became almost unbearable. Helen wrote a short piece for me about how those months were, when chemotherapy made life almost intolerable. She wrote:

'How did this news affect me? Being a doctor, I absolutely believed her. I could not think how the end would be. I had not the energy to think of, let alone do, things I always hoped I would do, had not done. Long hours thinking about my past, mostly good things. Kept my front door unlocked so it would be easier for whoever found me. Started to give things away so that a) they would be useful to someone and b) my brother would have less to do: sewing machine, sewing things, paintings. Had already made a will but did it need updating? Sister in law took over my money and bills, taxes. Co-housers had a rota, and a spare rota, to get shopping, washing up etc. Everyone in co-housing and everyone I knew in this town offered to help...

'No one knew how they could help, and nor did I – I was completely swamped by them. Had to put a notice on the front door saying 'too tired for visitors'. It was often ignored. Every day I woke up amazed to be still alive, but how was I going to get through another long day? Could not do anything, even water tasted sweet. It was winter and dark morning and early afternoon. I had to learn to accept help, no showers because of bandages for eight months...I was so preoccupied thinking about how to get through each day, getting through the days and nights, I didn't often think about death, but occasionally thought it *would be better than the time I was having... each person has to deal with it in their own way...*

'In March 2016 I happened to meet Dr. P in the hospital corridor. She looked very startled to see me. And I looked her in the eye and said, "still here, Dr P" and walked on.'

I am glad Helen 'startled' Dr. P by still being there. She said Dr P is no longer on her case. She told me of how the chemotherapy regime had been changed several times, but nothing helped, in the end the side effects were too much for her. 'Because of terrible, terrible side effects, I just sat here like a pudding I couldn't think or do anything.'

I am very grateful to have heard Helen's experience, which has added some balance to what others have told me. Eleven months after coming off the chemotherapy, which appears to have halted the cancer, despite what the doctor told her, she is very much alive, and life seems very much better than death could be.

'I finished chemo in June 2015, and gradually got better from all the side effects; my hair grew again; the huge blisters on both legs went. My feet not painful to walk on, my sense of taste returned; my hands became much more flexible, mouth ulcers and discomfort went.'

She has gone back to being the optimistic, creative person she was before: perhaps even blossoming. 'You get up with a degree of optimism, do normal things.'

But she said she still cannot do very much. '

There's a lot I can't do, my leg is quite battered. I can't swim, and walking is quite difficult... Doing little things, making little things, writing to people, I can only do one thing a day really before I get exhausted, maybe two.'

Helen's humour, her matter of factness and her obvious optimism and creativity suggested to me that perhaps she did not need to think about death to live more fully, she was already living fully.

Hannah had told me, as described in the previous chapter, of the 'absolute peace' of the death of her mother's friend in her arms when she was seventeen. I said that this sounded rather different from the blossom.

> 'I don't see this as an opposite. Peace is about relaxation. If I'm relaxed enough, it is easier to accept what is happening. When I'm relaxed I'm actually seeing life as it really is, in all its sparkling luminosity, but I'm rarely relaxed enough to see that reality. Unfortunately peace has become a flat word, but peace is very alive, so it's the same as the blossom. Definitely.'

I asked if anyone she had cared for had mentioned something like this.

> 'I can't remember, but it is well known that the opportunity for a shift in perspective is there from moment of diagnosis: your focus and perspective can change in an instant. So suddenly what seems to matter is put into a more real perspective. That's why Buddhists engage in lengthy practices about death: feeling that death is always on your shoulder, going to the burial ground and watching corpses decompose. It's about brining that reality to life, before you are actually dying, because that's the way to live.'

Rosie, who took a course on preparing for death, said when telling me of the stages of life that the final stage before death could be a very creative time.

In the two hospices I visited it seemed that the aims of both included facilitating blossom. Those involved in each of them told me that their hospice is a place of life, of love, of laughter. This may be in part due to the fact that those who go to a hospice have accepted that they are going to die. But, as I was told, a hospice is not a place to go to die, but a place to live more fully to the very end. I heard this in both hospices, and in the film *Seven Songs for a Long Life*.

The Welcome Hospice offers, among many other therapies, 'diversional therapy', and employs a diversional therapist who gives patients the opportunity to be involved in a wide range of creative activities. Jenny, who volunteers in the art room said,

'It's a lovely atmosphere. I get so much out of it. It's the people who come here, and seeing what they do, especially in the art room: we have people coming in who've never painted before. It's amazing what they can do. When they do something here they open up, and it's not all doom and gloom about their illnesses. They open up and they do amazing work. If there's a few in the art room there's laughter and they are not thinking about death and it's just lovely to see. People say to me "how can you work there? It's so depressing." But it's not at all – I get a lot of joy out of it and I love it... people think a hospice is all about dying, but it's not.'

Isabel, the nurse manager of that hospice, said the hospice offered a chance for patients to

'Just be themselves... The word hospice conjures up certain images, doom and gloom, but actually when people come for day care they have a lot of fun, a lot of laughter, it's all very, very gentle, but the word itself can be frightening.'

Her hospice organises open days so that the public can come and find out what really goes on in a hospice. She spoke of the privilege of working with people at such an important time of their lives, and the joy. One of the joys is helping people to discover creative talents within them that they never knew they had. She gave me some examples including a man who was invited to take part in the art group, but said he didn't have his reading glasses. He 'forgot' his glasses for the next six weeks, then one week he brought them and was taught to paint on silk. He did a lovely picture of roses, which Isabel took to his widow just before Christmas. She was delighted, and it is now on her wall. She said, 'that's the first Christmas present he's given me in nearly 60 years.' All those at that hospice remarked on the quality of the art work produced by those in the art room, most of whom had never done anything like this before. Isabel also said,

'Everyone here is passionate about what they do. Life for the patients is widening in a sense at a time when most might think life was closing in.'

Once again I heard the echo of the Quaker phrase 'to live more fully.'

Iain, the patient at the Scottish hospice, said that great art work goes on there too, with one patient becoming a really good painter, who had never painted before. Iain himself has become a weaver since coming there. It took him two years to learn to use the loom properly.

'I like to make things people can actually use, such as a scarf... People are creative, produce things that their family can look at afterwards and be very proud of. It also helps people to have something to focus on and take their mind off their illness. They feel they have achieved something special that they can enjoy now and have something to remind them of that person after they have passed away... I want to continue with hospice, it's part of my life now, part of what I do. The hospice have said they count me as part of the staff now, as I'm really good with new people when they first attend.'

I wondered if you needed to have a life limiting diagnosis to realise that.

Iain replied,

'That's very true, people think their life can be hard at times, but they don't realise how hard life can be for some who are constantly battling an illness. I sometimes think if they knew what it was like life wouldn't be so hard for them after all.'

Iain also told me of some of the realities of living with MS:

'I'm in constant pain, 24 hours a day for fifteen years; there is nothing they can do. The hospice has reduced it a bit, but they can't get rid of it, but you get used to it. There's no other choice... one of the things I hate about this illness, I forget things; people say something and I can't remember what they said. It's very frustrating: that's the illness, it's really annoying that that happens... [when first diagnosed] I was very angry, I was a very fit young guy, doing a lot of things, very sporty. It was very hard to learn, but eventually I learnt the lesson that that's how it was going to be.'

He also said that the hospice made it easier because, 'It's very hard, but it's good in a way because you're not thinking about your own problems, you're thinking about other people.'

Iain reminded me of the young man Sister Ally told me of at the Hospice of the Many Names of God who wanted to mow the grass. When I asked Sister Ally what her hospice provided, she said,

'We ask them how they really are. We offer assisted bathing, complementary therapies, home cooked meals, counselling, apart from that: a place just to be themselves, they don't have to put on a brave face – they can just be; and we try to look after everything practically. Just to be with them, to love them, to just sit in silence

with them... actually it's the ethos, the love, the energy that comes with everything that we do, because we invite the Lord into every aspect of that. Before I go to the hospice I ask God for his grace to flow through us, into them, and give them strength. "May your grace flow directly to those who need it, or may you use us as an instrument of your will, may thy will be done and may you guide us."

This hospice has a website where one of their patients, Winnie, talks about what it is like to be cared for by them. She talks of how important it is to her to be greeted with a hug ('We don't shake hands here'), which enables her to be calm, relaxed. Like Sister Ally she uses the phrase 'surrounded by love', and speaks of the happiness, the laughter, how massage helped her to feel 'happy inside'. She also tells of how, like Iain, she helped another patient, who was very anxious, but Winnie shared her problem. She says that at the hospice, 'You can just relax, and when the time comes you can go peacefully and calmly, the best way you can.' She appreciates the quietness and the fun, saying she didn't want to be 'occupied – we're not gaga', what she wants is understanding not sympathy.

I have used the word patient for those who come to a hospice, but Isabel said other words could equally well be used: client, guest, user. However, she told me of someone who said,

'I don't want to be called a client, that involves money; I'm not a user, the drugs I use are all prescription drugs; I'm not a guest because I would rather not be here. I'm here because I'm ill, so call me a patient. That's what I am.'

So that is the word I am using. However, Isabel also told me of one of the first patients at the hospice, who said, 'Make it as homely and as friendly as possible, and never forget me: whenever you're dealing with anyone remember they're a person, not a patient.' I feel hospices follow this advice to the letter, whatever they call the people they serve.

Gill, another of the Welcome Hospice's volunteers, said working at the hospice was 'really wonderful.' All those connected with both hospices said things along these lines, and I think perhaps what they meant was that those in their care were living through the blossom time of their lives. Isabel gave me a promotional DVD about the hospice, where several of the patients spoke briefly about hospice care: some of initial nervousness about coming, but all of the happiness, the caring, the love they found there. One said it was a bit like starting school, but once she got used to it, she gained confidence through its loving care, 'it's so kind, so welcoming.' There was great praise for the staff, who were said to be a special kind of person to do what they do. One patient said that she was very nervous about coming, she had lost interest in most of the things she used to enjoy, but the hospice had 'reinvigorated her'; she returned to old hobbies, and learned to use a computer, which was something new for her. Others spoke of doing things they'd never done before. The hospice was described as: most wonderful, so welcoming, so friendly, happy, caring. One said, 'It's my home.' Another, 'If you want tlc, this is where you'll get it.'

Helen, however, found that the local day hospice was not for her. This was not the Welcome Hospice. I had made several attempts to talk to those involved in this other hospice, but although I was always told they would 'get back to me' they never did. Helen said she went there 'reluctantly, but did not really enjoy it... too many people and too echoey... Horrible Benjamin Britten music.' However, she also said it was a 'wonderful place, particularly for those who live alone and have no one to talk to.' This is not one of Helen's problems, living in co-housing as she does. She described those who worked there and the volunteers as 'immensely kind and good people,' but she no longer goes there. She said when she did, she tried to hide behind a newspaper, and the door, but a volunteer would find her and want her to talk. Not about her death, about 'anything.' They were interested in the co-housing. She made some stained glass and other things at the hospice, suggesting that creative activities go on there, as in the other hospices; but Helen has always been creative, and did not need the hospice for that.

The Dying Matters' poll found that most people say they would like to die at home, but most die in hospital, seen as the worst place to die, but often inevitable. Hospitals do their best to provide a peaceful environment for the dying, but often this is just not possible, largely because there are not enough staff. Hospices seem able to manage pain better than hospitals, possibly because all involved have accepted death as the outcome, so they can ignore any possible long term side effects of the drugs. A hospice can provide all the benefits of modern pain relief, without the alarming, and frequently fruitless, technology of the hospital that it is hoped will enable the dying person to live just a little longer. Hannah said,

'It's a more peaceful environment. They're not looking at life saving, but being alongside.'

In the film about the Scottish hospice we see a patient admitted to the residential wing of the hospice, for her unbearable pain to be managed. We are told that many patients do not want residential care, because they fear they will not go home again. In fact, many have their pain relief managed, and are then able to go home, as was the case with the patient we see in the film. The aim is to get them back into the community, which is possible with modern syringe drivers.

The Welcome Hospice, like many day hospices, has a 'Hospice at Home' service, for those so close to their deaths that they can no longer make the journey. This sounds to me like the best of all options, to be at home, where one wants to be, yet to have all the benefits of modern pain control.

Hannah, who also worked in hospices, told me,

'When the first hospice was founded by Dame Cicely Saunders, there was very definitely a strong spiritual input. Unfortunately, since those times, as our society has become more and more materialistic, this is reflected in the way dying is handled. I'm absolutely behind anything that helps put people into the driving seat, when it comes to their own mortality. It should be possible to die as I have lived, in my own way, on my own terms.'

Unsurprisingly, it is the Hospice of the Community of the Many Names of God that is the more openly religious of the two I visited, but the Welcome Hospice has a voluntary chaplain, who will discuss faith with those who want to. The Hospice of the Community of the Many Names of God provide the spiritual input, but do not press it on patients. Swami S said of that hospice,

'They are not just there to die, they are there to live, and to live each moment, and for each moment to be a new experience: an uplifting experience. We're not just going to deal with practical-ities of that ill person, we're going to enable and empower that person to live joyfully... To be able to look after people who are dying, to play any part in helping to bring about that manifesta-tion of love and of grace in that person's life, that is the privilege of being involved in palliative care. And any little part you can play in that, that creates the opportunity for that love and that grace is an amazing thing. That is why we are passionate about it.'

Sister Ally said working in the hospice had totally changed her view of hospices.

'It's not about dying – it's about living. Well it is about dying, because they are dying, they are facing a lot of things, and facing their own mortality, what they're leaving behind, their losses, and the people around them. But what hospices do is to help people to really live before they die, to get the best out of their last months or years.'

Jenny, a volunteer at the Welcome Hospice said,

'People think it's about dying, but it's not about dying, it's about getting on with your life – living: you come here get your confidence and you live.'

Iain said of the Scottish hospice,

'People newly diagnosed, are very scared of coming to the hospice, and I can talk to them and try and make them feel more comfortable. They think they're going to die, but it's not like that; some people manage to get the right treatment and go on to live a longer life than they first expected. Any more time you can get is a bonus.'

What can be seen in the film 'Seven Songs for a Long Life', and what I think happens in all hospices, is people living until they die; people living more fully; perhaps even experiencing the blossomest blossom. The film looks at the lives of the patients: their homes, families, their everyday enjoyment. They all know that they are dying, but death is mentioned little in the film. One spoke of 'missing out' on life, but then said that perhaps when she has died she won't feel that she is missing out. It is those that will survive her that make her sad: her children will need her, and she won't be there. Others discuss the dilemma of not knowing how long they have; should they spend their money or preserve it in case they live longer? One says we don't talk about money or death. They do both.

The Scottish hospice is perhaps unique in that they all started singing (hence the title of the film) when one of the patients, asked by Amy if he would like to talk to her, said he didn't want to talk, but would sing. He said he had once won a medal for his singing, which was the thing he was most proud of in his whole life. Amy recorded his song, and made a DVD for him. He was delighted with it, and asked for copies to send to all his relations (he said he needed about 40). The other patients loved it too, and wanted their songs recorded. In an interview, included on the DVD of the film, Mandy, one of the nurses, who is also a singer, said she found that song allowed her to connect deeply with the patients, and that it was one of the last things to go at the end of life. She said they were singing for themselves, and for each other. They are doing it together, because in the words of one of the songs sung in the film, 'Everybody Hurts.' This song was sung by one of the patients, a young mother; it was incredibly moving to hear it sung by someone who was hurting so badly. But the message of the song is that we all help one another, which is explored in chapter nine.

Mandy also said that, as nurses, one of the hardest things to learn is that one can't fix everything: sometimes one can only listen. The film, while showing the joy of those in the hospice, did not shy away from listening to the sadness and the grief. In one memorable scene a patient breaks down in tears, and the nurse first puts her arm around her, then climbs onto the wheelchair beside her to hug her. They cry together.

Yet the film does not dwell on their sadness, although some patients talk of the uncertainty about how long they will live: should they spend all they have, or save it? Once they started singing, the director of the hospice asked a voice coach to come and coach the patients, to give them confidence that the singing would always be their 'best voice'. It seemed, from the faces on the film as they sang, that here was more than living fully, it was blossoming.

Other songs the patients sing on the film include 'Wouldn't it be Lovely,' sung by a patient doing her physiotherapy exercises; an elderly woman after talking about her late husband, sang very sadly the beautifully haunting 'Eriskay Love Lilt,' with it's Gaelic chorus ending, 'Sad am I without thee'. Like so many of those I talked with who work in hospices, Amy said, in the interview on the DVD of the film, 'To me they're still living.' Even though they are dying.

After the showing of the film which I watched, Amy ran a workshop, which was intended to use the energy produced by the shared experience of watching the film to allow us to get closer to our own fears and desires around end of life. We were invited in pairs to consider five questions:

- What makes a good day for you?
- What are the qualities you would like to be remembered by?
- What action do you take to express these?
- What would you change if you have a life limiting illness?
- Are these new actions?

The aim of the film, especially in its use of an expanded sense of cinema, that includes working with the audience on a one-to-one basis after the screening, is very much the aim of this book: to enable people to be able to think and talk about death, including their own deaths. And to show that life does not end with a life limiting diagnosis. In fact we all have life limiting diagnoses, we are all going to die; but we can all live until we die. We can live more fully, even, perhaps, experience the blossom. This may be preferable to living a little while longer, but in a hospital, wired up to all the devices of medical technology.

We do not need to die in a hospice to be able to live more fully. Julie, the Marie Curie nursing assistant, said, 'my job is to help them to live until the point when it finishes and they no longer live. To that point they are still very much alive, very much a spiritual being they're a person.' (Julie told me she was not religious). She said,

'*There are certain things you can do to try and make people realise that they are still living, and their existence is still valid, and important, and it has an effect... people in my job need to understand that. I think a lot of people lie there and think they've got nothing left to give.*'

She told me of one particular patient.

'*She couldn't get out into the garden, and she loved her garden, so I went out and took photographs of all the flowers, it was spring time. I brought my laptop in, and put it by the bed and scrolled it through, so she could still see her garden; and then she proceeded to tell me how deep you're supposed to plant this bulb, and that bulb, and I think it was lovely because it felt that she still had something to give.*'

Some of those facing imminent death have been able to write about it. One is the moving account, written originally as a series of articles for the *Observer* newspaper, *Before I say Goodbye* by Ruth Picardie, who died of cancer in her thirties leaving twin sons aged two. She writes of the hurt of losing the future: not being there for her children as they grow up.

In March 2016 the *Guardian* newspaper published a remarkable article by Max Edwards entitled, 'I'm 16. Five months ago, I was diagnosed with terminal cancer.' He suggested that it might be rather like getting his GCSE results. But they turned out to be a pleasant surprise, unlike being told he was going to die. His article ends with a wonderful piece of teenage philosophy – everyone is going to die. He urged his readers to get over it. Less than two weeks later the paper reported his death.

The blossomest blossom can, of course, be experienced anywhere. Dennis Potter was at his home in Ross when he saw his blossom. The singer Wilko Johnson reported something very similar. The rock and roll artist was diagnosed with inoperable cancer, but refused chemotherapy. A film called 'The Ecstasy of Wilko Johnson' shown on the BBC television as part of their *Imagine* series, shows his blossoming.

In an interview with the *Guardian* he said that after his initial diagnosis he felt a kind of transcendence, with insights and ecstasies, which he said made it almost, but not quite worth his diagnosis. However, later he was offered an operation, which seems to have cured the cancer. The ecstasy did not last.

More recently the death from cancer of the singer David Bowie two days after the publication of his first album for ten years, has led to some speculation as to whether it was the diagnosis that prompted this late creativity. An article in the *Guardian* newspaper spoke of a final, focussed burst of creativity.

In 2016 another book on death was published, *When Breath Becomes Air* by Paul Kalanithi, a neurosurgeon. He did not live to finish the book, his wife had to do that. He says that one of the choices confronting a dying person is to live life more fully (perhaps to experience the blossom?), but for those dying of cancer, the illness takes away the energy to do that. Yet in the final paragraph, which is addressed to his eight month old daughter, he writes about the joy she has brought to him at the end of his life, a joy such as he had never before experienced. Could this be his blossom?

In his book *Meetings at the Edge* Stephen Levine writes of children who die, but who seem to have blossomed shortly before they died.

Also in 2016 BBC TV showed a film, 'How to Die: Simon's Choice', about Simon Binner who had motor neurone disease and went to Switzerland to die. The film, which shows him enjoying final parties with his friends his delight in his friends and the parties, clearly shows his blossom.

Caroline, whose son died, reported a very similar experience when she saw the most exquisite roses she'd ever seen. She said 'it was as if everything was intensified.' But in her case it was grief at the death of her son that produces that intensity.

I felt very privileged that M, who supports the newly bereaved, told me of her depression, which sounded very similar to a bereavement, and how she coped with it, which, I thought, sounded very like living more fully.

'I may not feel happy, but I can experience things and try and live in the moment; with depression I have learned to live in the moment. That is how you cope, how most people learn to cope with long term depression, it's a long term disease, not something you get over, you cope with it. On the days that you can go outside with the simple things: you see the beautiful flowers, and the buds on the trees growing into leaves, and beautiful blossom, and feel the sun on your face, and go to the park and listen to the children laughing, hear the dogs chasing each other, and very little things can lift you if you let them. You do have to get in the habit of doing things like that to be able to start to feel the emotion of happiness, and you learn to live, to live each day and live in the moment... Life is to be enjoyed. Life is not to be suffered, it's to enjoy.'

For some the nearness of death seems sometimes to bring with it a unique dimension to life. Would it be possible to experience this if one was not facing death? When I asked Annabel, a retired nurse, if she thought it was possible to experience this nowness and the blossomest blossom when one was not approaching death, she was doubtful.

'...because of that level of intensity. I think we can live intensely but not all the time, I'm not sure I'd like to live like that all the time. It is the being blessed with these windows of intensity that make it so potent. Experiencing despondency, sadness and sluggishness is all part of the richness of being human I think. We

pass from one state to another, being in one state all the time sounds a bit unreal, life is always in movement, change and flux.'

I asked Pammy the same question. She replied,

'Oh yes well I suppose I do sort of agree with that. Once or twice I've been really ill. Once I was very ill and remember that it wasn't always a bad time – I felt very alive, and I remember in particular a heightened degree of sensory things. I remember thinking, 'Oh isn't life wonderful – isn't the sun wonderful aren't all the colours wonderful… well that's for me; if I can keep death in mind then I can live better.'

Perhaps we cannot live our lives in a permanent state of intensity, but, in the words of the Quaker advice, 'Accepting the fact of death, we are freed to live more fully.' I suspect that the blossomest blossom is more than 'living fully'.

This is very different from Dylan Thomas's view of death in his poem 'Do not Go Gentle into that Good Night', which is in *Poems for Funerals*. Yet perhaps the burning and the raving which Thomas writes of could be seen as blossoming?

Every death is unique: the blossom will not be the same for any two people and, of course, for many is impossible. We may choose life, but we cannot always choose to have a good death. The books and the courses on dying well all seem to involve living well. For some, life will always be unbearable and they may choose to take their own lives, perhaps contacting the Samaritans about it. For them the last days, weeks, months are the very opposite of blossoming. The next chapter will turn to this darker side of death and look at some of the very different reasons to choose to die.

*   *   *

'He is made one with Nature: there is heard
His voice in all her music, from the moan
Of thunder, to the song of night's sweet bird;
He is a presence to be felt and known
In darkness and in light, from herb and stone,
Spreading itself where'er that Power may move
Which has withdrawn his being to its own;
Which wields the world with never-wearied love,
Sustains it from beneath, and kindles it above.
He is a portion of the loveliness
Which once he made more lovely

(Shelley, from 'Adonaïs')

8 Going gentle

Just Cope With It!!

I don't know what's going on in my head
I have to struggle to get though the day
Maybe i would be better off dead
I'm up all night, then spend all day in bed
Not that i do anything anyway
I don't know what's going on in my head
I feel no results from the pills i've been fed
A waste of the taxes sane people pay
Maybe i would be better off dead
I've forgotten what my counsellor said
That i should do when i feel this way
I don't know what's going on in my head

Now most of my friends have quietly fled
They didn't know how to help; what to say
I don't know what's going on in my head
Maybe i would be better off dead

(by Yanna Gunn – who took her own life just before she
  was 30, not one of the contributors, the daughter of a
  friend.)

Despite God's advice in Deuteronomy, to choose life, and despite
society's view of it as the worst possible misfortune, death to some
can seem inviting. Some choose it, for a variety of reasons. In the
poem 'Death and the Maiden' by Matthias Claudius, set to music by

Schubert and the theme of the second movement of his string quartet no 14, the Maiden says:

> 'Oh! leave me! Prithee, leave me! thou grisly man of bone!
> For life is sweet, is pleasant.
> Go! leave me now alone!
> Go! leave me now alone!'
> But Death replies:
> 'Give me thy hand, oh! maiden fair to see,
> For I'm a friend, hath ne'er distress'd thee.
> Take courage now, and very soon
> Within mine arms shalt softly rest thee!'

Some, like Yanna, whose poem is printed above, take their own lives for reasons that I think are very obvious from her poem. A friend told me she was amazed to hear a Catholic priest say, at the funeral for a young suicide, 'Don't forget that Jesus chose to die'.

In chapter five I reported how many people, mysteriously, seem able to deliberately choose the moment to die. Advanced Directives can enable people, not necessarily at the point of death, to have some choice as to what they do and do not want at the end of life. There has recently been a debate within society, as well as in parliament, about whether the medical profession should be allowed to assist people who are dying to 'go gentle', in the words of Dylan Thomas. Passions are expressed on both sides of this debate, including among some of the contributors to this book. In this chapter I shall report first on what I was told about suicide, before looking at Advanced Directives, and finally considering different views on assisted dying. I will not enter into the debate on this, only report what I heard in my conversations with contributors. I think I am still as unsure of my views as I was when Phoebe asked me for them, before sharing her experience of taking her father to Switzerland for an assisted death.

Ellen, whose son died of pneumonia aged eight, said that she thought that the loss of a child was probably the worst thing one can go through. But there is an additional pain if that death is self-inflicted. Although it is no longer a crime, stigma lingers around suicide, with unanswerable questions, guilt, and sometimes shame as well as grief. Ellen told me that two in her Caring Friends group at one time had children who had taken their own lives, and some of the group objected.

> *'It got quite difficult and they stopped coming, because there was one lady whose daughter passed away and she got quite upset because these people's children had taken their own lives, and she was on the opposite side of the fence. Her child died not wanting to, theirs was self-inflicted.'*

This suggests that 'grieving with' involves someone who shares our experience in quite specific ways: for example not just having lost a child, but lost a child who did not choose to die.

J's son took his own life. She told me how hard the attitude to suicide is when it comes to telling people that her son killed himself. She is concerned for her listeners.

> *'After telling many people in one day, I learned how to be careful, to explain it slowly, so that they might, just before I tell them, guess what's coming, and survive the hearing of it. It is such an awful thing to tell, and shocking to hear, when it is suicide. And this doesn't go away. Each time you meet someone new, you know they will be very shocked. You are aware that it will be difficult for them to react, and you cannot be sure of their attitude towards those who kill themselves. It is anticipating the reaction that is most difficult. Though I have always been moved by the compassion shown.'*

In the past, when it was a crime, the coroner's verdict of suicide frequently added 'when the balance of his/her mind was disturbed.' This form of words no longer seems used: the stigma of mental illness is presumably greater than that of suicide. Yet suicide, even more than death, remains under an overwhelming taboo. Although it is no longer a crime, nevertheless those who kill themselves are frequently said to have 'committed suicide', as if it is still a crime: it is crimes that are 'committed'. Some contributors used that phrase. Suicide has not always carried stigma: in Roman times it was seen as honourable. In Shakespeare's 'Julius Caesar', act five, scene five, Brutus asks several of his companions to hold his sword while he runs on it, rather than be captured. Honourable suicide also was important in the past in Japanese culture.

According to the NHS website, suicide is 'The act of intentionally ending your life'. This website also list 'high-risk warning signs', which include threatening to kill themselves, talking or writing about suicide, and looking for a method, such as hoarding pills, as well as a long list of other signs. The Samaritans' link that comes up when one googles suicide gives a list of 'myths' about suicide, and tells the truths about them. One common myth is that those who talk about suicide don't do it. The reverse is the case. Another myth is that those who attempt and fail are unlikely to try again, it is said to be 'just a cry for help'. The truth is that those who have attempted suicide are more likely than the rest of us to try again. Yet another popular myth is that there is nothing that can be done for someone who is determined to kill themselves, and that it is not a good idea to talk about suicide. But it is possible to help someone who is feeling suicidal: talking about death could be life saving. As with the whole subject of death, we need to break the taboo of silence surrounding suicide.

I was surprised that among this small sample of contributors, so many had experience of suicide. As well as J, Sarah's daughter attempted suicide; the nurse M's brother may have done so, it was an open verdict, as with Caroline's son; Annabel, another nurse, told me that there had been four suicides in her family; Jean, the carer, told me of a friend who killed herself.

> 'She read it up, she did a lot of research, and was in contact with people in other countries, about end of life and suicide. There was an organisation called Exit. I think she had a lot of contacts and she was very good at networking. She organised it very thoroughly, and because she was afraid of it not being successful she asked someone to be present. A veil was drawn over it, and, because she wanted to protect her friends and carers, the name of this person is unknown to any of us.'

Exit is an organisation founded in 1997 which, according to their website, 'Believe that it is a fundamental human right for every adult of sound mind, to be able to plan for the end of their life in a way that is reliable, peaceful and at a time of their choosing.'

Annabel, who has seen many deaths as a nurse, told me,

> 'Suicide is even more shocking because the person has made a choice to end their lives... I've had a lot of experience of unnatural deaths in my family including four suicides, so suicide is something I'm very conscious of. The present suicide rate is high, particularly among men, four times as high in men as in women, especially in men under 50... Suicide seems to run very strongly in some families. When I was younger I was very aware of a selfdestructive streak in me... I know that my sister has had a fascination with suicide when she is in a low place, so there is something in the family and that's slightly unnerving. My sister disturbs me, it feels like it's hovering there somewhere, it feels like a bit of a bug in the system somewhere. It feels like a trauma in

*the family system, like something unhealed, a festering wound or
something, something that needs healing...*

*'I think suicide is often around feeling deeply disconnected
both inside and outside. That's not a well state, because in the
well state you are connected, part of the whole. If you feel disconnected that seems dangerous, and I don't think that the world as
it is now, particularly in modern, Western culture is conducive
to connection, to us all being part of a bigger, healthier picture...
There is also unbearable pain, emotional pain, which makes
people commit suicide. If they are in very difficult circumstances
that they can't think of getting out of, that are so hideous, that
they feel they can't live; life feels it's so restricted, it feels like a
walking death.'*

Sam, the Samaritan, would agree with the need to feel connected:
she told me that one of her aims when talking to the desperate was
to help them to feel less alone. Connectedness is the subject of the
next chapter.

I wanted to speak to a Samaritan because I thought I might hear
how they would dissuade someone from choosing death, or at least
suggest how someone on the point of suicide might be induced to
change their mind. I was fortunate that Sam agreed, and had a very
important conversation with her. She told me that Samaritans respect
the individual's choice, which as I said in the previous chapter,
includes choosing to die.

*'Because that is embedded within everything that we do.
Ultimately it's an individual's choice as to what they do. That's
not what you want, but that's what the person has chosen, and
regardless of that you stick with them in that decision.'*

When I asked her about the theory and principles behind the
work of Samaritans, Sam answered without hesitation: 'I think being

non-judgemental is our main one. That's the biggest.' There was then a pause for thought before she went on,

> 'Open mindedness, there's a link there; an emphasis on creating a relationship with the caller, being empathic and using active listening is really important as well. Those are things which they stress from the moment you walk through the door... Some people who call who are feeling suicidal... can perceive it as being quite empowering. For example if they are in the late stages of a terminal illness, they've taken that choice when other choices have been taken away from them... it can be empowering for some.'

I said I supposed they rang the Samaritans because those caring for the dying person would not permit them to make that choice.

> 'Yes. Which is I think why they choose to call us in that situation. Of those I've spoken to in that situation, even if they are sure suicide is the right choice for them, it's still a scary thing to go through, there is a loneliness in death. I think a lot of people just want someone on the phone – to know there's another human presence there. I think it's up to that person to make their choice to have someone there if they want, in that capacity.'

This view of suicide as a form of empowerment surprised me, but seemed something that ran through more than one conversation. Sarah would have liked her daughter's choice to kill herself respected. She described the horror of the time shortly after her daughter's life had been 'saved'.

> '...and eventually a young doctor told me that the Glasgow Coma Score when she came in was 3, which I knew meant dead. So my husband and I spoke with the consultant and advised him that we didn't want her to be forcibly kept alive if she was going

to be severely disabled. We wanted to take her off the ventilator but he refused point blank. Whatever his reasons, if they were religious or otherwise, we'll never know. But there was one doctor who was incredibly kind and would pick me up off the floor and speak to me on my own. We didn't know that Imogen's consultant had activated a POVA on Imogen (protection of a vulnerable adult) and tagged her; we were then watched all the time when we were with her. We had no idea that this had happened and the sympathetic doctor was the only one who would speak to us without a witness being present. He would take me off into a room to talk to us and he showed us great kindness and empathy throughout the time Imogen was in the hospital. He advised us that the only thing we could do was to sign a nil resuscitation form. So my husband and I duly signed it, only to find that it had been overturned the next day by Imogen's consultant. He said that there was nothing we could do, she didn't have a living will therefore we had absolutely no rights, while she was "under his care". The previous evening as I waited by her bed I vowed: "I'm going to get you out of here and let you die peacefully at home," and that's when her consultant activated the POVA.'

Sarah's story is told in full in appendix two.

My own father also chose to die; he was more successful than Imogen, but his was not a good death. When prostate cancer spread to his spine, and he was unable even to move from his chair to the commode without help, he decided that death was preferable to a nursing home. So he stopped taking the digitalis that was keeping him, a lifelong smoker, alive. I only discovered this when the warden of his sheltered bungalow told me of it a couple of weeks after his death. As a doctor he should have known what death from heart attacks could be like. Then I wondered how many people he had seen die, as I watched him. Death for a doctor means failure, relegated to nurses, as the doctor moves on to someone they can cure. When he chose death rather than nursing home care, did my father fully understand what he was choosing?

Years before this, my mother may also have chosen to die. She died on holiday with a friend in Sicily, after a trip up Mount Etna on a donkey. Years after this I went to Sicily, in part because I wanted to see the island where my mother had died. Like her, our group was offered a trip (by Jeep) up Mount Etna. The guide explained how the trip would be organised and then said something like this. 'Who have problem of heart or lung, not to accompany us on this visit to our Mount Etna. Could be danger.' My mother had a problem of her lungs, she had had TB for years in the days before drugs for it had been discovered. Half her lungs had been removed, and she was always short of breath. I wondered if she too, was warned that the trip up Mount Etna could be dangerous. Her marriage had been unhappy for years, and she frequently said, 'I wish I was dead.' I chose to ignore this at the time. On that holiday in Sicily I thought of it again: I should have taken her seriously. Did she go up Mount Etna, knowing it might kill her, because she really wanted to be dead? I tried asking the guide if such a warning would have been given fifteen years before. He did not understand me, or why I needed to know, only saying, 'my island no kill your mother.' Like many others, including Caroline and M, I will never know if my mother, like my father, chose to die.

The coroner's verdict on Caroline's son was inconclusive. Caroline said,

'It wasn't a conscious act, but he was taking himself on that route with acute alcohol abuse, so we had a long period of the chaos of that before it ended in his death, so it was a trauma.'

M, a retired nurse, told of the death of her brother many years ago.

'My father rang, and said my brother's body had been found on the beach at Beachy Head. It had taken four days for his body to

be identified by his boss at work. He hadn't turned up for a work meeting, and he never let people down, this was before mobile phones, so they went to the morgue and asked if there were any unidentified bodies, and they said yes, and it was him. That was a massive shock for all of us. It was either an accident, or he was pushed off the cliff or he jumped. The inquest verdict was open. My parents couldn't even contemplate it being suicide, because they're Catholic and until recently RCs still felt that if you take your own life that is the greatest sin. It's now recognised that for someone to take their own life they must be seriously ill. If they see no way out of the situation they are in, dying isn't a problem, but living is, they can't cope with living. We don't know what happened.'

There are, unsurprisingly, many books written by those whose relatives have killed themselves. Jill Bialosky, in her book *History of a Suicide: My Sister's Unfinished Life* says that bereavement by suicide is the worst kind of bereavement. I am not sure that bereavements can be measured in this way; certainly Tom would say that they cannot. He said that the pain of miscarriage was no less than that of stillbirth,

'If we start grading things, giving them a priority, that's wrong, because it's still a loss, and a loss is a loss; for a short period of time you thought you had another child, and that's a loss.'

Tom quoted the Quaker testimony on equality, applying that to loss. There can be no measure of the pain of bereavement.

Loss, like death and grief, is profoundly individual. Some relatives of suicides have written movingly on trying to understand this, perhaps the most inexplicable of actions. Tim Lott in *The Scent of Dried Roses* and Jeremy Gavron in *A Woman on the Edge of Time: A Son's Search for his Mother* both describe having lost mothers to suicide, search for a reason, but can never finally know. Ted Hughes's

Birthday Letters, published long after the death of his wife, the poet Sylvia Plath, attempts to make sense in poetry of his feelings of guilt at her suicide.

Carol O'Brien, in an article in the *Independent* in 2014, tells of a unique charity, the Maytree, which is a sanctuary where those feeling suicidal can go and stay for up to four nights and be supported, 24 hours a day, 365 days a year, to share their pain and be helped to find a way, other than suicide, to cope with it. Unfortunately Carol O'Brien did not find this charity until after her son's death by suicide. Once again, the solution includes talking, and listening.

Carol O'Brien writes that it is impossible to help someone to see that life is worth living, if they are certain that it is not, but that, for most, suicidal feelings are temporary; however, the suicidal need support to get through this time, when they feel a dreadful isolation. In a programme on BBC 1 in 2015, entitled 'Life After Suicide' relatives of those who have killed themselves talked of their unbearable pain. They told us that those who take their own lives do not in general want to die, but do want the pain to end. This seems the only way for that to happen. The message of the programme is that you can rebuild your life after suicide, but only with support and talking about it. The programme showed bereaved people sharing their grief at a meeting of the group Survivors of Bereavement by Suicide, SOBS: they found others to grief with.

The lawyer Michael Mansfield, whose son killed himself in 2015, inaugurated an organisation, The Silence of Suicide, to try and combat the taboo around suicide, to make sense of the motives that lead people to kill themselves, and bring compassion to those left behind. Like death itself, suicide is a subject about which we must be willing to talk, and to listen, for the sake of the living.

For some, for a wide variety of reasons, death, not necessarily by suicide, may be the right choice. There are many reasons why people

194 | The Undiscovered Country

might accept the view of Death, rather than the Maiden, that he is 'a friend, hath ne'er distress'd thee.'

Advanced Directives or living wills, made long before we are dying, enable us to say how we would like to die, and if there are any procedures we do not want to have to enable us to live perhaps just a little longer. We are now being urged by the NHS to make these directives, so that choosing death becomes acceptable: a rational decision in some circumstances. This should enable more of us to die as we wish, and make it possible to refuse treatments more easily. These directives, although not legally binding, are increasingly being followed, but relatives as well as medical staff need to know what we want.

Advanced Directives came up in several conversations: Phoebe made one after taking her father to Switzerland. Imogen, who tried to kill herself, did not have one, and Sarah, her mother, said, 'my friends have all advised me that our tragedy and the subsequent decisions made against our wishes, have prompted them to take out an Advanced Directive, because none of us knows what could happen when/if we go into hospital.' E told me how useful she finds them in her work at the Welcome Hospice, where she helps people to fill out the forms issued by the local NHS Trust. These are quite lengthy, more of a booklet.

'Sometimes when I go out and talk to people about the book, unless they've got a medical procedure they don't want to opt into, then it's more about opening up those conversations within the family, which is great.'

She talked about one woman who had six daughters and a long-term boyfriend whose opinions the daughters did not value.

'We actually just left the book in the house and it made for some very useful conversations between them about what was needed, what was wanted, what feelings were.'

The GP was enthusiastic about Advanced Directives and said:

'An Advanced Directive is incredibly helpful. You can refer to that and do it together with the family... So you have to help people to make the decision, but not make the decision for them, and that is quite hard.'

This reminded me of the days, long ago, when my father was a doctor, and people would talk about 'doctor's orders', and do as they were told. Today we have choice, and we need to use it.

The GP had heard Atul Gawande, surgeon, Reith Lecturer and author of the book *Being Mortal*, speak at a local literary festival. She told me that he had suggested useful questions that might be asked to open up the conversation, to get patients to a place where they are happy to talk.

'So you say something like "What do you understand about your illness?" Then they can tell you where they are at with it, and you can maybe push a bit further. You may find they are nowhere near understanding, so you roll back a bit. Then you ask what are the important things to you about living for the next however long. You try to understand. For some it might be very important not to go into hospital, for another it might be to live long enough to see relatives from Australia.'

Atul Gawande writes that intensive medicine has failed: those referred to palliative care live 25% longer than those in intensive care at the end of life. He writes passionately about making the end of life meaningful, living to the very end, doing what makes your life worthwhile to you.

Hannah, retired nurse, said

'The tendency is to prolong life at all costs, without establishing with the individual if they would prefer to have a nice day now,

or endure another procedure so that they might have a nice day later.'

I said that I thought Atul Gawande said much the same thing. She had heard the same talk as the GP.

'He is saying what I was saying 25 years ago. But he's a very gifted writer, a medic so he's respected in his own right as a medic. He embodies his Eastern roots, although he grew up in the United States. His grandfather lived to be about 105 in his village of origin, and was looked after by his family until his death. Gawande was very clear that the old ways meant the enslavement of family members, usually the youngest daughter. He's not advocating we go back to that, but he is saying that we are not there yet in terms of how we do care for the elderly frail in the West.'

Paul, a death café regular, said,

'I'm currently reading 'Do No Harm' by Henry Marsh. As he is approaching retirement, his attitude to when it's appropriate to surgically intervene is changing. Especially if it's repeated; is it worth doing something about this tumour, especially if it's only going to extend life by a matter of months? How useful, how valuable is that?'

Henry Marsh, CBE, a leading brain surgeon, is another medic, who feels that there are more important things than living as long as possible, whatever the cost. He tells us that to be human is to be limited: our lives are precious because they are finite.

Both Atul Gawande and Henry Marsh, like the GP, Hannah and others, stress the importance of living until one dies, even if this means that one dies slightly sooner: it is quality of life not its quantity that matters. We need to make our views known in Advanced

Directives, and in talking with our families. Paul said it was not just medics who want to keep people alive for as long as possible.

'Sometimes it's aided and abetted by relatives too... The medical profession is becoming more troubled with the way medicine has developed, but it starts out from a good place wanting to keep people healthy, alive.'

Jennifer Worth in her book *In the Midst of Life* tells poignantly of being locked out of the resuscitation department when her mother was dying, because the process is so brutal. She pleads for less use of resuscitation, so that more can die peacefully.

Paul Kalanithi's book *When Breath Becomes Air*, mentioned in the previous chapter, is endorsed by Atul Gawande on the front jacket, and on the back by Henry Marsh. Unlike these authors, Kalanithi is writing about his own death from cancer; as he had a baby daughter at the time, it is understandable that he was willing to endure anything that would give him the chance to share even a little more of her life.

Taking one's own life and making an Advanced Directive can both be empowering; some want to go even further, and be assisted to die, or have assisted dying. One cannot state in an Advanced Directive, 'I would like to be given a lethal injection when intractable pain becomes unbearable.' This is not only against the law, but many doctors (including the GP I spoke with) would find it impossible to do: doctors save lives. This is not even possible in Switzerland, where the person who wants to die has to be able to pick up and drink a lethal, and, I gather, extremely unpleasant, dose. In fact it is so unpleasant, that patients first have to take medication that will prevent them vomiting it up. The patient must not only know what they are doing, but still be physically able to put a cup to their lips and to drink.

Before she told me of her experience in taking her father to Switzerland to die, Phoebe asked me for my views on assisted death.

I was slightly uncertain. I said I believe in choice, but I did not think I would choose it for myself. Certainly not if it meant going to Switzerland. I had seen a TV programme on this, and said I thought the Dignitas clinic came over as rather cold, like a hospital death. Phoebe soon put me right:

It's not a clinic at all, not a hospital, it's just a living room in a house. And there were two people accompanying, who were the most compassionate, warm, loving people you could wish for.'

Since 1961 we no longer imprison those who try to kill themselves and fail. Today we have more sympathy with the suicidal, but it is still illegal to help people to kill themselves. Which is why, when Phoebe returned from Switzerland she found the police in her mother's flat. She told me about it:

'I knew that we satisfied all the criteria not to be prosecuted, but when we came back we found the manager for the housing association had let the police into my mother's flat. That was a very difficult time for us...this is the irony of the lack of a clear law in this country: the investigation can only take place after death, when its too late to do anything about it, if a person is being pressured. It causes enormous distress for the grieving family. It didn't last long, because there was no evidence suggesting that it wasn't done for compassionate reasons, but we could have done without that... at that time. It didn't bother us as much as you might think, we had half expected it and we felt confident that we met the conditions not to be prosecuted. Actually, if I had to go to prison I would still have done it, because I loved him and wanted to support him in his decision. But I knew that wouldn't happen, because I was so confident that what we did was OK, but also somehow that sense of peace and that sense of perspective, of what really matters was with me as well afterwards... it didn't

have as massive an impact as you might think, or I might have thought.'

The lack of clarity is due to the fact that, while assisting suicide is still illegal, the Director of Public Prosecutions has said that if this is done out of compassion there will be no prosecution. It is acceptable to take someone to Switzerland to die, but what Harold Shipman did is a crime. The GP said,

'Shipman has made us very defensive about those kind of conversations. It's made them more difficult; there's a feeling that we have to justify ourselves, and be very careful about the conversations we have, not to be seen to be hastening people's demise... He has cast a shadow, even to using morphine for people with severe pain; some people are very suspicious of that, so that is something you have to handle that very carefully.'

Euthanasia, where a doctor causes death either by administering a drug, or withholding treatment, is illegal in most countries apart from the Netherlands, Belgium, Ireland, Colombia and Luxembourg, and then only with safeguards including that the dying person has requested it. Assisted suicide, helping someone to kill themselves, is legal in Switzerland, Germany, Japan, Albania and some states in the US.

Sarah spoke of when her father was a consultant, and would help the dying to die peacefully; in his day Imogen's misery would not have been allowed to happen. She said,

'They were able to administer large doses of morphine, and, with the family's consent, to end a life which had become intolerable. It was just accepted, and people were previously not kept alive at any cost.'

Julie told me of one the first dying people she went to as a nursing assistant.

> 'The doctor came and said "Is there anything else you want?" and she said "You know what I want, doctor," and the doctor said, "I can't do that. If you were an animal I could take you to the vet, but we're not allowed to do that. But what I can say is that what will probably take you is what's in your syringe driver – we can't put that up because you ask for it, we can only put it up if you're still in pain," he said it very clearly, "or if you've got terrible anxiety – you know what I'm saying?'" "Yes." I had a chat with the lady and I said, "You understand what the doctor's saying? Basically tell the district nurse that you're still in pain or you're anxious. Because otherwise we can't put the morphine up." Otherwise they can't. I've never known a case where the drug in the driver has gone up by more than a small amount based on my clinical observations of pain and anxiety, so I've never witnessed a doctor do that. Nobody should have an end in pain, nobody should be in pain.'

John, the humanist, said,

> 'There's no doubt that doctors administer powerful painkillers to their patients knowing the effect will be not only the relief of pain, but also the shortening of life. This is recognised as the "double effect": as long as the sole intention of the doctor is not to hasten death, then it is likely the doctor won't get a prison sentence of up to fourteen years. If the doctor thinks (as does many a vet) "This suffering has gone on long enough, time to call it a day," there is a serious risk of the doctor being prosecuted.'

The UK bill that would have made it legal, in certain carefully defined circumstances, for a doctor to assist someone's death was defeated by a large majority in parliament in 2015. This despite the fact that the majority of the population are in favour of it. A Populus poll for Dignity in Dying in 2015 found that 82% of the population supported a change in the law; 79% of those who saw themselves as 'religious', and 86% of those who considered themselves 'disabled' also supported the bill. Around the time of the parliamentary debate there was much discussion of the topic in the media. Coincidentally this was the time that I was having the conversations for this book, so assisted dying came up more than it might have done at another time.

A local MP invited his constituents to a debate on the issue, with a representative from Dignity in Dying, who campaign for a change in the law, and Living and Dying Well, who are against a change. (Other groups campaigning include SOARS – the Society for Old Age Rational Suicide, which wants the law changed, and Not Dead Yet, disabled people opposed to this.) It was at this debate that I met John, who was an enthusiastic supporter of the campaign for a change. He later came and told me of the humanist view of death, as well as his reasons for favouring a change in the law. He said,

'Suicide is the result of wanting to die. Many people who wish for assisted death might say "I don't want to die, I love life too much. But I am dying and I want that on my terms".'

John quoted George Carey, the former archbishop of Canterbury, who said, 'There is nothing sacred about suffering, nothing holy about agony, and individuals should not be obliged to endure it.' He also told me something, which I think I had heard before, about the death of King George V.

'Many people know that when George V's physician (Lord Dawson) issued an evening bulletin stating, "The King's life is moving peacefully towards its close", Dawson could be sure his prognosis was accurate, because he was about to inject his royal patient with morphine followed by cocaine. The King died at

midnight, which meant the death was made public in newspapers such as The Times; for the king to expire later (say in the morning) there was a risk the public would have been informed by a tabloid such as the Evening Standard.'

Decca Aitkenhead in *All at Sea* reports that her mother, when dying of cancer, was given pills to enable her to choose when to die.

Julie said:

'You hear "You'd put a dog down," well you would, but maybe a few years down the line that might be something that's available to us humans, but that's a hard one to do, because they've had enough. My personal view is that when you've got to that stage you should be given something like morphine, which can allow the body just to stop. We're not talking about barbiturates with stomach cramps or anything like that, I'm just talking about putting the medication up over a 24 hour period to allow someone to be dignified enough to have their family around, if that's what they want, for them just to pass.'

M also compared the situation for people and animals. She said,

'As a Christian I should not believe in euthanasia, I don't agree with killing somebody who is suffering from a disease that they think is too hard to live with any more, and wanting to die, even though they could have many years of healthy living ahead, and I say that as someone who has had serious depression from time to time and who has thought of suicide quite a lot. I don't believe it's right to end somebody's life unless they are dying, but I do feel that there are too many people who are just kept alive for as long as possible, for the sake of I don't know what. It's as if living is sacrosanct, you must live as long as possible.

'But if somebody's quality of life is zilch because they're lying in bed, they can't feed themselves, they're in pain, they can't move

themselves, they need 100% care and they are dying, and they know they are going to die in the next few weeks. I don't see why at that stage they can't be given something so that they can say farewell to their family and then go to sleep and die... I do wish there was some way that people who are really physically dying and do not have much longer to live, could be put out of that agony. It takes an enormous faith, I'm not sure in what, for me as a Christian it's faith in God, but for other people it's a different kind of faith by them to say, "No – I want to die now, I am ready, I just want to slip away and die." You wouldn't let an animal live in that sort of pain. I've only felt that way since I had a dog that had to be put down. It was the kindest thing to do.'

Nicola, the counsellor, who had told me of Phoebe's experiences, and put me in contact with her, said,

'Assisted dying should be available in this country for people who are already suffering. I'm definitely in favour of it.'

The bill, defeated in parliament in 2015, would have permitted assisted suicide only with important safeguards, including that the person wanting to die should be terminally ill, and not expected to live more than six months. Phoebe's father would not have qualified in this country had the bill passed. He was in the early stages of Alzheimer's Disease, which did not disqualify him in Switzerland, where one does not have to be terminally ill. But he had to go when he still knew what he was doing, and not suffering from depression. Phoebe told me,

'He knew absolutely what he was doing, because it was the early stages. He went through very thorough psychiatric examinations. He still knew what was happening when he went. If he had not known, Dignitas would have sent him straight home. You have to go while you still have sound judgement.'

This stipulation means that those in Phoebe's father's situation have to die before they are really ready to do so, because if they wait until their quality of life is such that they don't know what they are doing, they no longer qualify. Sarah said,

'People would have a longer happier life knowing that there was a painless and efficient way out at the end. It seems that, in this country, we treat animals better than we treat people in terms of a good death.'

The prime aim of Dignitas is to save lives that can be saved. Phoebe told me,

'There was one piece of research that showed that of the people who get the provisional green light, (which means that the doctors have looked at all the medical records and the psychiatric reports and said that this person is eligible for an assisted death, subject to two satisfactory medical assessments when they arrive in Switzerland) only 30% actually go over there. Just the knowledge that they can is reassuring, that's one of the reasons I'm so supportive of a change in the law.'

Phoebe also told me that it costs thousands of pounds to travel to Switzerland and have a Dignitas death, so it is not an option open to all. She added,

'But I read that Dignitas help those who can't afford it. But that's why the law needs to be changed in this country, because at the moment it's only available to people who can afford it. I really feel it should be available in this country.'

Desmond Tutu was quoted at the Bristol Museum exhibition on the right to choose, saying that while he revered the sanctity of life, he would not want his own life prolonged, and wouldn't mind assisted dying.

Simon Binner (in the television programme mentioned in the previous chapter) chose to go to Switzerland to die, although his wife disagreed and initially said she would not go with him. She changed her mind when he tried unsuccessfully to hang himself, which she thought was even worse. His death, surrounded by his wife and mother, sounds very similar to Phoebe's father's: dissolving into love. It contrasted strongly with that of Paul Kalanithi, who ended his days in the intensive care ward of a hospital, but refused a ventilator, which would have kept him alive a little longer, and died with his baby daughter in his arms. Neither were able to die at home, which I suspect both might have preferred. Love surrounded both deaths, both tragically early in life.

Those opposed to a change in the law often talk of a 'slippery slope' that leads from the right to die to the duty to die, perhaps for the convenience of relatives. The disabled are frequently cited as those who might be prematurely dispatched had the bill passed. But the Dignity in Dying poll showed overwhelming support for the bill among this group, suggesting that concern for them by others is misplaced, possibly 'disablist'. Disabled people deserve the same autonomy as the able bodied. However, none of the contributors to this book was, as far as I could tell, disabled.

The reasons given by contributors who were against a change in the law were mostly rather different from the slippery slope argument, and more spiritual. For Swami S, of the Hospice of the Community of the Many Names of God, it was so that the soul could receive the grace he had seen his father receive as he died. He said,

'There's been a lot of talk about assisted dying. To anyone who had walked into that situation, seeing my father very distressed saying, "let me go, let me go, let me go", that was somebody who had 24 hours to live, perhaps 48, clearly he was someone who would fall into the category as eligible for assisted dying: someone who at the outset was able to express themselves, was able to say,

"I've had enough, I don't want to live any more". But if someone had come in and administered morphine to kill him, he would not have received that grace.'

I asked if he was suggesting that assisted dying might make a good death more difficult, or impossible. 'Yes, I strongly suggest that.'

Assisted dying did not come up in my conversation with Father P, but as a Catholic, who takes the traditional line, I knew he must be against it. It did not come up with either B, the Buddhist, or C, the Rudolf Steiner priest; again I suspected they would probably not be in favour of assisted dying. Both described a slow departure of the soul, or the mind, from the body. I emailed Father P, B and C, to ask how their faiths considered assisted dying. B said that in view of the Buddhist conception of the mind taking so long to leave the body, no Buddhist could accept assisted dying. She emailed:

'My sense is that most Buddhists would feel that it would be wrong – or at the very least unwise and misguided – to delib-erately hasten their own death. Death is seen as a profound spiritual opportunity and gateway. Suicide is, of course, always very difficult. But those who take their lives in this way are often so troubled in their minds that they are not making clear or wise decisions. In those circumstances this is then viewed with love and understanding. On the other hand to take your own life with a clear mind is a very grave act.

'Whilst I have no wish to impose my particular beliefs on others I am deeply disturbed by the idea of a change in the law which would allow assisted dying. My objections fall into the 'thin end of the wedge' arguments. Whilst supporters of change say that this would only be allowed in the most carefully explored circumstances, and I am sure they believe this, I think it is a dangerous move. It shifts the boundary of the preservation of life – who knows where it may lead. We know that many people

at the end of life feel they are a burden. We also know many old people are treated badly and, indeed, may be exploited. The subtle shift in national thinking would make all this worse. Our efforts as a caring society should go into improving end of life care not shifting the protection of the law.'

C replied to my email that she would like to come and talk again. The question of assisted dying was not something she wanted to comment on in an email. She said that there was no 'official' anthroposophical teaching or dogma. Each one should use the principles of anthroposophy as an aid to their understanding of questions concerning life and death, and then decide for themselves.

'We need to understand the purpose of life, which includes suffering, pain and death. Suffering, pain and death all have meaning in our lives.'

In an echo of what Swami S had told me about the death of his father, she said 'if a life is cut short, it may not fulfil its destiny and the challenges an individual needs to meet in their life in order to grow and develop will have been missed.'

Father P emailed,

'To do justice to this very important subject I would need to do quite a bit of reading and reflecting. I am clear about the general position of the Church, but the different views on assisted dying spring from fundamentally different views on the meaning of life; whether our existence here on earth is part of a larger reality; whether we are just organisms which come into existence and then die and cease to exist etc. And I would want to have the whole context clear in my mind before I could do justice to the Church's position. Unfortunately I am rather snowed under at the moment and will not be able to do the reading and thinking.'

Another powerful argument against change is that doctors would not be willing to assist.

The GP said:

'I think for me it just feels too much: I wouldn't want to be that doctor. Although I do feel quite strongly that we should make decisions not to extend lives that are of very poor quality, I don't feel comfortable with that at the moment. Although I have total sympathy with people who do, and have admiration for people who do help in that situation. But that couldn't be me... There are a lot of doctors, like me, who are in favour in principle, but wouldn't be the person to do it. There are a lot of concerns about coercion, or people making decisions for the wrong reason that make it very difficult. Most of the cases in the media are very clear cut, but it's never an easy decision to make. A grey area will emerge that will make it really hard. And the whole question of trust is difficult as well, that sense of having this dual role: how it that going to affect your relationship with your patient? So I'm slightly sitting on the fence in a way, but for people who have made that decision, and then have to go to Switzerland, that's a cruel thing as well.'

Talking of doctors in Switzerland and the Netherlands who were prepared to be the doctor to do it, the GP said,

'I admire them in a way... But there are a lot other things you can do in those circumstances where you don't actively strive to prolong life, without having to make that big decision about actually ending life.'

Hannah was also doubtful about assisted dying.

'I, Hannah, think it's dangerous stuff, it's sort of quick-fix mentality. I'm intuitively suspicious of it, because it could so *easily backfire and make things even worse. But that doesn't mean that I don't wholeheartedly agree that we need to care for, and have the services for, people who have life limiting conditions. There's massive room for improvement, that's what would make a difference. In a way it's a cop out, the assisted dying thing. It's not really addressing the problem, which is that people are not given enough support of the right kind to manage whatever they are being asked to manage at the end of life, or with chronic conditions where there is little hope of further medical help. This will require a cultural change, where everyone begins to take more responsibility for the dying process in their communities. What can be offered by health professionals of any kind is limited by many factors.'*

Annabel was similarly uncertain about her views on assisted dying.

'Let people do what they want to do, if that's somebody's journey. We're all so different. I can see why people oppose it, because where do you draw the line, often people feel they are a burden, people have to care for them and they can't stand it. I'm not clear about it myself, because the line is not clear, it could be abused. Beneath the radar people do it anyway. Doctors will help somebody along without it looking criminal. There are a lot of sticky ends around it. Nothing is clear cut.'

Hannah suggested that palliative care is actually assisting the dying:

'You could argue that this is what good palliative care could be. If assisting someone to die means assisting that person to die with dignity, then just as a midwife will assist a woman in labour, you offer support for someone to die. But that does not mean that you're making interventions that are out of step with the natural

course of things. You can ease, you can relieve pain, there's a lot you can do that assists the dying process. You can comfort, make sure their spiritual beliefs are taken into account, but it has to be live, happening in real time. The only real problem is lack of communication.'

When Dylan Thomas urged his father not to go gentle into that good night, did he not want palliative care for him?

Once more communication is the key. Is lack of communication all that prevents the dying being assisted to die with the law as it stands? In all the three types of choosing death that came up in these conversations, communication and empowerment seemed important themes. If, as many of these conversations suggest, death is not be feared, may, indeed be welcomed, then we need to listen to those who, for whatever reason, choose death. Contributors expressed different views, particularly about assisted dying, but there seemed to be a broad consensus that choice should be respected. Perhaps the most important thing is to respect the individual as an individual until the very last moment of their life, as hospices strive to do: to ensure that we all live until we die.

*   *   *

The Laws of Biology End Here

Inside me
Is a black hole, a vacuum
Sucking light and strength
Sucking from anything
Fool enough to enter my orbit

Inside me

Is an iceberg, a glacier
Freezing my life
Freezing my energies
Preventing me from thawing my numbness

Inside me
Is a maggot, a canker
Eating my mind
Eating my feelings
To bloat itself by shrinking me

Inside me
Is a spark, an ember
Trying to burn
Trying to survive
Trying to get out
To make me human again

(Yanna Gunn)

9 Oned in death

No man is an island,
Entire of itself,
Every man is a piece of the continent,
A part of the main.
If a clod be washed away by the sea,
Europe is the less.
As well as if a promontory were.
As well as if a manor of thy friend's
Or of thine own were:
Any man's death diminishes me,
Because I am involved in mankind,
And therefore never send to know for whom the bell tolls;
It tolls for thee.
(John Donne, Meditation xvii Devotions upon Emergent
   Occasions)

This chapter was to have been called 'Involved in mankind', in the
words of John Donne. However, while writing it I came on a book on
meditation by an unknown mystic dating from around 500 AD called
*A Book of Contemplation the which is called The Cloud of Unknowing,
in the which a Soul is Oned with God.* I was immediately struck by the
word 'oned'. Like J's use of grief as a verb, when she wanted someone
to grief with over the death of her son, it uses the word 'one' as a verb,
which somehow seems to be much stronger than saying 'made one'.
We are more than 'involved' in mankind, we are oned.

For Swami S, of the Community of the many names of God it was
oneness that he experienced at the death of his father:

'An amazing meditative oneness... everything was just one beautiful harmony, unity and oneness in the room'.

In this this chapter I will look at what contributors said about how we are oned in death, through love. Death makes all one.

Caroline, whose son might have killed himself, and Annabel, the retired nurse who said there had been several suicides in her family, both used the word connection, to describe a healthy society. Disconnection, Annabel said, can be one of the causes of suicide; for Caroline and for Pammy, organiser of the death café, it is our disconnection from nature that makes us unwilling to contemplate death. It was through a new connection to the human race, that some contributors seem to have found a life after death, a way to go on living after bereavement. For most of them this seemed to involve some form of service to the wider community, whether organising a group for bereaved parents (Ellen) or a poetry group for older people (J) or becoming a bereavement volunteer with Cruse (R): all these found themselves involved in mankind, or oned, in new ways. Hospices enable those nearing death to be oned with a group, through which they may blossom.

Accounts of near death experiences (NDEs) suggest that at death, as we lose our connection with the living, we may find new connections. For SA it was his connections with the living that decided him to return to his body to live after his NDE; other accounts suggest that it is connections with those who have died, that sent them back to life. Ellen's mother met her grandson (Ellen's son, who died of pneumonia) who, in her NDE, told her it was not time for her to die.

In her email to say that I could use what she had said, Corinna, the doula, wrote,

'What is interesting to me is that what you are doing is a way of bringing people together, not literally like meeting at a party,

but you bring peoples' experiences and their humanity together...
perhaps dying is a social act?'

I was puzzled at the time, saying only that this was something I would have to think about; but after many more conversations I think I know what she meant. Even if we want to be alone as we die, we are not alone. Perhaps at death we leave one set of connections for another.

B, the Buddhist, talked of the Buddhist concepts of interdependence, or connection.

'We are all profoundly interconnected with each other and with all of creation. The living and the dead. So a lot of suffering is about thinking that we're alone, that we're separate, and during the dying process all those you are connected to can help you on that journey. So it's really important for Buddhist practitioners to pray for people who are dying and have died. That is about their connections: so it's not prayer in the sense of prayer to a God who will step in and help, it's a prayer about connecting with those enlightened energies, and your connection with that person to help them on their journey... As Buddhists one of our main duties is to pray for people who are dying, who may have connections to our compassion.'

This sounded reminiscent of Jung's collective unconscious, and B confirmed that Jung had taken a great interest in Buddhism. I also wondered if this might explain the experiences some people report of being aware that someone has died, even though they were not with them at the time, or did not even know they were ill. B said, 'I've had that experience, and people often feel more connected to somebody in the immediate aftermath of their dying... it's more a real feeling of connection with that person.'

Annabel, reported such an experience when a close friend died:

'I wasn't able to be there when she actually died (I saw her the evening before) but early in the morning I had a clear sense of a visitation from her. When she actually died she came to me and I felt it very strongly; I felt that my whole body opened up to something completely other. It was love really and I knew that it was her. It was very memorable and touched me very deeply.'

Annabel also told me of someone she had done massage for, who died at the age of 97,

'I felt that the essence of her came back to me after she died, when I was in contemplation and remembering her.'

Anne had a similar experience after the execution of her death row pen friend, which I reported in chapter three. She spoke of a peace that came over her,

'It was like a soft glow. I had a knowledge that he was there and was OK: he was at peace.'

Caroline said,

'I also have very intense experiences of my son's presence: it wasn't memory, he was there, absolutely there. I remember the first Christmas after he died, I wasn't thinking of him, I was on my own in my bedroom opening a few presents and suddenly I knew he was in the room. It was like he was saying to me, "You didn't think I wouldn't come on Christmas day, did you?"'

J said that the bereaved have to find ways to reconnect and live with the person who has died. After his suicide, 'T [her son] had to become part of me in a new way.'

A poem by Caroline expresses this beautifully:

The qualities you had
That I loved

Are slowly, silently
Finding their gentle way
Into me
And I am glad.

GKP, the Hindu, spoke of how all faiths are seeking the same thing, connection:

'We keep creating separation. You have various prophets, Mohammed, Jesus, thousands of them, they all came to show us that there is no separation, and what we end up doing is wor-shipping that person, that creates separation... For me we are all human beings and we are searching for the same thing: we want to understand, and who doesn't want to live in harmony?... a sense of oneness with everything, that's the essence of who we are.'

Shelley writes something very similar in his poem 'Adonais', a lament for the death of Keats, part of which is quoted at the end of chapter seven:

The One remains, the many change and pass;
Heaven's light forever shines, Earth's shadows fly;
Life, like a dome of many-coloured glass,
Stains the white radiance of Eternity.'

Rosie, who attended William Bloom's course on preparing for death, recommended, among other books, one by Ervin Laszlo she was reading where he said that humanity came from a oneness, oneness with the earth.

'I'm a very keen fan of Lazlo – he writes a lot about how we're all connected. I've just read a book of his called "The Immortal Mind"... somebody, a near relative of someone who's died, comes and speaks to you.'

Iain, from the Scottish hospice, said,

'We all try to help each other, which is a good thing... It's good to come together, we've all got something in common so that's a good starting point, we're all in the same situation, in different degrees, but we are all there for the same reason... [When he first went to the hospice] I was not in a good position at all, I was very ill. In a bad place. The hospice has helped in very many ways, with medication, helped me understand my illness, manage my pain... I keep my fingers crossed, and hope they'll let me keep on coming. I get so much from attending each week. when I'm there it takes my mind off what's wrong with myself for a while, instead you think of other people.'

Nicola, the counsellor, recommended a novel, *The Universe versus Alex Woods* by Gavin Extence, which is the story of a 17-year-old taking a terminally ill and reclusive old man to die in Switzerland. It is sad and funny. Alex remarks how 'Mr Peterson's' life became more sociable when he needed carers.

While we may need to be alone at the actual moment of death, dying alone is not seen as 'a good death.' Christine, the artist, said of her brother's death, 'I did feel he was alone, and I didn't think that was right... he had to face it on his own. That was a bad death.' Sam said of calls she took in her Samaritan shifts,

'The ultimate aim for me is to alleviate that sense of loneliness for a short while: so when they finish the phone call, they feel they've been understood, that someone is trying to share their experience as much as they can, for a short time....there are lots of lonely people out there in all different walks of life, who feel no one listens to them, and I think that doing this they have somewhere to go to. The communality of issues and feelings about death that

I've come across in all those walks of life is very similar, and that's said a lot to me about human experience.'

It is to save people from dying alone that she, and all Samaritans, stay on the phone to be with those who are determined to kill themselves.

B said,

'A lot of suffering is about thinking that we're alone, that we're separate; during the dying process all those you are connected to can help you on that journey.'

This sense of oneness in death is expressed in the beautiful song, *John O' Dreams*, written by Bill Caddick to a tune by Tchaikovsky.

When midnight comes and people homeward tread
Seek now your blanket and your feather bed
Home comes the rover, his journey's over
Yield up the night time to old John O' Dreams.

Across the hill, the sun has gone astray
Tomorrow's cares are many dreams away
The stars are flying, your candle is dying
Yield up the darkness to old John O' Dreams.

Both man and master in the night are one
All things are equal when the day is done
The prince and the ploughman, the slave and the freeman
All find their comfort in old John O' Dreams.

When sleep it comes the dreams come running clear
The hawks of morning cannot reach you here
Sleep is a river, flows on forever

And for your boatman choose old John O' Dreams
And for your boatman choose old John O' Dreams.'

(copyright Bill Caddick, Rough Music)

The sleep of death unites: it comes to us all, and in death all are equal, 'the prince and the ploughman'. We may fear the darkness, but get our comfort from Old John O' Dreams.

For Hamlet these dreams can be fearful, 'In that sleep what dreams may come?' And for Shakespeare's Prospero:

We are such stuff
As dreams are made on; and our little life
Is rounded with a sleep.'

Rosie told me of the dreams Jung had about death, and her own dreams,

'I do believe it is possible to have warnings in dreams... in so many of my dreams I have I'm either teaching or I'm in a class learning. It fits with where I'm at, where my soul is.'

On the edge of a small Cotswold town are two cemeteries: one dating from the nineteenth century, the other from the twentieth. The older of the two has two chapels, joined at the roof, one for those belonging to the Church of England, the other for non-conformists, neither now in use. And there are two entrances to the cemetery: one with fine wrought iron gates, wide enough to admit a horse and carriage; the other, hidden behind the chapels, out of sight, is narrow, wide enough only to take a handcart from the local workhouse, bringing the wretched to paupers' graves. It dates back to the days when death might have been spoken of, but rich and poor were at opposite ends of the cemetery, as of society. Ostentatious tombs for some, an unmarked grave for others. Yet those with and those without a headstone share the same Cotswold limestone. Paradoxically it was as such differences became less acceptable, and we were encouraged to believe that class had withered away, that death itself became a taboo subject.

The twentieth-century cemetery opened because the other was full, the old one is now a nature reserve. The new one has just one entrance, big enough for a hearse, accepting that in death we are all one. If our Victorian ancestors could not tolerate this in the way we do, they could accept death, in a way we seem unable to.

Today there are other very tangible ways in which we are one. About a week after my heart operation I woke up at around 3 a.m. as one tends to in hospital. I cannot now remember if these words came to me before or after I woke, but I do remember that I sat up and frantically looked for pen and paper to write them down before they disappeared, as mysteriously as they had appeared.

On surviving the operation

Because I did not die,
Two strangers continue to live in a world of darkness.
Another two more to suffer the half-life offered by dialysis.
All made poorer by my survival.

As I continue on my way through life
I must remember these,
And countless others, unknown to me,
Who await another's death.

How can I justify my place
In the great web of life,
Which we all share?

I must live this sacred life,

Each day,
Until I die.

Organ donation, mentioned in chapter two as one of the most practical reasons for talking about death, in that it could save lives, is perhaps the also most tangible expression of John Donne's being 'involved in mankind.' We are all diminished by another's death, but in the twenty-first century, unlike in the sixteenth, some may be made whole by it.

In the UK, unlike Singapore, Israel and a number of European countries, one needs to actively 'opt in' to organ donation. Unless we are on the donor register, or carry a donor card, it is unlikely that our organs will be used after our death. In December 2015 this changed in Wales, where, with certain safeguards, it is now assumed that a dying person is willing for their organs to be used, unless they have opted out of the system. After six months, it was reported that already dozens of lives have been saved: 60 organs were transplanted in that time, compared with 23 in the same period a year before. The BMA is in favour of a similar system in the rest of the UK, which could save even more lives. There is currently a move for England to follow Wales in this. We need to recognise that we are oned in life as well as death.

Julie, the Marie Curie nursing assistant, is sure her relatives will not prevent her organs being used when she dies. She called organ donation

'The cheap option...I give blood and I'm on the donation register. I had a heart to heart with my daughter, and said when I'm dead my body's no use to me. I call it the cheap option because if they take the whole body you don't have to pay for a funeral, and that's important, because her dealing with her grief is more important than whether they've got a cadaver. She said they'll

have a memorial service, they'll still have all that, there just wouldn't be a coffin.'

I asked B if the fact that it takes three days for a Buddhist's mind to leave the body would have any implications for organ transplants.

'I have heard eminent teachers say, very reluctantly, that that is problematic – because if the person who is dying doesn't have adequate compassion and the ability to let go, if they are clinging to their organs, then it can set up anger and real problems in their progress. There are others who say this is the summit of compassion, and of course we should encourage it.'

Increasingly more and more of our organs can be used to save others after our deaths, or in some cases, before we die. Some give one of their kidneys to save the life of a relative dying of kidney failure. Others even do this for strangers, just like blood, although it involves a major operation with all the attendant risks. Why? Because we are all part of something greater than ourselves: we are, in the words of John Donne, 'involved in mankind.' No one is an island, no one a stranger. As the Roman playwright Terrence famously said, 'Homo sum, humani nihil a me alienum puto: I am human, and nothing human is alien to me.' Even islands, somewhere in their great green deep, are connected, all one. We are oned in death and in life.

Richard Titmuss's book *The Gift Relationship* is a fascinating study of blood transfusion systems in different countries, which concludes that the UK system of free donation is superior to those where blood can be bought and sold. This is not only because of the quality of donated blood is better, as there is no temptation to those who should not give blood to do so for the money, but also, and more importantly, because of the relationship between the individual donor and the society to whom blood is freely given. This is the gift relationship: a recognition of our common humanity, something almost mystical.

Can this tell us anything about the mystical unity of death? We all share a common life, and a common death.

In his book *No Future without Forgiveness* Desmond Tutu writes about South Africa's Truth and Reconciliation Commission and explains the African concept of 'Ubuntu'. This is not readily translated into English, but is about the very essence of being human: a person is a person through other people. Ubuntu means being involved in mankind. Organ donation, and blood donation, seem the epitome of ubuntu, of our mutual interdependence, our oneness. Satish Kumar says something similar in his book *You Are, Therefore I Am*. The last chapter of this is a 'declaration of dependence', which starts with a quote from the Buddhist Thich Nhat Hanh, which suggests that the idea of our separateness is an illusion.

Are our lives a journey from separation to oneness? At birth we separate from our mothers' bodies, then gradually throughout our lives we learn to integrate with others to a greater or lesser extent. We may learn to listen to the sorrows and separations of others, perhaps learn to grief with them in their loss, perhaps we might be oned in grief. Mary Oliver's wonderful poem, 'Wild Geese' (in *Staying Alive* edited by Neil Astley) has a line about sharing grief. Perhaps it is through sharing grief that we become a person through other people.

For most, our journey takes place within a human family, which so frequently is the scene of our grief. Hospices care for families, as much as for the dying. The chaplain at the Welcome Hospice and Julie and others who care for people as they die, told me that the family around the dying person also needs their care and support, and to have the death process explained to them. Annabel said, 'The family dynamics around the dying process are also very individual.' She told me that suicide seemed to be something that runs in families, including in her own family. 'It feels like a trauma in the family system'. It is in the family that we learn to love.

Love is what keeps us alive: as tiny babies we were all once totally reliant on a parent's love to sustain us; when we die, we seem to need our loved ones to leave us alone, their very presence holds us to life. It is not only for food that as babies we rely on our parents, we need their comforting presence, their love. John Bowlby's seminal book *Child Care and the Growth of Love* showed that babies need love, that intangible, spiritual care, as much as food. They need to be, and to feel, attached. Bowlby has his critics, nevertheless his work has changed our understanding of what children need. Children who grow up in the care system, without secure attachment, sometimes appear to be unable to make attachments in later life, and to suffer from a wide range problems. They may not feel involved in mankind, as we need to be if we are to be fully human.

For Swami S as for Sister A, of the Community of the Many Names of God, love is the most important thing. Swami S said, 'Every human being has love within them, and that expression of spontaneous love is a manifestation of their divine nature.' Later, talking about care for those in the hospice, he said, 'You just treat them with deep love, and that vibration of love is something they can respond to.' He talked of those who are dying, troubled by the unfinished business and regrets of a lifetime, and said,

> 'If they come to a place of sanctuary, a place where they feel safe, a place where they are not judged, where all they encounter is that vibration of love, then that vibration of love starts to heal those unresolved issues. That creates a safe place for them to manifest and to be resolved, and to enable the person to transform that feeling into one of acceptance, and ultimately to one of freedom... love is a language every single human being can understand and can relate to.'

Love leads us to connectedness, to being oned. In chapter six 'a good death' was defined as 'dissolving into love'. This was Phoebe's description of the death of her father at the Dignitas clinic in Switzerland, and echoed by Sister Ally, who said the dying 97-year-old sister 'radiated divine love', which grew and grew as she was dying. Sister Ally spoke of the 'immense peace and stillness and freedom and love' that was palpable in her room. In her book *History of a Suicide* Jill Bialosky writes that no one is really dead if we go on loving them.

Isabel, of the Welcome Hospice, told me that it was often easier for those approaching death to talk to someone outside the family. The hospice supports the family, but at the same time it is a place where the patient can get away from family pressures. She said the hospice offers an 'opportunity to have deep and meaningful conversations about the end of life, if they feel the need.'

Corinna said that, as a doula,

'You work with the family because it's not just the one person, you work with the whole psycho-social context.'

Sister Ally told me of patient who had great difficulty in telling her family she was dying.

'Recently there was a lady who couldn't for a long time accept it. You'd say, "How are you?" and she'd say, "Great" – we'd think, "No, you're not". It was always an extreme reaction, which was difficult for her. There were a lot of things going on in her family – her mother didn't know she was dying. Finally she told her mother and after that there was an amazing release. Finally, she could admit – yes that's what's happening. It was very, very difficult.'

R told me of his training as a bereavement volunteer.

'One of the things you get from the training is the influence the death will have on family structures and family relationships. Actually I can speak from personal experience here as well. What

happens, much more than people realise, is that all the issues
you had within in the family before the death, all the concerns,
all deep-rooted feelings you might have are expanded like you
wouldn't believe at the time of the death – so if there was a dys-
functional family in the first place they will be even more so once
that person dies. And all those years and years of pent up anger
concerns, issues, whatever it might be, will become more acute,
will become critical at the time of death… sadly each death,
expected or not, impacts on a number of people in a family – not
just the spouses, it may be parents, child, friends even… talking
to people in terms of their experience of bereavement, there is a
heightened awareness of the issues that underpinned that family,
for generations undoubtedly.'

I asked R if his experience of being bereaved as a teenager helped
him to cope with his own children when his wife died.

'I don't know, it would be presumptuous to say, you'd have to
ask them. [I assured him I would not.] It's probably fair to say
that it can't have done any harm. When your own wife dies, you
are going through your own grief at the time they are grieving at
having lost their mother. A lot is going on at the same time, and,
as is invariably the case, the kids are going through adolescence,
or exams or all the hard things kids have to go through these
days, that's not a winning combination of events…I would have
sought some counselling had I known about it.'

Sarah told me of the 'immense pressure' put on the rest of her
family, by her daughter's survival from her suicide attempt. Caroline,
similarly, told of the problems the death of her son had had on her
other son. It sounded to me as if one can be oned with negative
energies as well as the positive.

Tom spoke of mutual family support after the death of his ex-wife,
who had had so many miscarriages as well as a stillbirth, 'We're very

much looking out for one another.' However, he felt he had not been able to support his wife adequately when they accepted the advice that she should have a pregnancy terminated as the scan showed spina bifida.

'Again my wife was very brave and I felt the lowest of the low and I just felt I'd failed people in the family at that point.'

Ellen told me that child bereavement destroys whole families. She has met many in this position over the years through her Caring Friends group.

'The number of relationship break-ups – it just completely demolishes your whole family. Very few marriages stay together – often you're just on different planets. Prior to my son passing away we had an ideal life, we both had good jobs, two children a lovely house, everything you could want, and all of a sudden one click of the fingers, and your whole life has gone. That's why life is precious.'

Iain told me of how he helped others at the Scottish hospice.

'We try to help each other, we've all got problems of some kind... but we all try to help each other, which is a good thing... It's good to come together... If they have someone coming in who's struggling, they ask me to help them out... I can talk to people about how they feel about coming. Sometimes people struggle with it, the first time, and a few times I've been able to talk to people about coming, how they feel, and make them feel confident, and it's good to come. So I can give back to the hospice some of what they've given me, they've helped me a lot. It's good I can do that.'

Similarly Swami S said that at his hospice,

'They can have a laugh, and be with other people who have similar problems and support each other.'

Rosa, the Jew who goes to the death café, told me of the documentary film *The Griefwalker* about Stephen Jenkinson, who said that what people are most afraid of before they die is that they won't be remembered. Those who mourn do not forget. Remembering those who have died is an important duty of the living. Each November the dead in two world wars are remembered. In Mexico there is an annual 'day of the dead', a public holiday with carnivals and jollification. I know that ancestors are important to Druids, but Nimue, the Druid, and I did not get round to discussing this. I emailed her later about this, and she replied,

'Ancestry is important to many Pagans. It's perhaps of greatest importance to people who follow shamanistic paths. But all Pagan traditions are to some degree inspired by what we know of ancestral practices, and that makes them very present in our lives, one way or another.'

Rosa told me of the importance in the Jewish tradition of remembering those who have died on the seventh and the thirtieth day after death, and thereafter on the anniversary, when a candle is always lit to burn for 24 hours. James, the undertaker, told me of how he saw his mother, after her death, as an ancestor.

'She was now an ancestor and she stood on the shoulders of her mother, and, and, and, and back into for ever. So that felt like an important thing to remember: ancestry and the experience of saying good bye to something, which is, after all, natural.'

Iain talked of his weaving and other patients' art work which they could give to relatives to remember them by after they died.

Jean talked of her mother's heredity.

'For me it's about passing on. When we were clearing out her bungalow (I'm not embellishing this at all) the last box of papers I tipped into the recycling container and thinking that's that – the last paper, and then a bit of paper fluttered down and landed at my feet, it couldn't quite make it through the slot. So I picked it up and it was a poem by Thomas Hardy called 'Heredity'. It's about what's passed on, the voice is heredity itself, heredity talking. And I thought it's all just coming together, isn't this amazing – coming together at my mother's death. So I felt poetry was a channel and I felt I was being channelled very powerfully.'

Heredity

I am the family face;
Flesh perishes, I live on,
Projecting trait and trace
Through time to times anon,
And leaping from place to place
Over oblivion.

The years-heired feature that can
In curve and voice and eye
Despise the human span
Of durance — that is I;
The eternal thing in man,
That heeds no call to die.
(Thomas Hardy)

The Welcome Hospice's chaplain told me of the moving ceremony, held just before Christmas, to remember all those connected to the hospice who died the previous year. The first Christmas after bereavement is always a difficult time for the bereaved. If we wish to live more fully as a result of contemplating death, as the Quaker Advice suggests, we need to recognise our part of the totality of human life, that we are 'involved in mankind'. As Philip Larkin says in the 'Arundel Tomb' (in *Collected Poems*),

'What will survive of us is love'

These conversations suggest to me that in a very real sense death brings oneness. It ones us. There is a deep longing in human beings to be part of mankind: we are social animals. To me, the conversations reported in this chapter suggest that death is not so much an end of relationships, as a moving on to new relationships and to total oneness.

* * *

My pen friend, who has been on death row for 30 years, currently in San Quentin Prison, sent me a photograph of himself and his sister in the visits room. They were in front of bars, like a cage in a zoo. He wrote in his letter, 'we live in cages.' He had ended a previous letter:

'Have a wonderful week. Smile and think of positive and beautiful things! Enjoy your freedoms! Don't take things for granted!'

Putting these two together the following came to me.

Caged

Behind bars. In cages.
Row upon row, they wait for death,
Humanity's rejected.
Behind bars. In cages.

The will to live drives them

To fight for years,
Against their deaths.
Some win, only to spend
Longer years
Behind bars. In cages.

Some lose. Drugs, electrocution
Put an end to their suffering.
Giving some victims some comfort in revenge.
But the world is poorer
With each death,
  as
Another family mourns one who no longer lives
Behind bars. In cages.

All life is sacred.
We all die a little each time
We take a life,
Or condemn our fellows
To live out their lives
Behind bars. In cages.

We who do not live
Behind bars. In cages
Must rejoice in the freedom
They cannot have, who live their lives
Behind bars. In cages.

They cannot feel
The sun on the face,
The wind in the hair,
See rainbows,

Watch snowfall.
All these are ours,
To savour for those who live their lives
Behind bars. In cages.

They are caged for us,
We must live for them.
For all are one, the free and those
Who live their lives
Behind bars. In cages.

10 In sure and certain hope

'A number of blind men came to an elephant. Somebody told them that it was an elephant. The blind men asked, 'What is the elephant like?' and they began to touch its body. One of them said: 'It is like a pillar.' This blind man had only touched its leg. Another man said, 'The elephant is like a husking basket.' This person had only touched its ears. Similarly, he who touched its trunk or its belly talked of it differently. In the same way, he who has seen the Lord in a particular way limits the Lord to that alone and thinks that He is nothing else.'

(Hindu version of a story that can be found in many
faiths).

When I first embarked on writing this book friends suggested people I might talk to, two of these were priests: Father P and C, respectively Catholic and Rudolf Steiner. They were some of my first conversations, and I was primarily interested in what they wanted to say about death, rather than about their faiths, although Father P could not separate the two. Early on I asked contributors if they thought having a faith helped in coping with death. There were different responses: some saying it made it much easier, others that they felt it made things worse. Christine, the artist, said her Christian faith was useless when her brother died; Ellen, too, lost her faith on the death of her son. M, nurse and a lay minister, said,

'I think for some it makes a huge difference, a massive difference… for Christians their faith is that strong that they can die at the right time.'

When I asked Julie, who looks after the dying with Marie Curie, if she thought if strong beliefs helped people when they were dying, she said

'I think that's very true. The Jehovah's Witness was quite at peace because she believed that when you die you're buried, that's where your soul or spirit stays until such time as Jehovah comes back; then everybody will be risen from the dead.'

Later I realised that I should include what other faiths have to say about death and its rites and rituals, for we now live in a multi-faith society. A friend said she thought this would really involve me in writing another book, rather than another chapter; I think she was right. But I decided to go ahead and try, listening to what those of the faiths had to tell me. Father P and C are both full time priests, and I also talked to the Chaplain at the Welcome Hospice, an Anglican priest, and Chris, a volunteer there who is also a lay reader in the Church of England. This, inevitably, means that I have far more on the Christian religion than on other faiths. Several of my contributors are Christians, M as well as being a lay reader herself is married to a vicar, and some had other faiths. I had a choice between scrapping the multi-faith approach, or justifying the lack of balance on the grounds that the UK is, officially, still a Christian country with an established church. I have chosen to do neither, I will simply report what I was able to hear. Some readers may prefer to leave out this chapter, others will know far more than I was able to learn about some or all of these faiths.

As well as the four Christians listed above I was able to talk to B, a Buddhist, who said she was in no way an expert, but was compiling 'practical suggestions to help Buddhists who are preparing to die in the West, where the Buddhist teaching on death is not widely understood'. I also talked with Nimue, a pagan, a Druid, who celebrates Pagan funerals; John, a humanist who celebrates Humanist funerals, and is currently Chair of his county Humanists; Kalsoom, a Muslim, who said she was not a scholar or an expert on Islam, but just an ordinary person who follows the Muslim faith to the best of her ability; GKP, who grew up in a Hindu family, so he is knowledgeable about Hinduism, but not a practising Hindu; and Rosa, who grew up in Israel, in a cultural but not a religious Jewish family. I knew Rosa through the Death Café, and she suggested that there were other Jews who might know more about the Jewish faith. However, I failed to find any willing to talk: I was referred to a Rabbi, who referred me to books. I decided not to go to books, as I would then feel I had to do this for the other faiths, and would indeed be writing another book. Inevitably this has meant that I learned less about Hinduism and particularly the Jewish faith than about the other faiths. This is simply the result of the way I have chosen to write this book.

I did not ask Swami S or Sister Ally about the faith of the Community of the Many Names of God, as I was there primarily to hear about their hospice, and they were both very busy, as were the other members of their community, but I attended most of their pujas (worship) over two days.

I have listed these contributors, and will report on their views, in what I think is their order of involvement with their faith, which is also the order of how much I learned from them. I will outline very briefly what I what I was told of each faith's beliefs about death, including funeral practices. In the following chapter I will look at similarities and differences, and consider how far the Undiscovered Country is revealed by faith. Some readers may be surprised that I have included John, the humanist, who says that there is no God; however, he seemed at least as sure in his belief as any of those with a religious faith; humanism includes the acceptance that there is no good reason to believe in gods, yet has an an ethic that is remarkably similar to that of most religious faiths, and an apparent need to spread that belief, or non-belief. All faiths have something to say about death.

Christian

Father P's thoughts about death were an integral part of his Catholic faith.

'When Christ died on the cross and rose to a new life, he established a new reality, and the whole of the New Testament is quite clear that Christ came that we might have eternal life with Him and His Father. The life we have here is a preparation for our homeland in Heaven – that's where we belong. Christ came to teach the human race what it means to love one another; to love somebody is to reach out and to become a bearer of life to that person, because God is love... Love of God and love of neighbour are inextricably linked. To live in Christ is to live more and more open to the Holy Spirit flowing through us to other people... [Christ] came and walked with us on this earth, and His journey leads to eternal life... And so there's this journey through life to the fulfilment of life which is the whole context of our view of death... Saint Benedict said in his rule "keep death daily before your eyes" which to some sounds morbid, but in fact it's reality, and in a good sense it's the day we meet the Lord in fullness, this is what we're here for.

'So to be a Christian is to be a bearer of Christ's life and love to others, and to be a bearer is to make Christ present, with the invitation and promise of eternal life... In the Catholic tradition those who have died are part of the body of Christ, as are those of us here on earth: we are all part of one body – so death is just the

transition from the life here to the kingdom of God, to the fullness of that life in Heaven.'

Speaking of funerals Father P said,

'If the funeral has been celebrated as it should have been, for the mourners it's been a rite of passage, when they emerge they are not in the same place as when they went in. There's always hope, somehow with the ritual they've been able to express something. It doesn't mean the grief is wiped away, the grieving has to take its natural course – but this has been a way of expressing something essential in their loss and their grief, it expresses both the loss but also a hope and a recognition of the reality. It's an end, it's a loss, but it's also saying it's not the end. So this is the shape of a Catholic funeral.'

He went on to tell me what happens when a monk died in the monastery of which he is a member.

'We are a group of monks, living together in the monastery. When one of the monks is sick, as far as possible, we nurse them in the community and when it is clear that he is near death we sit with them – the infirmarian is in attendance, but the rest of us take it in turns, and when it's clear that death is near the bell is rung and we gather with the abbot for the prayers for the dying. When a monk dies, we have to get a doctor and a death certificate, but basically the infirmarian washes the body lays out the body and the body is strapped to a board laid in an open bier, because we don't use coffins. When all is ready we go in procession from the sick room to the church singing psalms and anthems, and the body is brought into that part of the church where we sing the Divine Office seven times a day, the first one is at 3.30. We watch with the body day and night until the funeral... On the day of the funeral we have a solemn mass or Eucharist. Eucharist means

thanksgiving... The Liturgy is focussing on the person who's died, and at the end come prayers of committal: we pray for the person who's died just before we move off to the graveyard. We then process solemnly from the church to the graveyard, with the bell tolling and singing psalms and anthems. The monks will then say prayers, and they lower the body into the grave, after we've walked with him, watched with him. Then the infirmarian goes down into the grave and puts a cloth over the face, and then puts a turf on top, and then, while going on singing, we fill in the grave.'

He told me that some time ago families were invited to funerals at the monastery, but they found it too upsetting, because,

'In our society people just don't do death... The scrape of the shovel and the earth going in are part of the reality of burial, but a reality which is hidden away from most of us in our society... this is reality'.

Father P said the back-filling of the grave,

'Brings something home which we shut out from our society – this is reality.'

There is only one certain reality: one day we will die. Max Edwards, the 16-year-old dying of cancer, told us to get over it.

I wondered if it might also be the lack of a coffin that upset the family. Father P replied that this might contribute to it, but even with a coffin there is still the sound of the earth covering it up. He said that when he went to a crematorium he didn't like the way the curtains close at the end of the service:

'I felt "don't cut it off, we haven't finished the journey with them."... In the monastery, it speaks of the whole cycle, we walk with the person, say goodbye, we miss them, but through death

we pray for them. Prayers will be said for the first month, we have anniversaries and a day when we pray for all the dead, we have a list of members of the community who have died, some we knew, some going back to 1835, when the monastery was founded.'

I said that from films and plays I had the impression that unless a priest could be there to administer the 'last rites' a dying person could not go to Heaven, they would go to purgatory. Father P told me how wrong this idea was.

'No. What have been called the "last rites" are in fact the sacrament for the sick, one of the seven sacraments, and not only for those who are dying, it could be for someone in hospital. There are prayers for a person who's dying, anointing the sick and communion. If they are well enough they receive communion, it's called "viaticum" – "food for the journey".'

Anne, retired nurse, writer to prisoners on death row and Catholic told me,

'Neither of my children are practising Catholics, they know I want a Catholic funeral, and they know what I want. I'd like a place where people can go, and not just if they wish to say that's where the person's body is, though I want to be cremated. I've already said to my daughter, whose very good friend died, "you can always remember him, plant a tree that is in flower at the time he died, and you can remember him. That's what I would like, I'd like something beautiful over my ashes, could I be grand and say a chestnut tree? So every spring, and I love spring, it's my favourite time of year, every May the horse chestnut will come out – that's when you can remember mother; you get on with your own life."'

Most of my conversation with C concerned funerals in her church, the Christian Community, who follow Rudolf Steiner. She emphasised more than once that after death the soul goes on a long journey, taking many years and involving many stages.

She said,

'In our funeral ritual there are two parts: the first part takes place three days after death because that's how long it takes for the life body to leave the body of the person. At the end of those three days we close the coffin, an outward sign that the process has occurred. We say words that accompany the individual on that journey to the other side of the threshold between life and death. In those three days immediately after death we say that the person has a whole panorama of their life in front of them – many people who've had near death experiences describe something similar, "my whole life flashed in front of me"– that takes about the three days, and then the body is left behind completely, and the soul starts on its journey proper, which is a very long journey after death, and it goes into different stages of the life after death, the next stage lasts about a third of the person's life and that is what in traditional Christian terminology is described as purgatory. The funeral proper takes place any time after the departing blessing (the closing of the coffin).

'In the first part of our funeral service consecrated water is sprinkled over the body, and in the second part of the service con-secrated water is sprinkled over the coffin, which is also censed with incense. You could say they are both pictures of the process of the person who has died, the moving away. Perhaps the oft used phrase "rest in peace" isn't an accurate description of what happens in the life after death. Life goes on, just a very different form of life, and the incense helps carry up people's thoughts and prayers to accompany the soul on that journey.'

C was unwilling to share with me the actual words of the ceremonies, but took me through the funeral service:

'We have a funeral ritual the words of which are the same in every funeral. In the funeral service we speak of the soul and spirit of the person who has died. Of Christ who is with them on their further journey, assisting them on their journey. The Lord's Prayer is spoken and then we ask that this soul finds its way in the world of spirit. It is a journey on the other side, and as with any journey, you need some preparation and you need some help on the way. We believe that the funeral service gives some of the help that is necessary to the souls on the other side. In the middle of the funeral service the priest gives a eulogy, speaking about the life of the deceased. Towards the end of the service consecrated water is sprinkled over the coffin and then the coffin is censed. Some of the final words speak of the need to remember our relationship to the spiritual world, because of course we can forget that so easily, we are so caught up with our life on earth that many people don't think about death and beyond death.'

My conversation with the Chaplain at the Welcome Hospice was mainly about her role in the Hospice. She also told me of some of her problems as a Christian Chaplain within an organisation that is not aligned to any faith. Volunteers at the hospice told me that she was always prepared to talk to anyone who wanted to talk about their death, or their faith. She said she tries hard not to impose her views on them. She always wears her dog collar, to make it clear that she is a priest, but introduces herself with her name and saying,

'I come as a friend. I'm part of the volunteer team. You can see that I come as a priest, and I'm really interested to get to know you, you are very welcome. Would you like to tell me something about yourself?

'Many say, "I'm not a bit religious," to which I reply, "that's fine. I'm here for those who have a faith and for people who don't. I'm here to be a friend, and someone you can talk to about anything."

About seven out of ten people who say they have no faith, come round to discussing the spirituality which they have... Others say "I'm really glad to meet you, I'm a Christian, or whatever, and I go to whatever church." And I will say "I'm here for prayer, and there is a quiet room we can go to if you would like to talk." Some patients are so exhausted by the effort of going to the hospice, I will pray with them in their chair. Other patients are aware of this and it hasn't caused offence. If they are very distressed then we try and take them into a quiet room, which is a much easier environment, but I don't push that...

'I played cribbage with one man because no one else knew how to play cribbage, and that was the game he used to play. We played for two weeks, and the third week he was late coming in and he was much weaker, and I said "you look very tired today. Would you like to play cribbage or would you just like to sit and I'll sit quietly with you?" And he said "the only reason I've come in today is for my game." To me, I was the face of Jesus at that moment, but we didn't talk about religion, because he didn't have a faith. But I felt I loved him to the end... Sometimes it may be someone wants help with thinking about a funeral, that's the best lead-in I get into discussing their spirituality.'

She told me of another patient, who gave her great joy.

'A lady said, "I wanted to tell you that I have found my faith again." Hallelujah! I asked her to tell me about it... "I remembered back to my younger days, when I used to have a faith, but you get very cynical when life throws things at you, but I've re-found my faith." I said "Shall we pray?" and she said, "I'd like that." I came away six foot taller. '

She told of an unhappy experience at the annual memorial evening for those who had died.

'We have a long, long list of names, gentle music, children from local schools come and sing carols, and there is an act of remembrance where families can write messages on cards and hang on a tree, and light a candle. I read out the names with the other chaplain, every name, with space between so that you give dignity to that moment. There might be 120 – 130 names. Then a period of quiet afterwards, followed by a time of fellowship with mulled wine and mince pies upstairs for those who want to stay. There is a prayer, the serenity prayer, that is used and is acceptable. But the first year I did it, I blessed the people present, and someone complained that the evening was too religious, and didn't take account of those who were not religious. So last year I did not use a Christian blessing. We have to be there as an organisation for those with no faith; we must not be overtly Christian. That was a little sad, and difficult for me. But perhaps I'm being selfish. I can bless people quietly and I know that God will hear. It's very gentle, not a service but an evening of remembrance, and there are lots of tears, and I will just sit beside people in their grief.'

Buddhist

Conversations with those of other faiths were generally shorter and more confined to beliefs around death and funerals. B told me she was not an expert, although doing the work about death for her Buddhist Sangha. B stressed that there are very many different views among Buddhists.

'One thing the historical Buddha said is that there are 85,000 sorts of human minds so you need 85,000 practices to help them... Death is really important in Buddhist tradition. One thing people think about a lot in Buddhism are death and rebirth. This *isn't quite same as reincarnation – only about 50% of Buddhists believe in rebirth; I come from a Buddhist tradition that does. I think I do...*

'There are two important concepts: one is the acceptance of impermanence. The Buddhist view is that a lot of suffering is wanting to make things solid, holding onto things, not accepting impermanence. Death is obviously the big impermanence, so one of the challenges in death is to let go of all your feelings and attachments to everything, and just take the experience and the journey as it is to you... The other important concept is interdependence, or connection. We are all profoundly interconnected with each other and with all of creation. The living and the dead. So a lot of suffering is about thinking that we're alone, that we're separate, and during the dying process all those you are connected to can help you on that journey. So it's really important for Buddhist practitioners to pray for people who are dying and have died. That is about their connections: so it's not prayer in the sense of prayer to a God who will step in and help, it's a prayer about connecting with those enlightened energies, and your connection with that person to help them on their journey... Another thing is that we think death is more complicated than just the moment that the doctor certifies death: we see it as more of a process, that will begin before but go on afterwards. So we feel it's very, very important, if possible, to give a lot of respect to the body, not to touch it for three hours, for people to sit and meditate with the person who is dying or has died. Ideally you would leave the body for three days, but in this country that is really hard.'

She stressed that the three days was only approximate, it could be more.

'What is important is that the 49 days after a person dies are felt to be the time when it's really important to pray for them

and connect with their minds. At 49 days people usually have a ritual and another service, because it's about the mind letting go of the body. When the body isn't holding the mind, the mind can go anywhere. If you think of your grandchildren, you'll be with them, after you have died. You are in a transition, which is called the bardo.'

I was surprised that B called it the mind not the soul, but she explained that Buddhists have no concept of the soul,

'The idea of mind is bigger than just the cognitive mind, it may include the soul, it certainly includes the heart, and is often called the mind-heart or the heart-mind, involving feelings, emotions, connections as well as the cognitive.'

This sounded very similar to C's description of what happened according to her Rudolf Steiner church. This, I learned, is because Rudolf Steiner studied Buddhism.

'After 49 days, there is rebirth. The mind (you might call it the soul) then can, if you are an enlightened being, can deliberately choose where you will be reborn. If you haven't quite got there, you are reborn according to Karma. It's not exactly 49 days, because time is just another concept, but after that point you will be karmically drawn to another birth.'

When I asked if she would like to add anything, B said,

'The most important thing is the importance of the death process, of the significance of it, and how we can all help each other through that... The moment of death can be problematic (obviously some people die in accidents, and so on) but if someone is dying in bed, you can see that the body gradually goes. That is true of the mind as well, and that we should honour and respect that process. We help by using our connection, our meditation, our prayer, and

being inspirational and encouraging people. If people get worried that they haven't done all that they should or feel guilty about things, helping them to let go of that, "you've had a good life, now is the time to move on"'.

Pagan

Connection is also important to Pagans. Nimue is a Druid, who conducts funerals for Pagans of many different persuasions. She is very knowledgeable about Paganism and its history, which she said is

'Full of mad characters, some of whom were vicars. They enjoyed symbols, ceremonies, costumes, and having fun.'

Nimue has written several books on the subject, including *Spirituality without Structure: The Power of Finding your own Path.* She told me that the word 'Pagan' is a Roman word:

'It was coined as an insult, like calling someone a pleb; it's "rural idiot", people who are not sophisticated enough to be in the cities worshipping the emperors; then that was co-opted into Christianity, through Rome, and Pagans became "people who are not embracing Christianity." Now there are Christian Pagans, most of these identify with Celtic Christianity.'

At the last census 30,000 people in the UK identified themselves as pagans, but not so long ago you could lose your job if it was known that you were a Pagan. This is now illegal under the equality act, but some prefer to keep their Pagan faith private. Many untrue stories have circulated in the media about satanic rites, child abuse and sacrifice, most untrue, but believable enough to repel those of other faiths. As in all faiths, there are innumerable different strands of Paganism.

'The main focal point for most pagans is the cycle of the seasons, and seasonal festivals. So inevitably at this time of year, everything is dying and decaying and disappearing back into the soil, but at about midwinter there's the return of light. So we say, everything's going to die, and I think that's very helpful because it's just woven into what we think about the world, about living, about our experiences. Something is reborn in the spring. In terms of what do we believe happens, there is a wide variety of thinking because there is a wide spectrum of what we think about the nature of deity and the nature of reality. There are atheist Pagans, who say nature is everything, and nature is sacred, but there's nothing more: you live, you die and that's your lot. Very straightforward, no one is keeping a score, there's a certain warmth in that – this is what you get. You know where you are... The essence of Paganism for me is that it is a natural and human response to the experience of being alive... I think the desire for mystery is something that motivates a lot of pagans."

Because of this emphasis on nature, where everything dies, Nimue told me that Pagans are not afraid to talk of their death. Most of our conversation was about the Pagan funerals she celebrates.

'What happens in a Pagan ceremony will depend on the beliefs of the person who has died, and their family. Often you bury a Pagan with a whole lot of people who don't know what it's all about. And that's really tough...

'There is no specific ceremony or words, I need to establish the beliefs of the people involved. The funeral of an Animist will be very different from that of an Odin worshipper: it's a whole different reality. The important thing is to serve the reality, the beliefs and the priorities of the people whose ritual it is. The role of the celebrant is not to turn up with your own belief system, or to invoke anything that these people would not believe in, *because that would be massively disrespectful. It's to facilitate the things people need to do. Some things I do, because I feel they are helpful, for example to honour the four directions and the elements: that's very easy and very pragmatic. And in terms of settling people into the situation, drawing breath and saying here we are, it's really good. I would always in any ritual situation want to have people to be active participants.*

'I do what works for people, not using set lines because if that's what we do at this time, that can feel quite desperate. I ask: "what would help? What would be useful? What do we need to do here?" Every situation is different, burying someone who is old and has lived a full life and celebrating and honouring that life can be almost a joyful community thing, because you recognise someone who's lived. It's not agony, it can be the grief of loss; but that's not same as burying someone who was very young, there's the sense of unfairness and anger at the universe, that can be completely different. If something is difficult, if it hurts and is angry-making it's important to give people space to deal with whatever the situation creates.

'You need it to be OK to say "this shouldn't have happened, he died needlessly, and that's really something to get cross about." I think being able to be honest about that and having space for the kind of emotions that provokes is best, rather than having to soothe it all down – that's useless. When you are furious with reality, letting people express that is much more useful... No two lives are the same, no two funerals are the same. I think funerals need to be done individually rather than having a script... A funeral is so much about what the living need. I tend to start from there: what do you want? Whatever the dead are doing they are probably doing it, and we don't know. I suspect they don't need anything from us, but if they do, we don't know what it is with any certainty. With so many religions it's based on the idea

that we do know, in line with a set of beliefs about how reality works. I'm not sure how reality works.'

At the end of our conversation she came back to uncertainty, to what she called, 'maybeism':

'I try to approach everything in spirit of I don't know, but well you might be right. If it works for you that's fine, it's very releasing. Ultimate truth does not work... Forcing it into a shape that fits the tradition rather than the individual isn't helpful, and it's very easy to use to use at times of high emotion, which a funeral is, to reinforce a spiritual message, rather than cater for the needs of the people. For me it's much more useful to use the spiritual stuff to look after the people, rather than using the people to look after the spiritual stuff. That influences a lot of what I do.'

When I said I loved the term 'maybeism,' she said she got it from Philip Carr Gomm, but a lot of people are using it.

Finally she reminded me of the story of the five blind men and elephant, a version of which is at the start of this chapter.

Humanist

I did not detect much of Nimue's maybeism, or her spirituality, in John's humanist beliefs; he seemed quite certain that those who believe in any sort of deity are mistaken. He was wearing a badge which said, 'Happy Humanist', which he said he preferred to the other badge produced by the British Humanist Association, which says, 'Good without God', and which he finds more assertive. The theme of the ability to be good without a God, or the fear of hell or promise of salvation, came up repeatedly during our conversation.

At the end of our time together he summed up his idea of the humanist position as follows:

'Humanists accept death;

Humanists regard mortality as a reason for living well;

Humanists don't have any truck at all with the supernatural and therefore not with any idea of life after death, heaven or hell – (a lot of us reckon that has been to keep us in line).

Humanist funerals can be very beautiful, and usually are (Religious funerals, I think I believe, have picked up on this and are now more meaningful);

We are good because it's sensible to be good.'

He started by telling me of a survey of hospital chaplaincies which found that about 0% of them are secular, but when asked about patients' conversations with chaplains, a very small proportion of the time was devoted to religious issues. Although hospital and prison chaplaincy is officially changing to allow secular chaplains, there is some evidence of pressure to preserve what may be thought of as something of a 'religious monopoly'.

As to death,

'Humanists see no good reason to suppose other than that when we die we become dead, just as a frog (for instance) does when it dies. When you're dead that's it as far as your physical existence is concerned… Some of us take a slightly superior view of religious folk who say, "you've got to be good, otherwise salvation is not guaranteed". Not so many hundreds of years ago people were told every week by their priest "if you're not good, you'll miss out on salvation and you'll go to hell." So we do our best to live good lives without acknowledging any sort of god, the promise of heaven or hell doesn't work for us.'

As well as telling me of his reasons for supporting the Assisted Dying Bill, John seasoned his conversation with jokes, including Woody Allen saying that he was not afraid of death, but would rather not be there when it happens. Another was,

'A lad brought up in a Hindu family in India went to university and did a lot of reading and thinking, and said to his father, "I think I'm an atheist." His father said, "Good, that's a branch of Hinduism."'

He told me that he is sometimes asked to go into schools to explain the humanist view to A-level students of religion and ethics.

'At question time, one lad asked, "the lack of immortality – doesn't that worry you?" I said "what comforts me is I know I'm mortal therefore I must make good use of time". Another asked, "What if when you die you find yourself face to face with Almighty God?"'

I recall hearing Professor Richard Dawkins asked this question and his reply was 'I would ask God, "Now, which one are you?" as humans recognise so many.'

Like Nimue, John is happy that such ceremonies are not tied by any 'official' programme'. They are both free to construct a meaningful funeral specific to the individual who has died. Both were similarly critical of traditional Christian funerals.

Muslim

Kalsoom stressed that Islam is a way of life.

'A code about how to live your life on a day to day basis; it covers all aspects of your life, and so is vast. I practice as much as I

can, and I'm always learning new things, because the Quran is endless, every time you read it you find something new.'

I wanted to know if Kalsoom was a Sunni or a Shia Muslim, as, knowing only what I have learned from the media, I thought there was an important distinction. She replied,

'Well, I don't like these labels at all, as there are lots of different sects in Christianity so in Islam, but I don't like to associate myself with either. I follow the Quran and the Sunnah. The Sunnah is the way of the life of the prophet Mohammed (Peace be upon Him) and is what we follow. He was the last Prophet who came after Jesus. Allah sent him to us, a normal human, he lived and died just like a normal human being he had no supernatural powers. The way he lived his life is the way we should live our lives: prayer, work and all aspects of his life we follow. What I tell you is from Quran and Sunnah, nothing else...

'Death in Islam is very important, it's something we always have to remember as part of our daily lives, because it could happen at any time. In Islam this life is a test of how good a Muslim, how good a person, you are: the real life is the after-life, paradise or hell. It's in our prayers all the time about having a good life and a good death... by a good life I mean being a good person, living your life really well, and being honest – that is what a Muslim is: kind, compassionate, truthful, worshipping Allah five times a day, fasting, with the intention of pleasing Allah. If you live a good life you'll have a good death. If someone was a very, very good person, they'll have a pain-free death. My dad died about a year ago, he had dementia and slowly deteriorated. When it came to his death it was very easy – just a deep breath in and then out, and he was gone; we weren't even aware of it.

'What we believe is that the person who is dying can see the angel of death (he can't communicate with those around him) as

far as he can see, he sees angels lining both sides of his vision, and the angel of death comes and requests the soul to come out. If it's a good soul it will come out easily, like a drop of water dropping out of the person, the soul is removed, and the angel of death takes it. If it's a very bad person, the soul doesn't come out easily when the angel comes, and the soul is ripped out, because it doesn't want to come, it's so attached to this world, it doesn't want to leave. So the angel pulls it out, so it's a painful death. Islam is very detailed about death. So when a good soul is taken, away the angel wraps that soul in beautiful cloth from paradise, that has beautiful smells, and will carry it up to the seven heavens, (there are also seven hells). First they go to the first heaven: the angel in that heaven will smell the beautiful soul and ask who is this good person, so he can go up to the next heaven. He asks for the names people used to call him by, and then he goes up to the next heaven. And it goes on up to the seventh heaven. When it gets to the seventh heaven, Allah will record all his good deeds to be taken into account. We believe there are two angels on our shoulders all our life, recording every thing we do, the good deeds on our right shoulder and the bad on the left. Those records are kept for the day of judgement. When the soul reaches the seventh heaven, Allah tells the angel to put the soul back in the body. You don't come alive again, it stays in the body or next to the body, and then the body is buried, very quickly.

'*The funeral happens very quickly once the person dies. The body has to be washed by the close relatives, a ritual washing, men wash the men and women wash the women. It has to be done is a very modest way, so that no one sees the naked body. It has to be covered at all times. You have to wash the body under the covers, then the body is covered in two pieces of unstitched cloth, which is usually white, but doesn't have to be. Then there is prayer, it's very simple, the Imam makes prayers and everybody gets together and makes prayers for the person who has died.*

There are no speeches, the men take away the body – the women don't go to the burial. The body is then buried and another prayer is said, it is buried by hand. We don't have a coffin, usually the body is wrapped in a white sheet and placed in ground directly, because the Koran says we brought you to life from dirt and we will return you to dirt: literally putting you back in the earth. The people who are left have to reflect on that: this is the final destination you must be a good person; it's very hands on.

'*There is an old Arab saying that Death is like when you plan to meet a friend, you say, "I'll meet you somewhere" and you both leave the house at the same time, and you meet somewhere. Death is like that: it has already left its house and is going to meet you somewhere, and you're unconsciously walking towards it all the time... You have to do good deeds before you die so that you get to heaven. It's a stark reminder to the people who are left: this is all it is, all our material goods, what we strive for, are nothing. That's why our funerals are so simple, you could be a king, but the funeral is the same. When the King of Saudi Arabia died, one of the richest people in the world, his funeral was very, very simple. He was buried by hand, in dirt in two cloths. Death is death whoever you are: you can't take anything with you.*

'*Once the body is buried and everybody walks away, the soul can hear the footsteps of the people walking away after they've buried him; we know the soul is there. When they've gone and he is alone in the grave, two angels come and the soul will be asked to sit up, and the two angels will ask the soul three questions. This will happen whether you are a Muslim or not. The first question is: who is your lord? The answer is Allah. The second question is: what is your religion? Islam. The third is: who is the messenger? That is Mohammed (Peace be upon Him). If it's a practising Muslim he will answer easily, but if the person is not a good Muslim, or not a Muslim, they won't be able to answer. After that the soul is laid to rest, if they've answered correctly, they will be shown their place in paradise, and they will also be shown hell fire, because you are a good person, this is what you have avoided and paradise will be your place for ever. Alternatively, the bad person will be shown their place in hell, and the paradise they have lost. The good soul will want the day of judgement to come quickly, but the bad person won't want it. If it is a good person that grave will be vast – it won't feel constricting, they will have cool breezes and light from paradise, it won't be a tight dark grave, it will feel spacious, have scents, they will be rewarded, and at peace. The bad will have the opposite: a restricted grave, even punishment in the grave if they were very bad. That's just the beginning; as a soul you know at that point whether you are going to heaven or hell. The day of Judgement will come for all of us: on that day all will be resurrected, all life will end, the whole world will stop.*

'In our prayers we mention death five times a day: "give us best in this life and best in the next life." As Muslims we are taught to believe that we should be in this life as if a stranger, or just a traveller. Which means that this life is just temporary and that we should not get too attached to things in this life and that we are merely travelling through this life, collecting our good deeds, to our final destination which is the afterlife.'

Because of the Muslim emphasis on death, Kalsoom told me Muslims are not afraid to talk about it. She was appalled at the idea of people crossing the road to avoid meeting a bereaved person.

'It's the complete opposite to us: everybody will come to your house to console you, look after you and your kids, cook for you, bring you food. We have three days of mourning, from the day the person dies, and everyone who wants to give their condolences comes round; but it doesn't work out like that, they keep on coming for weeks... When someone dies or when we hear of someone who has

passed away, or when struck with any calamity, we are taught to recite a verse of the Quran "inna lillahi wa inna ilayhi raji'un" (Quran surah Baqarah 2:156) This translates as "We surely belong to Allah and to Him we shall return". A reminder of our inevitable return to our creator and that whatever we have is not really ours. It belongs to Allah, He created everything including our souls and bodies and everything will return to Him. Everything that is given to us, our children, health, wealth, power, poverty etc. all are given to us to serve as a test for us in this life. A test to see how we utilise these things, for example if we have been blessed with wealth, Allah tests us to see if we use that wealth to help the needy and stay humble and continue to worship Allah or if we will be greedy and just be concerned with accumulating more and forget about worshipping Allah. Just as easily as Allah gave us these things He can take them away from us. '

Hindu

According to GKP the Hindu view of death is rather different from that of Muslims, or other faiths, he told me,

'There is no death. The body, the vehicle, dies; but the essence of who we are is eternal. It lives on for ever, its aim is to return to Brahma. We are part of Brahma: our journey is about realising that we are Brahma, the creator, the created, this is just eternal... It is Atma... Atma is eternal, with no beginning no end. My personal view of this is that it makes sense for me. I can't know, but some of my experiences suggest this is so, the essence of who we are goes on for ever.'

When I asked what experiences led to this conclusion he said,

'Well, when I was very young, and since then, I've had experiences of being merged into a sense of oneness with everything, that's the essence of who we are. It's like the water, the river, and the sea – they are all one: you can't say this molecule of water is separate from the sea, but it does become separate as well. It goes through various stages: it's a cycle. That's exactly what our Atma is – a cycle.'

He told me a lot about Hinduism, but said he did not personally believe in it.

'It's important to understand that Hinduism, the word, didn't exist until the 1700s when archaeologists excavated in the Indus valley, and discovered a civilisation of the people of the Indus there. Before that there was no Hinduism. There was a way of life based on teachings of various philosophers dating back 5,000– 10,000 years or more. There were ritualistic practices based on metaphors and knowledge of how energy works. The simplest way of putting this is where mind is focussed, energy will follow... Hinduism is a word that has been coined, it has no real meaning: these people who followed a certain way of life are called Hindus.'

India is a vast country and Hinduism takes different forms in different parts, with different practices, and stressing different Gods. I asked about the large number of Gods recognised by Hindus. I had heard that this was because human beings find the concept of one God too much to comprehend. 'That is correct in the sense that is what we can relate to: not many people can relate to the concept that God is everywhere and in everything.' He went on to tell me of just a few of Hinduism's Gods.

'Kali is the goddess of death: the death of the ego. Kali is there to destroy that part of us that creates illusion; we live in a world of illusion and by destroying the illusion there is clarity.

Ganesh is to do with removing obstacles, that is the metaphor. An elephant will clear the path with great strength, you evoke that energy by connecting with the deity, the image of Ganesh... Lord Krishna was an incarnation of Vishnu, who is part of the trinity of Brahma, Vishnu, and Shiva. It's a trinity because it's about aspects of yourself which are seen as trinity, different layers of yourself: the physical, mental, spiritual aspects of yourself... Before the word Hinduism the philosophy is known as 'Sanatan Dharma', which is simply a way of life based on natural forces.'

There are of course many more aspects of God that are worshipped in different ways, in different regions. Temples from different regions of India can be very different, the dialects and traditions vary. Hinduism is a vast topic, and most of it has little relevance to this book. However, it links in well with other faiths' ways of making sense of death.

GKP went on to talk of the Hindu rituals around death:

'These rituals are to do with the body, and are aimed at really giving the soul a send off, whereby they can evolve in the most positive way. They respect that part of what was in the body... The ceremony itself is for the soul to continue on its endless journey of evolution.'

I said I understood that these rituals involve ashes being scattered in the Ganges, and asked why that particular river. GKP said,

'The Ganges is the most sacred river in India. In ancient myth there are three rivers: the Saraswati, the Jumna and the Ganges. The Saraswati river doesn't exist on the physical plane. There are many stories about these three rivers, from many millennia ago, where Lord Shiva harnessed the Saraswati so it is one of the three sacred rivers. I'm not sure why the Ganges is now seen as most sacred, I imagine it's because it comes from the top of the world.'

GKP said he did not think it was necessary for ashes to be scattered in the Ganges; for Indians in the West this could be 'quite a thing to do. Personally I'm not too much into pilgrimages, and places, because although some places have a quality of energy more than other places, it depends on your means.'

GKP has been to the death café a few times, because he is thinking of setting up as a funeral advisor who would help those who do not know how to proceed when someone has died.

Judaism

The last of my conversations about faith was with Rosa, to whom I am extremely grateful for telling me what she could remember from her childhood in Israel. The day I visited her was just after the memorial day for her mother.

> *'Traditionally you light a 24-hour candle in memory of the dead, on the anniversary of their death. I find this interesting because in one of the death café conversations we were told of a documentary film "The Griefwalker" about Stephen Jenkinson.'*

He has been with many dying people in his work in palliative care counselling, and showed the film locally, and gave a talk which Rosa heard.

> *'He said that what people are most afraid of before they die is that they won't be remembered.'*

This is less likely in Jewish families, and is one of the things that even secular Jews, like Rosa's family, practice.

Rosa lit a candle for her mother, but said that while such candles are easy to obtain in Israel and Jewish areas of London where they can be bought in any convenience store, in a glass, locally it is more difficult to get a candle that will burn for 24 hours.

'In Israel there is a religious organisation that takes over after someone dies. I don't know how it is in other countries. They would wash the body and prepare it for burial, cover it with a shroud, not a coffin, and then it would be taken to the grave and the oldest son would say a particular prayer, called a Kaddish. Nowadays girls, women, daughters, can do it as well in a progressive tradition, but traditionally it must be a man. And they would go home and sit Shiva. That means seven days, sit for seven days, not go out of the house, the close relatives and friends would come and visit. Traditionally they don't do anything for seven days.'

Rosa's family, although not religious Jews, observed Shiva after the deaths of both her father and her mother. When her mother died Rosa was living in this country.

'When my mother died we stayed at my uncle's house and people would come and visit and console… so that is so inherent in the culture.'

After those seven days, the next memorial is after 30 days at the grave. 'Sometimes they put up their tombstone after 30 days but usually about a year later: so there is the 7 days, and then the 30 days, and then the year memorial, and then every year.' All this makes forgetting less likely.

When I asked Rosa if she had anything she would like to add, she said,

'My father died when I was hirteen and the fact that he was buried and had a headstone was very helpful to me as a child. There was a place where I can go and sort of be with my father. Spiritually I knew he was with me at any time, any place, but the

fact that I knew he was buried in a cemetery, which was a very quiet, silent place, so I could get on a bus from the city and go and visit now and then, when my heart felt heavy. So I think the tradition of burial and a tombstone is quite supportive for those left behind.

'The tradition of burial was very supportive for me in my grief as a child. Every time I go to Israel I visit my mother's grave as well as my father's.'

Rosa was not able to answer my question about whether in the Jewish community it is any easier to talk about death than in contemporary UK. She thought that probably the general community's reluctance may also apply to those in the Jewish community. She agreed however when I suggested that having a faith makes talking of death easier. 'Perhaps death is not so threatening or frightening if there is faith.'

In addition to these conversations, when I visited the Community of the Many Names of God, I took part in their very lovely worship sessions, pujas. These take place in their three beautiful temples, and appear to be mainly a mixture of Hindu and Buddhist chanting, in different languages which I do not understand, but from time to time they break into English for 'Hail, Mary, full of grace…' then returning to an Indian language, or perhaps Arabic for Islamic prayers. It was not easy to know what was going on in another language, but there was a very special atmosphere that is hard to describe. Sometimes the chanting was very noisy, with gongs and bells, and everyone seeming to be trying to make as much noise as possible. Although it might seem the complete opposite of a silent Quaker meeting, for me the effect was very similar to an hour's silence. Sister Ally described it as

'What you feel here in the temples is that peace, that specialness, and it's all there the unconditional love, and the wanting to serve for no other reason than to serve, and to make people happy. It

allows people to have the space to digest things and just be comfortable, and able to talk about it.'

Peace, specialness, unconditional love, service seem to be the essence of their faith, which is an amalgam of faiths. Perhaps those in the Community are nearer than most of us to comprehending the nature of the elephant in the story at the start of this chapter.

In all the above faiths there are many different traditions, which most contributors stressed. In the next chapter I will compare what I learned about the views of death in these faiths, and what they can tell us about the Undiscovered Country, before going on to see what meaning these, and other contributors, may make of death.

*   *   *

Mourner's Kaddish

Exalted and hallowed be God's great name
  in the world which God created, according to plan.
May God's majesty be revealed in the days of our lifetime
  and the life of all Israel — speedily, imminently, to which we
  say Amen.
Blessed be God's great name to all eternity.
Blessed, praised, honored, exalted, extolled, glorified, adored,
  and lauded be the name of the Holy Blessed One, beyond all
  earthly words and songs of blessing,
  praise, and comfort. To which we say Amen.
May there be abundant peace from heaven, and life, for us and
  all Israel,
  to which we say Amen.
May the One who creates harmony on high, bring peace to us
  and to all Israel. To which we say Amen.

The Universal prayer for peace

Lead me from death to Life,
from falsehood to Truth.
Lead me from despair to Hope,
from fear to Trust.
Lead me from hate to Love,
from war to Peace.
Let Peace fill our heart, our world, our universe.
Peace, peace, peace.

11 The cloud of unknowing

'Everybody's wonderin' what and where they all came from.
Everybody's worryin' 'bout where they're gonna go when the
whole thing's done.
But no one knows for certain and so it's all the same to me.
I think I'll just let the mystery be
Some say once you're gone you're gone forever, and some say
you're gonna come back.
Some say you rest in the arms of the Saviour if in sinful
ways you lack.
Some say that they're comin' back in a garden, bunch of
carrots and little sweet peas
I think I'll just let the mystery be.'

Pammy, the death café organiser, and Paul, a regular attender, both
mentioned this song by the American country singer, Iris DeMent.
Paul, who described himself as a 'recovering Roman Catholic' (the
echo of Alcoholics Anonymous was intentional) said,

'That captures, in a kind of open way, the possibilities of whatever
may happen… Certainty can be dangerous.'

Pammy said,

'I don't have any of that certainty about death… I don't feel I've
got to know.'

Nicola, the counsellor, said,

'It's very important that we develop some kind of – religious for
some people, spiritual for others – we have something there to
hold us when something terrible happens. Where do we go for our

*resources, our support? We all need that. If there's nothing there
to hold us ... personally I'm not into religion, but I'm sure it really
helps – people who are Christians, or Buddhists or Catholics,
(Buddhism is bordering on religion) anything that helps you.'*

In this chapter I will report what contributors had to say about
Nicola's 'something'. The previous chapter looked at how six specific
faiths are concerned with death, and what happens after death, which
is important in all faiths, with varying degrees of certainty. How
far is the Undiscovered Country revealed by faith? How are those
who do not accept any of these faiths to make sense of death, and of
life? Death is not the end in most faiths. Yet there is something very
final about death; faith denies death's finality. Can we accept death,
embrace it, find peace in the idea without a faith? I suspect we can.
John, the humanist, seems able to; he seemed quite certain that there
is nothing beyond death. I was surprised at how similar were the
metaphors used by those with very different views.

The Chaplain at the Welcome Hospice, when discussing how
she approaches those who claim to have no faith, told me of some
training she had in spirituality for NHS staff,

*'I learned from there to ask "what is it that gives meaning to your
life?" rather than about spirituality. It's quite a good opening if
you can't get anywhere on the spiritual trail. It might be nature, or
family or whatever. I ask that question; I heard it from somebody
else so it's not original, but I use it and find useful.'*

Perhaps Nicola's 'something' is that which gives meaning. Victor
Frankl, a concentration camp survivor, wrote in *Man's Search
for Meaning* of the vital need to find some meaning in life. Those
who survived the concentration camps were those who could see a
meaning, and some hope for the future. Through his own suffering
Frankl came to understand that human beings can only be saved
through love and in love. All those I spoke with about their faith

found meaning in it, apart from Rosa, who did not embrace Judaism, but she was the only person I could find to tell me anything about Judaism.

Rosie, who attended the course on preparing for death with William Bloom, said she had also read a lot of Jung, who wrote of the importance of myth in giving meaning to life. In Jung's sense, all the great religions can be seen as myths. For Jung, who himself had a near death experience which had a profound effect on him, death is the goal of life, not its end. Jung divided life into two stages: morning and afternoon. From Shakespeare, who wrote of the 'seven ages of man' onward, and long before him, people have divided life into different numbers of stages. For most the final stage is seen as decline. But not for a Hindu and not for Jung. For Jung the afternoon is the most important, and its primary purpose is individuation, by which he meant finding out who one really is, and in so doing relating to others. I wonder if, when I suggest that we can be oned, we are oned in Jung's collective unconscious. Is it to the collective unconscious that we go when we die? Could individuation be what is going on in hospices?

M5, member of the Quaker Fellowship of Afterlife studies, said,

'When my first husband died, I was totally convinced he's gone to wherever he needed to go to at the time.'

Those of all the faiths I was able to talk with offered broadly similar messages; details varied, but they all had their own interpretations of the meaning of life and death. All seem to say that death is not the end; some believe in reincarnation, or rebirth, others in resurrection. Even John said,

'A lot of us think, consider, you might say we believe, that we do "live on" because people remember us; our children carry on how we have brought them up; each of our children has half of our genes; if we leave things behind, for example if we have

written a book, or built an extension to a house, created a lovely garden, something of us lives on, which is a comfortable thought. Therefore we don't attach any weight to the problem of life after death.'

I was quite surprised that he did not also include in his reasons for being an atheist the role that religion plays in perhaps helping people to come to terms with death, with promises of immortality.

Father P, the Catholic priest, talked of atheists who seemed to feel that death is not the end. He told of someone who said, after the death of her husband, 'I wonder what John's doing now. I wonder where he is.'

Father P commented,

'She spoke of him as if he still existed, instinctively this is part of the human condition; and looking at various cultures over so many centuries, it's not just an end, the spirit lives on.'

For millennia human beings have been creating, or inheriting, myths, in Jung's sense of the word, both about the creation of the world and about what happens after death. We need these myths. Some have been elevated into religions, about which some have a perhaps enviable certainty. Even John who rejects religion and any kind of deity, has joined with others who share his views and seems to work to promote them as much as those evangelical about a religious faith. Whether the humanists are right and human beings have created God in their own image, or whether there is a Creator, throughout history religion has been harnessed to politics, and we have enrolled God in our various projects to create the sort of society we want. Caste, class, apartheid and even holocausts have been, and still are, justified by religion. John said, 'Humanists don't have any truck at all with the supernatural and therefore not with any idea of life after death, heaven or hell – a lot of us reckon that has been to keep us in

line.' I would agree that in the past much of Christianity seems to
have been as a form of social control. The Victorian children's hymn
'All Things Bright and Beautiful' originally contained the verse:

> *'The rich man in his castle*
> *The poor man at his gate*
> *God made them high and lowly*
> *And ordered their estate.'*

That this verse is not now usually printed suggests that this may
no longer be one of the church's functions. It is not just Christianity
that tells us how to behave. Kalsoom told me that Islam is ' A code
about how to live your life on a day to day basis... You have to do
good deeds before you die so that you get to heaven.'

Perhaps the different faiths lie along a continuum from certainty to
uncertainty: a rather different continuum from that in the previous
chapter. Father P would be at one end, with Nimue, the Pagan, at the
other. John seemed at least as certain as Father P, although at the
other end of another continuum. Kalsoom also seemed certain in her
faith in Islam; B, the Buddhist, and GKP were much less so; Nimue
spoke of 'maybeism'; B spoke of '85,000 different minds needing
85,000 different Buddhist practices'. She said some Buddhists believe
in rebirth, adding, 'I think I do'. Pammy said, 'I'm a Buddhist, but
I don't feel I absolutely KNOW or totally believe in some aspects of
reincarnation and rebirth; I know some Buddhists absolutely believe
it.' She said, 'I would say that for most of us Death Café goers, we're
sort of exploring the mystery of it.'

Father P, talking about certainty said,

> *'You can't prove it. If you look at all the history of the human*
> *race in different cultures, all we know, there are other ways of*
> *knowing: intuition, and there's a certainty about it. This way of*
> *knowing is faith, but also as a human being, there are certainties*

which you have which are beyond just the rational. This is where the ambiguities and confusions come in, the difference between just surface feelings – I feel this and that – and the knowing at a deeper level... When Jung was asked if he believed in God, he said, "No, I know He exists." It's not intellectual – I can't prove it to you, but to deny it I'd have to be untrue to myself, to deny what I know to be true. So this dimension is something else.'

For Nimue, maybeism is important.

'There will always be people with very fixed beliefs, they pop up everywhere. There's always one who knows, is absolutely certain, about what will happen, but what they are certain about varies widely. A sense of mystery is very important to a lot of Pagans, so while there will be quite a lot of people who believe in a spirit living on, and reincarnation, but within that much more acceptance of the unknown and not knowing, and for the possibility of the unknown, something much bigger than we can imagine. I'm certainly not alone in holding ceremonies that include uncertainty, and being very comfortable with it. I think the desire for mystery is something that motivates a lot of pagans.'

Many people today seem somewhat averse to mystery and maybeism, there seems to be a quest for certainty, and the notion that science can explain all. Those in the media frequently seem to want scientists to say that they have proved something. Scientists themselves are far more cautious: hypotheses are proved until other scientists suggest otherwise; uncertainty lies at the heart of science. The history of science is full of stories where our picture of the world has had to change, from what we thought it was to new understandings.

The last of Elizabeth Kübler-Ross's stages of grief is acceptance, perhaps this can be seen as similar to acceptance of a faith. With acceptance perhaps comes freedom and fearlessness. To live fully we need to accept that our lives are finite. Acceptance is not easy: Hannah said, 'It's very difficult to let go and accept that actually time's up.' Sister Ally and Isabel both spoke of hospice patients who found peace once they could accept that they were dying. Sister Ally said of one patient at the Hospice of the Many Names of God, 'Once she accepted it, she was completely different.' Isabel's Welcome Hospice offers diversionary therapy which seems to make acceptance easier. Iain, of the Scottish hospice, found it hard to accept that he could never again ride a motorbike or be involved in sports, but once he did his life was transformed. Christine, the artist whose brother died, thought a good death is one where, 'The person dying has entirely accepted and embraced the leaving of life.' Similarly M, who works with the newly bereaved, thought that a good death was when 'The family have come to terms and accepted the death.' SA told of the lovely funeral of one of his homoeopathy clients who, 'Who refused treatment, because he accepted death.'

Nicola spoke of acceptance rather than getting over or moving on. 'We're not supposed to want to totally get over it, but there can be acceptance.' Swami S, of the Community of the Many Names of God, spoke of the vibration of love, which, 'Creates a safe place for them to manifest and to be resolved, and to enable the person to transform that feeling into one of acceptance, and ultimately to one of freedom.' B spoke of the importance in Buddhism of 'The acceptance of impermanence.' Nimue of 'Acceptance of the unknown and not knowing.' Ellen said, 'You just have to accept what happened and move on.'

Perhaps acceptance underlies this poem by Caroline, whose son died after abusing alcohol :

The Night he Died

The moon shines full tonight
Pure, clear, beautifully
He will not see it or any moon again

Not with human eyes that is
But dancing somewhere amongst the stars
Goes free my son
Free now, his journey done
His body gone
His spirit shining
Pure, clear, beautifully
Not fettered any more
By the body that he loathed.
(Caroline)

However certain or uncertain, all faiths, including Humanism, seem to attach considerable importance to funerals, and the rites and rituals following death. All have some idea, again with different degrees of certainty, that the person who has died is going somewhere, even if that is nowhere. Perhaps funerals are a stand against meaninglessness, as well as a link between life and death, an important rite of passage, and comfort for the bereaved. They play a part in our essential need to make sense of our lives and the lives of those we love. For some this meaning is in religion, for others in the life that has been lived. In Islam, as in Hinduism and Judaism, there is a need to bury the body quickly, while for Buddhists and the Christian Community the whole process around death is more gradual, as it takes time for the mind or the soul to leave the body; Buddhists have ceremonies after 49 days, after which the mind can be reincarnated. Reincarnation takes much longer for followers of Steiner: they must wait for one third of their lifetime.

Rosa's description of a Jewish funeral showed similarities with the Muslims: both use a shroud, or specific cloth, not a coffin, which Father P also said was the custom at his monastery. Both he and Kalsoom stressed the importance of the actual covering of the grave: for Muslims this is done by hand, meaning no shovel is used, in the monastery the monks do it themselves, rather than leaving it to a sexton. In most ordinary funerals (if there is such a thing) the mourners only throw a symbolic handful of earth, the actual burying is left to others. Rosa's account of sitting Shiva echoed Buddhists and the Steiner church, where there is a time for the mind or soul to leave, and the holding of ceremonies after a particular number of days. These faiths are also similar in that, traditionally, only men take part in the funeral.

Decca Aitkenhead in *All at Sea* also writes movingly of the sound when the family filled in her partner's grave; she says it felt like tucking him in. She later had a text from an old friend of theirs, saying how disappointed and hurt he had been that this had not been part of the actual funeral, so he had been unable to take part. He said the black community like to be able to put dirt on loved ones.

Rosa, Kalsoom and father P all mentioned the importance of ritual washing of the body before the funeral. For Jews this washing is also done by men, Kalsoom said that in Islam men wash men, and women wash women.

Jean, the carer and unbeliever, told me of the profound significance for her of washing feet.

'My friend, who had MS, asked me to wash her at the last. There's something profound about washing someone's feet – her feet hadn't been in contact with the ground for a long time, because she couldn't walk. I don't know if it was her who said it's really important to wash the feet because when you wash someone's feet it means that you're helping them to leave the earth. I don't know where I got that from, but last year I did live-in care for a man who actually wanted to die. He'd had enough and I washed his feet, and I know that was a really big thing for him and it was such a pleasure. It was not long before he died, and I feel that's a very profound experience.'

When I wondered if that had anything to do with the Christian ceremony of foot washing on Maundy Thursday, Jean replied, 'We're products of a Christian based culture.'

Funeral practices can also perhaps be arranged along the same continuum: Father P's Catholic rites, which seem to be clearly prescribed, through to Nimue performing individual funerals, designed for the particular person who has died. Somewhere in the middle is the Chaplain, who stressed choice but also mentioned the importance of the Liturgy.

She told me of someone who thought the 23rd psalm was compulsory. (That is the psalm that includes the words, 'Though I walk through the valley of the shadow of death, I will fear no evil, for thou art with me.')

'I said, "It's a very beautiful psalm and is often chosen, but there's no such thing as have to have. It's your funeral and you're planning it, and it's a great gift you give your family if you do plan it. It should be what has meaning for your memory, and would help your family."… I do three things at a funeral: I honour the memory of the deceased, I comfort the family and I commit the person to God's grace and mercy… at the committal you commit the body to dust to dust, in sure and certain hope of resurrection to eternal life. I take time and much thought in preparing for a funeral and in getting it right for the family.'

I once attended a funeral of a very keen gardener. Mourners had been asked to bring posies of flowers, and at the graveside the minister was asked not to say 'dust to dust, ashes to ashes,' but 'flowers to flowers', and we all threw our posies onto the coffin, which was cardboard, beautifully decorated with pictures of flowers. It was very moving.

John said, 'Humanist funerals can be very beautiful, and usually are; religious funerals, I think, I believe, have picked up on this and are now more meaningful.' Chris, the C of E lay reader who volunteers at the Welcome Hospice, told me he had conducted about 500 funerals over the last eighteen years. I asked him if funerals had changed in that time. He said,

> 'They've become more expensive... More and more people are now asking for particular pieces of music or poetry. That would have been almost unheard of twenty years ago. People's attitudes to services are becoming more personalised, which I subscribe to: I very much think a person's funeral should be personalised as much as the person and family wants.'

When I put to him John's suggestion that this was following Humanist funerals, he did not agree.

> 'I wouldn't say that at all. I was personalising funerals long before I'd met or even heard of a humanist. I agree with him in that sometimes you can go to a funeral that is absolutely featureless. In some nothing is said about the person, you could be burying a box of bricks. I will not do that, it's so impersonal. I have been to a number where they really have been so impersonal from start to finish. Some are over in fifteen minutes.'

It was just such a funeral that was a spur to James to start his own funeral business. He told me how he personalises funerals.

> 'In the ten days or so of arrangements prior to the funeral, I try and bring humour in – being a little bad, and irreverent with the rules, the bloody rules, about how to do things. To remove the bureaucratic formality and uncertainty about how to do it all. But when there's something heavy like that – needing to "do it right"- I begin to kind of put some air into this, by giving all the information and letting people know they can do it how they want to do it. So then we have a relationship. They're not feeling

they've been cornered by a bloke in black, saying "Shall we carry out our duties with the remains of the deceased in our chapel of rest?" (While counting the tenners with a wet thumb on the way out!) I give lots of room for people to think and to choose and as much contact as they need, keep it informal and the family can then come up with the best funeral they can imagine. And mostly it's simple, and beautiful and heartfelt that people want.'

Nimue's views were similar.

'No two lives are the same, no two funerals are the same. I think funerals need to be done individually rather than having a script... When we buried my grandmother there was the priest at the front, we just sat in rows and joined in when we were told to; that can be quite alienating, keeping the grieving people separate from what's happening. I prefer giving people time to speak, if there is something they want to share. I like toasting, which is predominantly a Heathen tradition of passing a mead horn round. You can't put a mead horn down until it's empty. It opens people up, because if you drink to the memory of somebody, if you honour them, say a few words of what's important. So you can keep up a flow of people saying what they want to share. If you can't speak, you can just make a physical gesture of respect, and be a participant. It's the very human things we come back to: sharing of bread, wine, cake; sharing the basics of life in a ritual setting. So many religions, for example Hindus, have some kind of participatory ceremonies with liquid, whether you are tipping it over someone, or sharing it. Mead is popular, but anything that can be passed round. Wiccans tend to favour wine, Druids favour mead, but it depends on what makes sense seasonally, it could be beer, or apple juice or elderflower cordial for those who don't want alcohol.'

Caroline told me of the very beautiful funeral for her son.

'It was incredibly uplifting, because he was so present. He had worked in the sorting office at Royal Mail and droves of them came in their blue shirts. I was determined that this funeral should reflect who he was, not some sanitised version. So we said "Come in casual clothes", because he absolutely detested getting poshed up for anything – he'd been to a funeral where everybody had shown up in suits and ties, and he got quite angry, he didn't often get angry, but he said, "That has nothing whatever to do with her, she wasn't that kind of person at all." So they came in their trainers, and it just seemed so him. They wanted to put their hands on the coffin, and said, "See you later, mate", and all this sort of thing – it was so real. People said afterwards, what an amazing experience it was. He was very emotional himself, very up front with feelings, which people used to find difficult, because he would just tell it how it was. One of his closest friends was an actor, and I asked him if he would start the sharing, because I thought he's an actor – he'll be able to hold it together. No – he's an actor so he didn't mind people seeing his distress, so he just stood there and wept throughout, and sort of saying bits in between. That allowed everyone else to come forward, and some were very tearful and others recalled things that made them laugh. It was a very, very emotionally honest day, which was a huge relief. Even my mother cried and she would never cry at a funeral. But she did at that one. It was quite extraordinary.'

Jean chose, very carefully, eight poems for her mother's funeral: poems that had meant a great deal to her during her life, and from which Jean had learned much. These included Masefield's 'Sea Fever' because, 'Her father was a ship's engineer, and her mother loved travelling with him.' There was also 'The Life that I Have.' Jean said

'I looked it up online and found it's a poem of the French resistance, I'm not sure if that's a myth or a fact'.

Jean told me of the importance of poetry in her mother's life as well as at her funeral. She read to her mother when she was dying; and they had enjoyed 'Jaberwocky' together when her mother was very ill following her first stroke. She said:

> *"Twas brillig and the slithey toves" while eating grapes! I thought that was brilliant... So I felt poetry was a channel and I felt I was being channelled very powerfully. The day before she died, the last time I saw her alive, I had a private word with her and I thanked her for everything, and I said, "That poem you taught me when I was a child, I carried it in my heart through my life, and it helped to form me." It's from Blake's Auguries of Innocence. She loved Blake, and it's that verse:*
>
> *"To see the world in a grain of sand,*
> *and heaven in a wild flower,*
> *to hold infinity in the palm of your hand*
> *and eternity in an hour".*
>
> *'I said to her "That poem has helped me so much, to see the world in a particular way – it makes me full of wonder, and you gave me that, you taught me that poem."'*

Neil Astley has published a beautiful anthology called *Do not go Gentle: Poems for Funerals*. There is also a much larger anthology of contemporary poetry, *The Book of Love and Loss*, edited by Rosie Bailey and June Hall.

Both Nimue and James spoke of the need for honesty at funerals. Nimue said,

> *'I've sat through other people's "Christian" funerals where, for various reasons, it has not been possible to be honest about certain things in their life, because that would be problematic. Not being able to own that at the point of death and say this is*

*who that person was, and this is what was going on, and having
to maintain a façade for a funeral – how can that conceivably be
doing anyone any good? Funerals are a time when honesty and
integrity are far more important than liturgy or ritual ceremony.
It is toxic if you have to pretend that certain things haven't
happened: you end up silencing things that can't be articulated.
If you have unspeakable things that doesn't do people any good.'*

James told me of a funeral he had conducted just the previous day.

*'A young man who was found dead in his flat after prolonged
use of drugs, so whether that was suicide or overdose we don't
know. At the funeral yesterday I was blown away by the parents'
attitude; what they didn't want was a sense of shame or secrecy
around this appalling situation; the young man's father was just
– I can't believe how open and direct he was with us: about his
son's life, the beauty, charm, early promise and success, the intel-
ligence, and then the tragic and looming underbelly of that which
eventually took him down to take his own life. Because the dad
was so open, it removed the secrecy and any lingering sense of
shame... the whole place was then open for them all to grieve.
This replaced the "Oh how awful, he took his own life," all that
stuff... His courage was an incredible gift to the people who were
at the funeral, who didn't have to suffer under the projection of
"Oh how these people are suffering" ... his dad did it – by being
straight with us. It can be done, but it takes real courage.'*

James would have liked a funeral for his father which 'Would have
made it a proper kind of "Farewell dad, warts and all."'

Perhaps the need to cover up hurt which James and Nimue talked
of is linked to the idea, maybe the need, to 'Never speak ill of the
dead: de mortuis nil nisi bonum'. When I read accounts in the local
paper of those who have died tragically, it is always stressed just
what an amazing dad, or mother or child they had been. I sometimes

I wonder if we might instead never speak ill of the living; what difference might that make to our lives? Which is the real person, the one we find it hard to relate to when they are alive, or the paragon they seem to become in death? I would suggest both, but not one after the other, in both life and in death they are both. It is interesting that the phrase 'loved one' seems to be used mostly of people who have died. When they are alive they tend to be relatives and friends. What is the difference? Can we only admit to loving someone after they have died?

Judaism and Father P's monastery stress the importance of anniversaries. Rosa said how comforting she found the headstone for her father in the cemetery, where she could go to visit his memory. Father P said each year his monks remembered all those who had died going back to 1835, when the monastery was founded.

John talked of passing things on to future generations, whether through one's genes, or in things we have created. I have already mentioned the importance to Jean of Thomas Hardy's poem 'Heredity'.

Love does not die when the person we love dies. Love seems to be the common factor running through all faiths, including doing good to others, which is important for Humanists. Father P had the most to say about love in Christianity, much of which is in chapter ten.

'Christ came to teach the human race what it means to love one another... All love begins in God... God the Father and God the Son are united by a bond of Love – and that Love is the Holy Spirit... We can think of loving someone as something I do, but a more helpful image can be to say that when I love someone the Holy Spirit flows through me to that person... in Western culture the word "love" has a range of meanings; in Welsh there are two words, in Greek there are four and in the New Testament when they talk of the love of God they use agape – which is not used much elsewhere, but it's given a specific meaning, and it means

the self-giving love we see in Christ on the cross . It's not about
romantic love or sex, but self giving love, so that you can lay
down your life for those you love, so it's demanding love... So to
be a Christian is to be a bearer of Christ's life and love to others.'

The chaplain said, 'I walk in the shadow of Christ and bring his love to this place'. Kalsoom said, 'Islam is a religion of peace and love.' Talking about the Buddhist belief in non-attachment, B said, 'so love people, but with an open hand, don't cling onto them for your own needs – that's what the attachment means, or non-attachment.'

Sister Ally talked of the ethos of the Hospice at the Community of the Many Names of God, saying,

'The love, the energy that comes with everything that we do...
What you feel here in the temples is carried over: that peace, that
specialness, and it's all there the unconditional love.'

She went on to talk of the dying sister who 'Radiated that divine love'.

Swami S, of the same community, said,

'Every human being has love within them, and that expression
of spontaneous love is a manifestation of their divine nature...
When you talk about spiritual care in palliative care, you're not
talking about Christianity, Buddhism, or any other faith, you are
talking about the manifestation of love: understanding that that
person is not that body, the body is the vehicle.'

While most faiths involve love and forgiveness, most, apart from Humanism, seem also to believe in some form of judgement at death, before some kind of immortality. John finds comfort in the fact that he will not face a judge when he dies.

Rosa and Kalsoom both spoke of the importance of the day of judgement in their faiths. For Kalsoom, this was also the end of the world, when the good would go to Heaven and the bad to Hell for eternity. Many Christians also support the idea of the separation of the wicked from the good after death, but this was not mentioned by Father P or C. Only Kalsoom had much to say about heaven and hell, and even she was vague about details. These are Undiscovered Countries, even to their believers. Father P suggested that it is impossible to know what life after death will be like.

> 'After death there is no time, you've got eternal present. In our material world scientists say that time is one of the dimensions: how do our minds come to terms with an existence, a reality, in which there is no time, just eternal present? So time doesn't have any meaning after death, it's just eternal present and we can't really get our heads round that, because we exist in time... C S Lewis wrote a book called The Great Divorce, it's nothing to do with marriage, but it speaks of those who've died and the divorce between those who've died, between Heaven and the fullness of reality, and those who can't quite come to terms with it. He gives us an image of people in a dark grey town and a bus going to the outskirts of Heaven, which you can see in the distance. I think he expresses very well the difference between the unreality in which we all live and the fullness of reality. Heaven and the journey into it, and the blindnesses we have in this wonderful world.'

Despite judgement, there is also the possibility of being forgiven by a loving God; Kalsoom told me that God has 99 names, 'One of his names means merciful, the most merciful, we hope that because he is the most merciful, that he will be merciful with us.'

For many Christians the soul goes to Purgatory after death. Father P said, 'It's not mentioned in Scripture so some denominations don't accept it, but it makes a lot of sense.' For those in the Christian Community purgatory lasts for about a third of the length of the life of the individual. Eve, a follower of Rudolf Steiner, though not a member of C's Christian Community church, said, 'For every hour you've slept you spend an hour in purgatory, which is roughly one third of your life.'

C said,

'What happens is the soul experiences all it has done from the point of view of those people it has had dealings with. They would feel what the other person experienced through their dealings with them. So it's not a time of punishment, but I would imagine if you have treated people badly you're going to feel bad at that time, you will feel what they have felt. And in the process of experiencing that the individual feels that next time round they will want to do better. This is not the final stage; the journey goes on for quite a long time. Eventually the soul will be reincarnated.'

For Hindus and Buddhists there is karma rather than judgement. B said,

'Karma [in Buddhism] doesn't mean quite the same as karma is used in other traditions: it's not just because of bad things in your past you suffer now, it's more connected with the interdependence of anything and everything, and everything has consequences. I heard the Dalai Llama say that karma is such a positive idea, because it means everything you do now has its own karma. That which is of good motivation, and is compassionate and giving, has good consequences, and everything that you do which has poor motivation has negative consequences, and that's just how things are. With appropriate practice and meditation you can affect to some extent the karma you have accrued. It's not about fate, but it is your karmic connections in the 49 days and beyond.'

GKP said something very similar.

'Karma is action. It's a misunderstood word, it's not that if you do something you will be punished, it's not about punishments or rewards, it's action. Actions have reactions: that's all there is to it. Karma is the consequences of action. These consequences can happen in another incarnation, because it's energy. Everything is energy.'

I said I thought this sounded very similar to what B had told me. He replied, 'When we are here on this earth we are learning. In one sense you could say the earth is purgatory. Not being reincarnated is the ultimate aim, to get to a stage where you can choose to be reincarnated or choose not to be because you have those abilities.'

Many Buddhists, Hindus and those in the Christian Community Church all believe in reincarnation. C and GKP both said that the aim is to reach a point where one has learned enough, and done enough good, not to be reincarnated. C said, 'When we've learned all we need to learn, then you remain in the world of the spirit – there is no more need to return to the earth.' However when I asked B if, as in Hinduism, the aim for the enlightened Buddhist is not to be reincarnated, she replied, 'I can't give a definite answer, but my feeling would be, because the core thing is working for the benefit of other people, it is unlikely that they would choose not to.'

Nimue said,

'There are quite a lot of Pagans who believe in reincarnation... some are greatly influenced by Eastern thinking in this, some believe in afterlives – the Norse traditions, Egyptian and Greek traditions that inspire people all have their own takes on what happens when we die. Some pagans are atheists and believe this is all we get. Some, particularly the animists, see our energy returning to the flow of life to become something, which has a literal truth to it, but its easy to think that spirit dissipates just as

*energy and matter do. Some of us, like me, are maybeist and have
no real idea and will deal with it when we get there.'*

Christine said she found the idea of reincarnation comforting.

*'Reincarnation makes it understandable that you can have a just
God.'*

Eve said,

*'I firmly believe that we will come back – reincarnate. I don't see
any point in having all these trials and tribulations other than
working towards something – other than just purifying the soul.
If there wasn't reincarnation, there'd be an awful crowd of souls
not on the earth, wouldn't there? I like to think that the soul is
re-embodied and comes back to use its experiences in some way
or other.'*

I wondered if when reincarnated, she would be aware of her
previous life.

*'Next time it's just possible that we might, but this time very few of
us do; one or two of my children know that they were in a previous
life, they've seen themselves in a previous life, recognised that,
and know they have been here before. My other children believe
in it but haven't experienced it. I haven't experienced it myself;
I've had no flashbacks to previous lives, but I am convinced that
there is such a thing, and that when I die – a lot of people believe
that you have a tableau of your life when you die, but I believe
that I will be able to look back, not only on this life, but on my
previous lives. You learn what you have to work at for next time,
and choose your next life so as to be able to do this.'*

Rosa told me that within Judaism there are those who believe in
reincarnation.

'It might be slightly different from other religions. They believe you reincarnate in the same family, same kind of circles. Not everyone believes in it, but it is there in the tradition.'

According to the *Tibetan Book of Living and Dying*, early Christians also believed in reincarnation.

For most Christians and Muslims, however, the life after death is resurrection rather than reincarnation. For them also life on earth seems to be a mere preparation for the life after death, which is the real life.

What of the majority who do not have a faith, what meaning do they give to death? Is it all mystery, lost in a cloud of unknowing? What about judgement, immortality, reincarnation? These only came up in conversations with those of faith, but others used metaphors which made death meaningful for them. The most common was that of the journey, which was used by several contributors, those with and those without faith. Death is a journey: an essential part of the journey of life. I was reminded of another Ewan McColl song, 'The Ballad of Accounting', which says that as we journey from the cradle to the grave we don't really notice the landmarks, we think our lives will go on for ever.

Sister Ally said, 'We look after them through their journey.' GKP said, 'Our journey is about realising that we are Brahma, the creator, the created, this is just eternal.'

Swami S said,

'It is understanding that the journey of life, the purpose of life, is for human beings to realise that they are themselves part of almighty God... a person's journey from the moment they've been given the diagnosis of a life threatening-illness, that moment of confusion, when they are confronted for the first time in their life with their own mortality... they can be helped through their

journey through that expression of love, and that comes from the spirit.'

B said,

'During the dying process all those you are connected to can help you on that journey.'

Father P, was very certain of his destination.

'There's this journey through life to the fulfilment of life which is the whole context of our view of death... This is our orientation, and this image of a journey is quite powerful. If we're going on a journey, the destination shapes the whole journey, the ticket you buy, what you pack, what you do; if you pack for the Bahamas and end up in Iceland that's silly . So on our life journey the destination, the purpose, where it's going, death is just part of the whole journey to life eternal, the transition.'

When describing what happened in his monastery when someone died, he said there was always someone with them until the funeral, 'Praying with them on their journey... So this is the whole context of the Catholic view of death – the journey.'

C emphasised more than once that after death the soul goes on a long journey, taking many years and involving many stages.

'We say words that accompany the individual on that journey to the other side of the threshold between life and death... Three days after death, the soul starts on its journey proper which is a very long journey... It is a journey on the other side, and as with any journey you need some preparation and you need some help on the way. We believe that the funeral service gives some of the help that is necessary to the souls on the other side.'

Anne, telling me of one of the conversation she had had with one of her palliative care patients in the small hours, said,

> *'I felt I had been sent to her for that reason for that one night. That was part of my journey and part of her journey. She died a couple of days later.'*

Talking of the execution of her pen friend on death row she sounded very similar to Father P (she is also a Catholic) when she said,

> *'He'd had his life's journey. He's now continuing his journey. I believe that's the journey we will all be making eventually; this life we are living now is the preliminary journey, the preparation for the real journey to come.'*

These were people of faith; the metaphor of the journey of life was also used by others. Father P's journey to the Bahamas sounded very similar to something Julie, the Marie Curie nursing assistant who said she had no religious faith, said:

> *'There was one man who was determined that he was going to take £20 with him when he died. He knew he was going somewhere, he knew his mum was taking him shopping on Monday, and he had to go somewhere. He died about a week later. He wanted money to play the slot machines while he was waiting, he wasn't too sure about where he was going... his wife said, "What does he want this money for?" I just said, "Let him have the money – you've got it to spare, he's not going to lose it". When he died it was in his pyjama pocket. He knew he had to go somewhere. When you go on a trip you make sure you've got everything you need. He didn't know what he was going to need. Do any of us know what we are going to need for the final journey? Life is a journey and death is a journey.'*

Rosie said that in William Bloom's course, death was seen as,

'Taking a journey into the clear light... Dying is being on a big adventure. I think in each one of us there is a person who is prepared to be excited by where we're going and what's going to happen next, and there's a person who is quite frightened at the thought of going on to something that feels like completely unknown. So there's fear and excitement; fear and excitement have the same physical body responses, don't they?'

Phoebe told me her father, whom she took to Switzerland, was an atheist.

'Interestingly, just when we were already in Switzerland a friend sent a text to me and said something like "I'm saying goodbye and wishing him a good onward journey". I read it to Dad, and it really touched him, tears came to his eyes. I didn't ask him directly at the end what he really thought, but yes, he was an atheist. I'm definitely not an atheist.'

Jenny Diski, writes in *In Gratitude* that she hated being told she was on a journey, but was forced to admit gradually that she was. Almost at the end of the book she writes of her journey home. She also says she did not want to die, but resented the idea that she should be fighting against her death. Many stories of deaths from cancer reported in local papers say such things as, 'After a brave fight.' Not all want to fight.

Sam, the Samaritan, Caroline, Rosie and Nicola all used the word 'explore', when discussing the need to be able to talk about death. For Sam, this exploration involved discussing the situation of the distressed caller and could lead to empowerment. 'We will give people space to explore what they're going through, and in doing that we can hopefully support them in developing strategies to help them better cope with situations.'

Caroline, Nicola and Rosie talked about exploring ideas: talking with children in school for Caroline, a book that explored later life for Rosie. Nicola said of counselling that it enables,

> 'The fear of death, fear of life to be really explored – I'm not saying that happens with everybody, but it can be taken and used in a constructive way: you're still, and taken into that area of what do you want to do with your precious life?'

For Christine the metaphor was the horizon that one may see on a journey, but not cross. She showed me some of the art work she was preparing for her degree as her brother was dying twenty years ago.

> 'There are three of them. This is the second: "21 places discovered on journeys from a chosen place to the horizon in the south west." Landscapes. You see it on the horizon. Some pages have holes in the middle, you catch a glimpse of what is on the next page but you can't see the whole till you turn the page. It's totally different from what you think it might be. It's about landscape, not about death, it was about the dying process. To me the horizon was a metaphor for death. You can look to the horizon, but when you get there, you can't get to the horizon. Horizon is just a nice way of bringing my interest in landscapes into working with what he was going through. The journey: I had gone there, metaphorically, and he had gone there physically.'

Christine used another metaphor from art: perspective. 'So you get a perspective on life,' from losing a loved one. Others used this also: Hannah, retired nurse, said it is,

> 'Well known that the opportunity for a shift in perspective is there from moment of diagnosis: your focus and perspective can change in an instant. So suddenly what seems to matter is put into a more real perspective.'

She said of the death café, 'it puts everything in perspective in a way that's quite rare.'

Pammy said,

'Dad's death really did make me think. I would like if possible to embrace my own death like my dad. I sort of realised that meant making the most of my life, and also constantly keeping death in mind, not in a morbid way, but sometimes in a very helpful way, if something difficult was happening I'd think, "Well, does this really matter?" In the end we're going to die, I'm going to die... very helpful in getting things in perspective.'

Swami S said that when his father died in a flood of the grace of God,

'I absolutely know... this life soul had been received by God, that made everything else fall into perspective.'

Kalsoom said that after the recent deaths of two friends,

'It has put my own life into perspective and this is what Allah wants from us.'

Sam said,

'I think being a Samaritan helps you to put things in perspective in your own life quite a lot. You can't even imagine what some people have gone through, and even six years on I still get moments of "I can't believe you've been through that". That kind of call puts a totally different perspective on your own life, whatever kind of issues are going on.'

She felt that one aim of calls was to help the caller to 'Come through to a new perspective.'

Phoebe spoke of the, 'Sense of peace and that sense of perspective of what really matters' after taking her father to Switzerland.

Paul said,

'Many writers have encouraged us to use death as a stimulus for looking at what's important. Rumi said something like, "Go directly to the moment of your death and see what's important." I think it's good advice if you can do it, it's challenging.'

C talked about the service in her Steiner Church to accompany

'The individual on that journey to the other side of the threshold between life and death.' That threshold is the one that no one crosses before death, not even those who have had a near death experience. The word *'threshold'* comes from the word to thresh – to separate out the chaff from the grain, or to move violently. Crossing the threshold is hard work, like threshing.'

Light was another metaphor used in conversations. Several contributors spoke of light in relation to the end of life. Tagore wrote, 'Death is not the extinguishing of the light; it is only putting out the lamp because the dawn has come.

Hannah spoke of seeing life 'As it really is, in all its sparkling luminosity.' When her mother was dying, Jean told me, 'There was a feeling of lightness in the air.' Of one of her clients who had HIV/ AIDS, 'There was this spiritual light, or depth, that I felt he had, so he could travel that path in a positive way.'

Rosie told me that the preparing for dying course she had attended encouraged participants to see death as, 'Taking a journey into the clear light'. SA told of the light that many see in a near death experience.

Quakers believe in the Inner Light, or 'That of God', in everyone. J said that her therapist 'Was helping me find some light within and outside myself... with therapy I have been able to find a new relationship with my son, and some light.' Rosa told of candles lighted on anniversaries, others of lighting candles for the dying, or for the body after death.

Life is indeed luminous, as Hannah said, it sparkles with possibilities and then it ends in a journey to another light. Rosie told of William Bloom's 'refrain about going into the clear light.' J spoke of finding a new light after the death of her son. Others mentioned lighting candles. However, Annabel said, 'The light goes out of the eyes' at death.

The journey, the horizon, perspective, the threshold, the light: for each of these contributors the perspective is different. Different perspectives, new understandings coming from very different journeys and encounters with death, in very different lives.

Swami S used the metaphor of drama several times; he talked of 'The drama of the dying process.' Describing his father's death he said, 'Everything was a drama'. He also said 'Part of life's drama is finding out who you are.'

However no other contributor used this metaphor. Corinna used the word 'dramatic' and said of those with a dying person, pretending they were not dying, 'All these dramas and these wonderful processes that are going on in the room, the elephant we don't talk about. But they are huge in the room, pretending doesn't work.'

Death is also a letting go. Perhaps letting go of the light of life. Both the dying and those who love them need to let go. 'Let me go' was what Swami S's father was begging shortly before he died. Sister Ally said the 90-year-old nun was 'ready to go'. Hannah said that particularly in Western culture, 'It's very difficult to let go.' Annabel said that some people just let go of all their thoughts and find peace when they are dying. Rosie talked of, 'Letting go of lots of thoughts of how we should be, how we used to be – it allows us to go into the future.' Paul told of his friend who was dying, 'She asked me to go off with her husband, to get him out of the way so that she could practice letting go with her two friends.' Sister S said, 'Letting go of the body is extremely difficult.'

Jean spoke of letting go of her mother.

'Later I buried her, I was one of those who lowered her into the grave, as with my father. That was very important to me as a child, the last tangible thing I could do for each of them, to put my parents in their graves, that last connection with their corpses in their coffins. The coffin was already on planks above the grave, as it was at a remote and stony cemetery. The strap was touching the coffin and in my hand, that act was very powerful, it's very meaningful when you let go. I think when I let go of my mother I turned to the world... Up until recently I've felt that my mother's death had such a profound effect on me, but now I can see it is her life that's also had a profound effect on me. And life is what she gave me. Sometimes I think I want to see my mother, and then I realise, oh she died: it's just that connection, that sort of joy – oh my mother, and then she's not here, but she is.'

B said,

'At 49 days people usually have a ritual and another service, because it's about the mind letting go of the body. When the body isn't holding the mind, the mind can go anywhere... the practice in life is to let go of those things. But that doesn't mean you shouldn't get close to people – you can be attached to people, but not in a grasping way, the issue is the grasping.'

The conflict between loving and letting go is beautifully expressed in Mary Oliver's poem 'In Blackwater Woods', in *Poems That Make Grown Men Cry*.

Death is the final letting go, it is moving on in the journey of the individual, even if we are not sure of the final destination. We have our myths, our metaphors of a journey, or as Rosie said, an adventure. Funerals are our rites of passage, to speed us on our way, a farewell from those who may, or may not, know where we are going. Whether or not we know our ultimate destination, we know that death is on our horizon; but until we die, we cannot see beyond that horizon, we cannot go through it before death: we view it 'through a glass darkly'. Ellen mentioned a Bible reading from her son's funeral, which I think must have been from one Corinthians 13 where 'through a glass darkly' is translated as 'Now we see only puzzling reflections in a mirror, but then we shall see face to face.' Another Christian had told Ellen that this life is like the back of a tapestry, with all the knots, after death we will see the finished picture. I asked if these were of any comfort to her.

'Not really, I don't want to wait. I don't know if I'll ever see my son and husband again. I will only ever remember my son as a nine-year-old. I was talking to a customer at work recently, he said he had been at school with T, "We'll never forget him." It must have taken a lot of guts to say that: I got some comfort from that, "We'll always remember him."'

We can only see 'through a glass darkly,' or 'puzzling reflections.' Perhaps the only certainty is that there is no certainty? For Paul, certainty is dangerous.

Listening to those contributors who had watched someone die, it seemed to me unlikely that death is the end. Something significant seems to happen at the moment of death: even Jean, the 'sceptic unbeliever', said, 'something left her' when her mother died. Others talked of the atmosphere in the room following a death as one of some beauty. If something leaves as we die, surely that goes somewhere: to an undiscovered country?

Rosa said, 'Perhaps death is not so threatening or frightening if there is faith.' This echoed what I heard from other contributors. Kalsoom and B, both thought that in their faiths death was not the taboo subject it appears to be in Western society generally; they are able to talk about it freely, so it may hold less terror for believers. But

John and Julie, who had no religious faith also had no fear. From these conversations I thought that fear of death seems more to do with one's experience of it than one's faith.

Personally I remain a maybeist, with Nimue. Like Pammy and Paul, I am content not to know. As for life after death I will 'let the mystery come.' As for reincarnation or immortality, I recommend the film 'Jesus of Montreal', where a modern Jesus is resurrected through transplant surgery: others live on after his death, they are oned by his death. The song Joe Hill says that Joe did not die – he lives on in the working class movement.

I do firmly believe in life before death, which was the Christian Aid week slogan one year, and seems to be the conclusion of many of these conversations: the need to live more fully. The next chapter will look at what contributors had to say about this.

*   *   *

Not how did he die, but how did he live?
Not what did he gain, but what did he give?
These are the units to measure the worth
of a man as a man, regardless of birth.

Not, what was his church, nor what was his creed?
But had he befriended those really in need?
Was he ever ready, with word of good cheer,
to bring back a smile, to banish a tear?

Not what did the sketch in the newspaper say,
but how many were sorry when he passed away.

(Anon – 'Poems for Funerals)'

12 Living more fully

The Joy of living

Scatter my dust and ashes, feed me to the wind
So that I may be
Part of all you see
The air you are breathing,
I'll be part of the curlew's cry and the soaring hawk,
The blue milkwort and the sundew hung with diamonds.
I'll be riding the gentle wind that blows through your hair,
Reminding you how we shared
In the joy of living.
(written by Ewan MacColl, reproduced by kind
    permission of Ewan MacColl Ltd)

The above lines are the last verse of the song *The Joy of Living,* which Ewan Mcoll wrote halfway up a mountain, when pains in his chest forced him to sit and wait while his wife and daughter went to the top without him. He realised that he probably did not have much longer to live. In the first three verses he says goodbye to the mountains, to his wife, to his children, before going on to this beautiful description of being oned with all creation. It is similar to a poem frequently read at funerals,

Do not stand at my grave and weep
I am not there. I do not sleep.
I am a thousand winds that blow.
I am the diamond glints on snow.
I am the sunlight on ripened grain.

I am the gentle autumn rain.
When you awaken in the morning's hush
I am the swift uplifting rush
Of quiet birds in circled flight.
I am the soft stars that shine at night.
Do not stand at my grave and cry;
I am not there. I did not die.
(Anon in *Poems for Funerals*)

This book is about death. But from the first I knew it would be as much about life, and living it more fully: life and death are inseparable. Death is the end of life, but also, as Kalsoom and Father P said, it is its destination; its goal, according to Jung. The Quaker advice tells us that we are 'freed to live more fully' if we can contemplate death. Do we only contemplate death when we are confronted by it, perhaps with a life limiting diagnosis, or the death of a loved one? What does it mean to 'live more fully'?

What have these 45 conversations told me? What, if anything, have I learned? Can I now better contemplate my own death, and live my life more fully? What does this mean? We tell ourselves stories, create myths, as we try to make sense of death; our stories about death reflect what we understand of the meaning of life.

Each of us needs to make our own sense of death: inevitably these chapters are written from my point of view. I have chosen what to highlight, which concepts that arose in conversations deserves a chapter. You, the reader, may well disagree with my interpretations. I have often quoted contributors at length, which I hope may help you to reach your own conclusions. All the contributors are atypical in that they are willing to talk about death, perhaps this is why it is important to listen to what they can tell us; for no one is typical. Perhaps, after reading these conversations you will feel you want to talk to others about death. If you do, this book will have achieved one of its aims. Perhaps you, and possibly those you talk to, will find ways that you, and they, can live more fully. This was another aim.

Life is a journey, or as some said, an adventure; our destination is death; it is on our horizon, as Christine showed in her art work, but until we die we cannot see beyond it, or cross the threshold as C called it; we go into a clear light, according to Rosie; now we see only puzzling reflections, as a friend told Ellen.

Until death comes we live, and how we live our lives seems to me more important to me than what happens at the end. Yet contemplating death could make this life more fruitful, more fulfilling. While this is a message I was perhaps looking for, it is what I heard in these conversations.

In listening to contributors' accounts of death, I was struck by the spirituality of the end of life. Jean, 'a die-hard sceptic and non-believer', said 'something spiritual happens when someone dies'. Christine also talked about 'something spiritual' leaving her mother. For some this 'something' is a soul going to a God. The unbeliever who met the journalist in the Dignitas clinic asked for the window to be opened, in case she had a soul that needed to fly out. For others, perhaps, that something is what makes us who we are, and links us, in ways which we cannot comprehend to all humanity, or all creation. GKP talked of 'A sense of oneness with everything, that's the essence of who we are.' We are oned in death, even though, or perhaps because, every death is unique. Are we perhaps merged, oned, into Jung's collective unconscious? I once heard a scientist say that all human beings consist mostly of water, with some common chemicals; the rest is Star Stuff from the Big Bang. GKP said that we are all one, 'Like the water, the river, and the sea – they are all one.'

Both Jean and Annabel mentioned the atmosphere when someone dies. Jean said, 'The quality of the atmosphere changes when someone dies.' Annabel spoke of, 'The quality of the atmosphere… it can feel like there's a spirit in the room.'

Those who witnessed deaths told me that the experience was a privilege. I have been privileged to have these conversations. I hope I have done contributors justice, and apologise to any whose contribution I have inadvertently missed, or misrepresented.

I seem to have used the word 'moving' rather often in previous chapters: it seems the most fitting adjective to describe many of these conversations. We need to be moved by the fact that our lives are finite, to be aware of every moment. How can we be moved to live more fully, to be oned with others, to experience the blossomest blossom? The word emotion comes from the Latin word to move: we need our emotions to move us and to live more fully, before we move from life to death: a uniquely moving experience.

Nicola suggested that perhaps we can only live more fully if we know that we are going to die: she described this as 'deep knowing'. Where does such knowing come from? I suggest it is from our emotions, which can move us to move on, to a fuller life.

Swami S said,

> *'It's about recognising the embodied divinity in every life, and treating each life as sacred. It is understanding that the journey of life, the purpose of life, is for human beings to realise that they are themselves part of almighty God.'*

Paul said, 'Contemplating death can help to enrich life.' Tom told me that it was through his experiences with still births and miscarriages that, 'I learned to embrace life in a fuller way.' This included being able to come closer to other men.

Those who go regularly to the local death café, including myself, say they come back month after month because they find it helpful, life-enhancing, energising. Death can illuminate life.

Pammy said, 'If I can keep death in mind then I can live better.'

Talking about death plans, and how they might have to be abandoned, Hannah said,

'To have had the opportunity of trying to prepare for it [death] is a gift, because it's really about life.'

Iain added to my report of our conversation:

'I would just like to add that it's really important to keep a positive attitude to life because no-one knows what's ahead of them, we just need to be grateful for what we have.'

Ellen showed me a poem her son had written, before he died. He was eight:

My magic box

I will put in my box the silk in the middle of a chestnut.
The gorgeous scent of chocolate melting down your throat.
The first sight of a baby.

I will put in my box a cuddle from a friend,
A chat with a nearby relation,
And the best Christmas ever.

My box has the glittering look of a star in the midnight skies.
It is made of steel,
Solid as a boulder
And ice that never melts.

I will remember my box
When I am sad.
It will help me to enjoy my life.
I don't think I will ever be sad,
Because of my glittering box.
(Ellen's son, T.)

304 | The Undiscovered Country

He was living fully until he died. Perhaps children can do this in a way adults cannot, just as I was told that children are more matter of fact about death. Ellen said,

> 'You've just got to strive for what you think is important. You've got to get out there and live your life.'

No contributor was very specific about what living life fully might mean: there is no prescription, each must find their own answers. Perhaps I should be living more fully myself, rather than talking about death, writing about it? Have these conversations given me any ideas about how I should live more fully? I have decided that, for me, at this time in my life, writing this book is my way of living more fully, even though I seem at times immersed in death. At times I wondered if, in writing about it, I was escaping from my own fear of death, by concentrating on the thoughts of others, being comforted by what I was hearing. Perhaps my fear of death was replaced by a fear that I might not finish this book before I die. Possibly.

These conversations have moved me in many ways. I was particularly moved by those who work or volunteer in hospices, who are involved in enabling others to live fully and to blossom before they die. Isabel said, 'Life for the patients is widening in a sense, at a time when most might think life was closing in.' She also spoke of the joy in the hospice. Sister Ally, and others, said, 'It's not about dying – it's about living'. Hospice patients live their lives to the end: they find creativity, they talk about their fears, they share with others.

What I saw at both the hospices I visited, and in the film *Seven Songs for a Long Life*, was living fully through the happiness of creativity: whether this was music, as in the Scottish hospice, art in the Welcome Hospice or being with an elephant, in the Community of the Many Names of God. Perhaps even more importantly, each hospice is a community, where patients and staff can be oned and, perhaps, through this they may find Jung's individuation. Iain said, 'we all try to help each other,' and spoke of how he was able to help new patients at his hospice; those involved in the other hospices told of patients' support for one another. I was reminded of Wordsworth's poem 'Tintern Abbey,' where he writes of:

'*..that best portion of a good man's life:*
His little, nameless, unremembered, acts
Of kindness and of love.'

Thoreau famously said, 'The mass of men lead lives of quiet desperation and go to the grave with the song still in them.' Could finding, and singing, one's song be what Jung meant by individuation? For those at the Scottish hospice their songs are most certainly not still in them when they die, they are literally sung for all to hear: they blossom. Those in the other hospices find other songs, things within them they did not know they had. Perhaps they are finding individuation, inextricably linked to the concept of the collective unconscious, what I have called being oned. Jung said, 'From the middle of life onward, only he remains vitally alive who can *die with life*' (his emphasis). Those in hospices seem 'vitally alive', perhaps because, in Jung's words, they have died with life, accepted death.

The word which perhaps sums up much of what I heard is acceptance: acceptance of death, including one's own; acceptance of finality; for some, perhaps, acceptance of pain; acceptance of loss; of the blossom; of oneness; of the collective unconscious. Acceptance of death frees us to live more fully: to live in oneness, to blossom. Both sister Ally and Isabel gave examples of patients for whom acceptance made all the difference. Acceptance brings peace. Winnie, the patient at the Hospice of the Community of the Many Names of God, was talking of acceptance when she said,

'*You can just relax, and when the time comes you can go*
peacefully and calmly, the best way you can.'

I see this acceptance as very similar to forgiveness: giving up on a better past, accepting a limited present, and thus enabled to live more fully in whatever future there may be. Today, very many people seem unable to accept the reality of death, unwilling to talk about it. Are they missing something very precious in life?

For some, accepting a faith enabled them to talk about death and to be less fearful. Others have found other ways of incorporating fearlessness into their lives, living more fully. Phoebe said, after taking her father to Switzerland, she felt comfortable about her own death.

Rosie, who said that dying is being on a 'big adventure', spoke of each of us having within us someone is excited by this and someone who is quite frightened. I hope I can find the person within me who feels excited rather than fearful of the adventure that is death; I suspect most of those I talked with have done so.

I hope I have not painted too rosy, or too cosy, a picture of death: we blossom before dissolving into love, oned in death. This is what I heard. Death can also be horrendous: I heard too of the enduring pain of bereavement, of isolation, of sickness. Helen told me of the dreadful side effects of chemotherapy; Iain of the reality of living with the constant pain of MS; Ellen of the horror of finding her son collapsed and dying at the foot of the stairs, of giving him mouth to mouth, but being told 'he's gone.' Caroline spoke of the unbearable pain of being told that the hospital had been unable to save her son. Some die alone, unloved. I heard too of fear, but this was mostly that contributors had less fear of death than previously.

In chapter three, 'Someone to grief with', and chapter nine, 'Oned in death', I have used the noun 'grief' and the pronoun 'one' as verbs; this seems to me to give them greater power. Sometimes we may need to adapt language to fully express our meaning when talking about the incomprehensible. Nimue talked of maybeism; J of 'gone-ness', as well as griefing; Dennis Potter of nowness, and the blossom being the blossomest; Pammy spoke of the 'blossomiest', which I think I prefer to Potter's word. These words were created because no words in the dictionary say exactly what we mean. Tom used the poignant phrase 'a childless mother', which I have never heard before, to describe his daughter after her stillbirth.

Sometimes, however, prose, even using such words, is inadequate, which is why poems and songs seem to appear increasingly in this book. Caroline was told, 'Your poems put words to what I felt but couldn't say.' Poems can reach a place where prose cannot go. Wordsworth's 'Intimations of Immortality from Recollections of Early Childhood' ends with the words:

> 'Thanks to the human heart by which we live,
> Thanks to its tenderness, its joys, and fears,
> To me the meanest flower that blows can give
> Thoughts that do often lie too deep for tears.'

Poetry uses words to touch these thoughts too deep for tears, emotions impossible to put into prose, which is what these conversations involved. Some contributors wrote poetry to express such thoughts. I have quoted poems by J, by Caroline, the daughters of friends (Yanna and Lilli), Ellen's son, as well as published poets. There are some poems that can, according to the title of a lovely anthology, *Make Grown Men Cry*.

Chris said most funerals now seem to include some poetry. Jean told me of choosing eight poems for her mother's funeral, reflecting the important part poetry had played in her life. Poetry can teach us what matters most in life.

It seems fitting that it was a poet, Michael Symmons Roberts, who choose death as his topic for the Sunday morning programme on Radio Four, 'Something Understood.'

I can draw no conclusion from these 45 conversations, none is possible. I have been enriched by them: touched and moved by the depths from which contributors were willing to share. Yet death is still enveloped in the great 'cloud of unknowing'. Only one certainty emerged: we must live until we die. However short the time we have, we can live it more fully; the rest is uncertainty. The Undiscovered Country remains undiscovered. I think these conversations confirmed my maybeism. Nimue said she tried to approach it in a 'spirit of I don't know.' B spoke of '85,000 different minds needing 85,000 practices'. As Pammy said, 'It's a mystery to me.' This mystery includes Nicola's 'deep knowing' and Father P's 'certainties which you have which are beyond just the rational.' Finally I am convinced that Julian of Norwich was right: 'All shall be well.'

Perhaps, instead of a conclusion, I can refer you to the poem by Mary Oliver, *When Death Comes* (in *Poems for Funerals*). Like many of these conversations, it is a poem about life. Yet Mary Oliver cannot have the last word. Sometimes even poetry is not enough; only silence will do. Sister Ally talked of just sitting in silence with hospice patients. 'You just sit with them, and let them know you are there, and that you know they are still there.' The Chaplain of the Welcome Hospice said that with a good death, 'There is not a huge outpouring of grief at that moment of passing, but almost a silence and stillness'. A silent passing through the threshold, passing from one reality to another, something both mysterious and mystical, spiritual, sacred.

Another of the Quaker Advices and Queries says, 'We seek a gathered stillness in our meetings for worship so that all may feel the power of God's love drawing us together and leading us.' I think both Sister Ally and the Chaplain were describing a 'gathered stillness'. Is this the stillness of the collective unconscious? Is death a journey into the stillness of silence, into a gathered oneness? Silence is surely where all faiths, and none, can meet.

When I was a Quaker prison chaplain I organised a weekly silent meeting for those of all faiths and none. I was surprised how popular the meetings became. Those who came appreciated the silence, which was usually deep. There were frequent references to the noisy environment of the prison; our meetings were the only place they could find quiet. Visiting Quakers often said the meetings were truly gathered. I felt there was a quality to these meetings based on a shared suffering and despair, which is not often found in Quaker meeting houses. In discussion after the silence, men would share terrible problems, others would offer sympathy, support and suggestions: they had been there. They understood. They could grief with one another, could be oned. Silence is not solitude. One can be alone in a noise, and gathered with others in silence, in oneness. We can blossom in silence.

Different people respond differently to the absence of sound. For some it may be frightening, even threatening, they feel it is empty and needs to be filled. For others, the same silence is comforting, welcoming. We talk of an empty, a threatening or a pregnant silence; the silence of the grave, the silence of death. When I came round from having been unconscious for many hours, I felt I was surfacing from the silence of peace. Could the silence of death be the living silence?

In his posthumously published book, *The Silence at the Song's End*, Nicholas Heiney, a brilliant student, poet and tall ships sailor, who after much mental suffering, killed himself at the age of 24, wrote a poem which ends with the words:

> "...I sing, as I was told,
> inside myself.
> I sing inside myself
> the one wild song, song that whirls
> my words around
> until a world unfurls
>
> my ship's new sail
> I catch the dew

and set a course amongst the ocean curls

The silence at the song's end
Before the next
Is the world"
Nicholas Heiney (1982-2006.)

God is Silence is the title of a small book by Pierre Leconte, a Catholic who became a Quaker before returning to Catholicism. He writes:

'Words split apart. Silence unites. Words scatter. Silence gathers up. Words stir up. Silence brings peace. Words engender denial. Silence invites even the denier to find fresh hope in the confident expectation of a mystery which can be accomplished within.'

The hymn 'Dear lord and father of mankind' has the words, 'the silence of eternity, interpreted by love.' The psalmist wrote, 'Be still and know that I am God.' (Psalm 46).

Gerald Manley Hopkins wrote of 'Elected silence,' singing to him, when he decided to become a monk. John Henry Newman wrote the beautiful prayer:

'May He support us all the day long, till the shades lengthen and the evening comes, and the busy world is hushed, and the fever of life is over, and our work is done. Then in His mercy may He give us a safe lodging, and a holy rest and peace at the last.'

The word 'peace' came into most contributors' descriptions of a 'good death.' Father P said of a good death, that there is 'a peace, and whole sense of "Yes, the time has come."' Julie, talking of the death of one of her patients who had been in terrible pain for a long time, said, 'When he passed he was at peace.' I heard of making peace with the family, peace with God, peace filling the room. Corinna spoke of sharing the peace with the dying.

At the end of the film *Seven Songs for a Long Life*, before the applause, there was an amazing silence in the hall when I watched it. Was this 'the silence at the song's end, which is the world'? I felt moved; I think we were all moved, perhaps we were all thinking that some response other than applause was called for. As we did not know what this would be, eventually we applauded. I suspect I was not the only one in that hall who found this almost crass. That brief silence was the acknowledgement that we had all been deeply moved by the film. Sometimes silence is the only possible response; that very brief silence in that hall had an almost spiritual quality. Even in the most secular of gatherings, perhaps a football crowd, when someone has died, silence, perhaps a minute, sometimes two, is called for; the quality of those silences can be, and was at the end of the film, something approaching the silence of the Quaker meeting. A living, holy silence that is far more than the mere absence of sound: those who share such silences are oned in something greater than themselves, something awe inspiring.

There can be no conclusion to this book. At the end, all there is is silence. A silence all share. I can only end with Hamlet's dying words,

'*The rest is silence...*'
(Hamlet, act five, scene 2)

Appendix one: Contributors

Annabel: used to be a nurse and has worked both in a hospice and in an anthroposophical clinic with dying patients, so she has seen a lot of death. 'I really enjoyed working with the dying.'

When I asked her why, she said: "I think that it affirmed the spiritual dimension of life…I really enjoyed working with the dying.'.. It is a privilege to be around that sort of mystery.'

Anne: writes to American prisoners on death row. Her professional background was palliative care; she worked in nursing homes and hospices, and on retirement for Marie Curie.

B: is a Buddhist, who is doing a piece of work for her Buddhist Sangha: practical suggestions to help Buddhists who are preparing to die in the West, where the Buddhist teaching on death is not widely understood.

C: is a priest at the Christian Community Church, which follows the teachings of Rudolf Steiner.

Caroline: Caroline's son died 14 years ago from alcohol misuse. She has written about grief, both poetry and prose and works in therapeutic writing.

The Chaplain: is a volunteer chaplain at the Welcome Hospice.

Chris: is a volunteer at the Welcome Hospice, he is also a lay reader in the Church of England, and as such has conducted many funerals.

Christine: is an artist, who told me very movingly about the death of her brother, twenty years ago, when she was just finishing her degree in fine arts.

Corinna; is a naturopath and nutritionist. She has just completed the demanding training to become an end of life doula.

E: works in the Welcome Hospice's outreach service, where she encourages patients to talk about death.

Ellen: Ellen's son died twelve years ago of pneumonia, just before his ninth birthday. She then started a self-help group for bereaved parents, Caring Friends, which is still functioning twelve years on.

Eve: is 86, probably the oldest contributor. She has six grown up children, 21 grandchildren ('10 'opted – ie. direct descendants – 2 adopted, and 9 co-opted – ie. came with partners), and eight great grandchildren. She is a follower of Rudolf Steiner, particularly his ideas of reincarnation,but not a member of C's church.

Father P: is a Roman Catholic priest, a monk currently the chaplain to a small community of Bernadine Cistercian nuns.

Gill: is a volunteer at the Welcome Hospice. She does Reiki, Qi Gong and works in the art room, which she thoroughly enjoys.

GKP: grew up in a family with a 'Hindu' background, and while he is not himself a practising Hindu, he knows a great deal about Hinduism.

The GP: has seen many deaths in her work. She described herself as being 'slightly evangelical' about the need to have conversations about death before death, so that the dying can die as they would wish. She has had such conversations, but they are not always easy.

Hannah: is a retired nurse who has worked both with Marie Curie and in a hospice, and is a regular at the death café.

Helen: was given six months to live about a year before I talked with her. She did not really want to talk about death, saying 'there is not much to say', but kindly told me about the dreadful months of living with chemotherapy.

Iain: has been a patient in the Scottish Hospice for eight years. He has Primary Progressive MS.

Isobel: is the manager of the Welcome Hospice, who was extremely welcoming. When I went to one of the hospice's open mornings and explained that I would like to talk, she let me record her then and there.

J: is still grieving after her only son took his own life eight years ago, and much of our conversation was about grief. She gave me the phrase 'to grief with'. She began writing poetry to honour her son, and now runs a poetry group for older people.

James: is a funeral director 'with a difference', and runs a business called 'Family Tree Funerals,' which specialises in creating meaningful and personalised funerals.

Jean: is a carer, who has cared for many clients at the end of life. Her mother died about three years ago, and she described this to me most movingly.

Jenny: has been volunteering at Welcome Hospice for six years; she helps the diversional therapist in the art room, and loves the work.

John: is a retired teacher, a humanist and currently Chair of his county humanists association. He came to give a humanist view of death, and humanist funerals, and also his views on the Assisted Dying Bill then going through parliament.

Julie: welcomed me to her home, despite being in the midst of selling it, and having just learned that the process has fallen through. She was bubbling with life, with her three noisy dogs and her butterfly tattoo; it was easy to see how with her warm openness and friendly smile she gives comfort to dying people in her work as a Health Care Assistant for Marie Curie. She loves her work, and said she was 'passionate' about it, and quite happy to talk about death.

Kalsoom: is a Muslim who said she was an ordinary person who followed the Muslim faith to the best of her ability. When two of her friends of around her age died it made her even more determined to to continue to strive to be the best possible Muslim and to show other people that Islam is a religion of peace and love.

M: is a nurse who has worked in intensive care, coronary care and with cancer patients, and seen many deaths. Now, the wife of a curate and a lay minister herself, she finds herself caring for the recently bereaved. She told me of some 'amazing' deaths she had witnessed.

M5: is a retired aromatherapist, and a member of the Quaker Fellowship for Afterlife Studies (QFAS). She told me of some strange experiences with messages from people in her life who had died.

Martin S: wants to help people to weave their own caskets for when they die. He ran a weekend workshop for this with an experienced basket maker. He is a death café attender.

Nicola: is a counsellor, who says on her website that she is a graduate of Core Process Psychotherapy because of her interest in Buddhism. She is also a trained Cruse bereavement counsellor, but said this is not her main concern in her work.

Nimue: is a pagan, a Druid, who celebrates Pagan funerals and has written several books on Paganism.

Pammy: started and organises the local Death Café. She is a Buddhist, a retired social worker with a special interest in death and dying and bereavement. She described her father's death as a 'turning point' for her.

Paul: is a regular death café attender. He described himself as a 'recovering Roman Catholic', and has thought a lot about death.

Phoebe: took her father to Switzerland to die with Dignitas. She works with Cruse.

R: is a Cruse bereavement volunteer whose mother died when he was fifteen, and his wife three years before our conversation.

Rosa: grew up in Israel. She told me what she could about Jewish ideas of death. She also goes regularly to the Death Café.

Rosie: attended a course called 'Passing over' with William Bloom on preparing for death.

SA: is a homoeopath who told me of his two near death experiences.

Sarah: Sarah's daughter attempted suicide, she was 'saved' but with serious brain damage: Sarah has lost the daughter she once had, now she has a toddler in her 30s. She is passionate about making realistic decisions about the end of life.

Sam: is a Samaritan. One of the youngest contributors.

Sister Ally : belongs to the Community of the Many Names of God, where she works as a carer in their hospice.

Swami S: also belongs to the Community of the Many Names of God, and said he was 'passionate about hospice care, end of life care.'

Tom: is the warden of a Quaker meeting house. His wife had six miscarriages, a stillbirth and a termination of a pregnancy on medical advice. One of his daughters had a stillbirth, the other a miscarriage. Some time after our conversation his ex-wife died, tragically and totally unexpectedly.

Violet: is a Quaker attender. She told me of a remarkable experience following her mother's death.

Appendix two: Sarah's story

I spoke to Sarah on the telephone because we live on opposite sides of the country, but her story sounded unique, so I was happy to do it on the phone rather than not at all. She is a friend of Phoebe, who put us in touch.

Eight years ago Sarah's daughter, Imogen, attempted suicide by hanging. She was saved from death, but is now so badly brain damaged that it she has very little quality of life. She is certainly not the daughter Sarah once had.

'My father was a consultant, and I grew up always with the knowledge that if people didn't want to carry on living for whatever reason, doctors would help them go in a peaceful way. And I'd always believed that this was true. My husband and I both had living wills that we took out years ago, to make sure that we couldn't be kept forcibly alive. But Imogen, just before her 24th birthday, tried to commit suicide for the second time in three years: she was suffering from severe clinical depression and she tried to hang herself. She was actually dead on arrival at the hospital – I only found this out later – but she was brought back from the dead and kept alive on a ventilator. She couldn't eat, breathe or do anything for herself. I've spent a lifetime working with severely disabled children as a teacher in special schools, and I recognised the signs of disability at once, as she was constantly fitting.

'I did lots of research on line and I found a piece of research in America, re people who'd tried to hang themselves. The piece of research was carried out over twelve years, so was very comprehensive. Anyone with a Glasgow coma score of less than 8 would, almost certainly, be severely disabled. I asked the consultant as

Imogen was under, to give me her GCS but he refused to let me know. My husband and I would take it in turns to be by Imogen's bed, and I would frequently lie on the floor sobbing. Imogen would constantly have tubes forced down her throat to draw out the saliva, because she couldn't swallow. She would be like a landed fish, threshing about, obviously in huge distress every time they carried out this process. It was horrendous to watch and eventually a young doctor told me that the Glasgow coma score when she came in was 3, which I knew meant dead. So my husband and I spoke with the consultant and advised him that we didn't want her to be forcibly kept alive if she was going to be severely disabled. We wanted to take her off the ventilator but he refused point blank. Whatever his reasons, if they were religious or otherwise, we'll never know. But there was one doctor who was incredibly kind and would pick me up off the floor and speak to me on my own. We didn't know that Imogen's consultant had activated a POVA on Imogen (protection of a vulnerable adult) and tagged her and we were then watched all the time when we were with her. We had no idea that this had happened and the sympathetic doctor was the only one who would speak to us without a witness being present. He would take me off into a room to talk to us and he showed us great kindness and empathy throughout the time Imogen was in the hospital. He advised us that, the only thing we could do was to sign a nil resuscitation form. So my husband and I duly signed it, only to find that it had been overturned the next day by Imogen's consultant. He said that there was nothing we could do, she didn't have a living will therefore we had absolutely no rights, while she was 'under his care'. The previous evening as I waited by her bed I vowed: "I'm going to get you out of here and let you die peacefully at home," and that's when her consultant activated the POVA. We didn't actually find out about that until she'd moved out of the *care of the consultant and into the rehab unit in the hospital. We couldn't understand why we couldn't take her out, even though she could now sit up in wheelchair and was speaking, but we couldn't take her out into the concourse for a drink because every time we tried to an alarm went off. The sister of the ward, who was very kind, said it was nothing her ward had done and we should speak to her previous consultant. Then I got a notice that I had to attend a meeting, with a group of people from the hospital, to discuss overturning the POVA. I was asked a few questions about my intentions towards Imogen, which obviously satisfied them and the POVA was duly overturned*

'The woman who chaired the meeting came and spoke to me afterwards and said the POVA should not have happened and she was sorry. While our nightmare continued, over several months, Imogen's consultant set up weekly Friday afternoon meetings. We erroneously believed that the consultant had done this out of kindness to us, to help us get through the ordeal and to answer our questions, but it was, in fact, part of the POVA requirement and every meeting was minuted. I was still teaching children with special needs and my husband was a senior manager for the county, and we were horrified to learn that, owing to the POVA, we were under threat of losing our jobs. Fortunately for us, the director of social services, and his deputy, were completely on our side and gave us their full support. We found it deeply shocking to learn that once you are through the hospital doors, unless your relative has an Advanced Directive or a living will, you have no power whatever. The medics can do exactly as they like. Imogen's consultant could have forcibly kept her alive on a ventilator for years, unless we went to court.

'The consultant wasn't used to dealing with parents/relatives who had strong views and opinions and he lied repeatedly to us, assuring us that Imogen would make a good recovery. He also

said that she would be nearly normal and able to live a near normal life. As we were so desperate to believe him, we accepted his prognosis. That was long before we discovered a POVA had been activated and just before she was moved out of his care into the rehab unit. The doctor who ran the rehab unit, came to examine her; he took one look at her, and said "She will be like a toddler for the rest of her life, severely brain damaged." I just fell apart again I asked to see Imogen's consultant again, and he just laughed and said, "Oh he's glass half empty but I'm glass half full. I believe she can live a near normal life." A year after Imogen left the rehab unit, which she moved on to, she sank into a deep depression again. I remember the consultant joking and saying, "I wouldn't recommend this as a cure for depression." I began volunteering for a charity called PAPYRUS – set up to try and prevent young suicides. I also did a lot of campaigning around improving conditions for people with acquired brain injury.

'A year after Imogen's brain injury, I wrote to her consultant to tell him what he'd left us with and how badly our lives were being affected, living with a daughter with a severe brain injury: Our son would have this burden for the rest of his life, and was deeply affected by the violent mood swings and rage which our brain-injured daughter frequently displayed and we were tied to Imogen who we had, in effect, lost. Her mind and personality permanently altered for the worse, but left in the body we still recognised, a mere shell of her former self. We would also never have closure. We watched, helplessly, as one by one, all her friends stopped contacting her and her boyfriend left too. We were left with Imogen who was nothing like Imogen we'd lost, who veered between extreme aggression, when she violently attacked people, to being very placid on occasion and often extremely sad, crying for days on end without knowing why.

'We have been through eight years of unimaginable hell as a result of the decision made by Imogen's consultant. We have regular contact with her; although she doesn't live with us, we have to make sure her finances are all in order and all that kind of thing – we're still very responsible for sorting out her everyday life, seeing her regularly and being on call if anything goes wrong. She lives in a flat with carers, but last year she suddenly became very violent to both her carers, (they had been with her for years and were wonderful) to the point where the police had to be involved on several occasions. We attended meetings with Health and Social Care but nobody put in any contingency plans; they just advised that we should phone the duty doctor in the event of extremely challenging behaviour, but the duty doctor can take three hours or more before he rings back, leaving us in a dangerous and impossible situation. In the meantime Imogen had become so aggressive, that she attacked the carer and tried to strangle her. She also attacked me, left the flat and couldn't be restrained even though she was walking towards the main road and was clearly a danger to herself and others. The police had to come out three times in a row, until she was finally moved into a temporary residential place. We have been through unimaginable hell over the years. It has put immense pressure on the rest of our family. I have friends whose son committed suicide years ago, a tragic death, but at least they have closure now and can get on with the rest of their lives, something we can never do.

'My father died in 1982. In those days doctors were much more revered, no one would ever have dreamed of following them around and they were able to administer large doses of morphine, and with family's consent, to end a life which had become intolerable. It was just accepted, and people were previously not kept alive at any cost. Now technology and medicine have moved on to such an extent that people can be kept alive for many years *in awful situations. I have worked in a special school where there was a teenage girl who was blind and strapped onto a bed or into a wheelchair, and who just screamed, cried and self -harmed. There was another boy who was blind, deaf and severely mentally retarded; he self-harmed all day and took chunks out of his face. The parents of children like this are left caring for them, sometimes for decades. The endless stress often causes the family to break up and badly affects the other siblings. Many more severely disabled children are being kept alive, who would not otherwise have survived, and we spend vast amounts on keeping them alive. The money that is spent on keeping people alive unnecessarily, and often in great distress, could turn the whole NHS around in a day. It costs a minimum of £10,000 a week to keep someone alive on life support. When I carried out my research eight years ago, I learned that the longest anyone had been kept alive was ten years. Imogen goes to Headway, and whilst there I have seen lots people with brain injuries in even worse states than her. It is absolutely heartbreaking to see people with such extreme brain injury that they are almost constantly distressed and/or have little quality of life. It seems that there are some doctors who will do anything, at any cost, to keep people alive, but then hand them back to their families and don't see what dire consequences their decisions have caused.*

'It's just a terrifying prospect that people going into hospital don't realise what they might face. It seems crucial to me that people should be educated properly about preparing for death, as we prepare for weddings and christenings and other significant life events. I don't think there's anybody I've spoken with who has not been shocked to learn the real power of hospitals and doctors, once someone is through their doors. My friends have all advised me that our tragedy and the subsequent decisions made against our wishes, have prompted them to take out an Advanced

Directive because none of us knows what could happen when/if we go into hospital.

'The power doctors have is frightening: I'd always had a great admiration for doctors, and believed that that they were amazing people, who always did the right thing; the experience with Imogen has, sadly, changed my view. We had to watch in a slow and agonising way, seeing all the friends disappear. Her friends gradually disappeared and fell by the wayside as they couldn't have a conversation with her, there's nothing left of the Imogen we loved apart from the physical shell. She has been left without either empathy or sympathy and is often cruel and vicious to other people. The daughter we once had was kind, sensitive and caring and all those attributes have gone for ever.'

Sarah went on to tell me of the case of Frances Inglis:

'It was headline news: her son was very severely injured when he fell out of an ambulance after a minor accident. He was left very severely brain damaged, bedridden and unable to speak. Frances was a nurse and she tried to kill him with a syringe of morphine, but was caught before she could administer it. She later tried again and succeeded and was subsequently sent to prison for eight years.'

We briefly talked about moves to change our law on assisted dying: 'Only people who are wealthy enough, and well educated enough to go to Switzerland and Dignitas can manage to arrange their own death' I mentioned the case of Phoebe's father who might have been able to live longer had assisted dying been legal in this country.

'Exactly – people would have a longer happier life knowing that there was a painless and efficient way out at the end. It seems that, in this country, we treat animals better than we treat people in terms of a good death. I remember my husband saying to the

consultant "What we don't want is for you to hand Imogen back to us as a severely damaged person, because that's what we fear most." He, of course, doesn't have to live with the consequences of his decision making. When I wrote to him a year later and told him what never ending hell he'd put us through he wrote back and said he didn't regret anything he'd done. We will never know what his motives were, but had we had a different consultant, who did not overturn our wish for "nil resuscitation" none of this would have happened and Imogen would have died. We have never ever been able to move on as a result, and will never have closure.'

Since all this happened, Sarah has done a lot of campaigning for PAPYRUS, the charity to prevent young suicides.

'Imogen used websites to tell her how to kill herself. We learned, to our horror, that there are people, "trolls", who encourage young people to kill themselves. That's why PAPYRUS was started. The parents who started it found that their son had been groomed by an internet consultant in his early 40s and encouraged to hang himself when he was severely depressed. They took him to court, but the judge ruled it out of court as inadmissible evidence because it wasn't face to face grooming. As the law stands at the moment in the UK it's legal to groom a young people to kill themselves, but it's not legal to groom them for sex. We still haven't succeeded, despite endless campaigning to persuade the government to force the internet providers to police their websites, and eradicate the websites which encourage suicide. Imogen was using our computer, just before she attempted to take her own life, and my husband checked the memory and found she'd been using suicide websites to find ways to kill herself. The law is a mess, and the decision not to police these websites will continue to have disastrous consequences.'

Appendix three: J's thoughts

I had a very pleasant conversation with J, who very kindly offered me an excellent lunch. J was an acquaintance of mine, but I did not think I knew her well enough for this to affect the conversation. J's only child, her son, took his own life eight years ago at the age of 33. J is still grieving and much of our conversation was about grief, how it feels and how difficult it was at the beginning and through the first few years, to find people willing to talk about it.

> 'Some friends were reluctant to talk of what had happened; though they were very encouraging and warm towards me. My own family, siblings in particular, were suffering their own shock: two were able to respond well while one couldn't engage with me about it and none of us were helped by our geographical spread, lack of regular contact – we had not for many years met at regular family events; they either didn't have children or none of similar age.
>
> 'Living alone, I faced an isolated bereavement. I longed for others to grief with, to hear others lamenting. Alone, it felt as if no-one else was grieving for T, though of course they were. For me it was all about wanting to hear praise for my son and hear how much he would be missed. From most people I sensed compassion for myself but I did not seek that. For a long time I was thinking only of my son's loss, not mine, to the extent that I wondered what it would be like begin to feel he had gone and to simply miss him...'

Losing a son is not something one can 'get over' or 'move on' from and yet those phrases were sometimes offered to her in response to her expression of loss and especially regret . Those who have not experienced such a loss find it hard to understand the need to regularly express regret and sorrow and some of the most harmful things that were said to J at the time were 'It is said one needs just 40 days of grief', 'You need to move on' and, within a few months, 'I didn't know you would still be going on about this'. One does not move on. Nor should one. J said, 'I thought that to say these things to me was inappropriate.' She went on to quote Julian Barnes, the writer who lost his wife and said that you don't move on and leave something/someone behind, you wouldn't want to do that anyway, and you will always be making your way round this awful event, finding ways to reconnect and live with the person.

J said,

'T [her son] had to become part of me in a new way. Any idea of moving on presents an image of detaching from the lost one; one already feels detached and reeling from this. With T it was as if he had disappeared entirely, his death being so unexpected and sudden, so much so that I couldn't anymore properly imagine him, he felt so utterly gone. To myself I used the word 'goneness'. 'I felt isolated from a normal current of life, life had indeed stopped. A poet, Denise Riley, said 'I live time without its flow'. Moving on, forgetting, putting it (T, his death) behind me, was unthinkable, frightening.' It was only in psychotherapy that I began to "see" T again, to see him in colour, see him moving. But no one would have guessed this.'

She told me that a bereavement volunteer had said 'It will feel like losing a limb'.

'I didn't think the pain of limb loss could equate with the loss of a loved one. J said, I wasn't asked what bereavement felt like. 'I wrote a poem about imagining my limbs floating away, with the lines 'It doesn't correlate with the marks you make, the space you leave.' I tried imagining being without a limb, and because of the

physical emotional pain I was in at that time, I couldn't imagine that the pain would be similar. T's absence was much bigger than his presence had been. The presence of a loved one is a familiar concept but the absence of someone can be of overwhelming capacity, doesn't have a relationship with ordinary scale. After many years, now I think they may have meant that without a limb one would have to negotiate any move, the absence would always be there, there was the risk of imbalance. This way of looking at it makes sense now. But was quite inappropriate at the beginning, there being no explanation or discussion.'

J mentioned other unhelpful things people had said to her eight years ago:

'A friend wrote to me, telling me about his brother who had killed himself and he said "We can be sorry for ourselves, but we really need to pick ourselves up and move forward." And I remember feeling alienated, thinking – I am an expert in terms of how I feel – why doesn't he ask me, learn from me, not make assumptions. I never answered his letter…. though he meant well. At the time I didn't have the capacity to accommodate that kind of attitude. I was altogether less tolerant.'

She told me of another friend she'd known for many years but with whom she had little contact.

'She rang me up just after T died, having heard from a mutual friend. She said, "I'm so sorry, they say, you'll need 40 days of grief". I simply moved the phone away so her voice was not too loud – I was very sensitive to sound – but it was the words which did not resonate with me, in fact I found them abhorrent. The length of grieving time was of no consequence to me. I was simply in the middle of it. Again, she didn't ask me how I was, what I might need. She offered to ring again and I said kindly I preferred

at the moment not to be called by anyone (I didn't want her to feel singled out), that I would ring at times best suited to me. I didn't ring again and then a few years ago I'd heard she had suffered great loss and I rang.

'She rings me for support. She has suffered emotionally and physically and is finding it very hard to re-establish herself. There is no mention from either of us about 40 days of grieving. I don't expect she remembers. I cannot be sure how helpful I am to her. We cannot know what others want, even if we ask, I suspect. But asking seems the best and humblest way to help. Which means of course, listening.

'The best experiences for me were with those who gave their time to me, with a quiet gentle warm presence, not those who bounded up enthusiastically saying "How are you?" That's odd, isn't it, to want to be asked how we are, and then to find it not always appropriate! Sometimes the way of asking seemed to preclude an honest answer. I probably wanted to give an honest answer. Another recently bereaved friend said how she disliked this breezy "How are you?" She preferred someone to greet her with "How lovely to see you".

'People who said, at the beginning, "I just don't know what to say. I'm really sorry. I can't imagine": they got it right.'

She went on to talk of the difficulty of telling someone about the suicide.

'This happened immediately after the death and after telling many people in one day, I learned how to be careful, to explain it slowly, so that they might, just before I tell them, guess what's coming, and survive the hearing of it. It is such an awful thing to tell, and shocking to hear, when it is suicide.

'And this doesn't go away. Each time you meet someone new, you know they will be very shocked. You are aware that it will *be difficult for them to react, and you cannot be sure of their attitude towards those who kill themselves. It is anticipating the reaction that is most difficult. Though I have always been moved by the shown.'*

One of the hardest things J has found is when she's meeting new people, and circumstances in which they say, 'Do you have children?'

'Children was another thing: I find very hard to look at children because, with the death of my son it was like the death of every part of his life. he was my only child. So children of any age reminded me of him.

'I had fairly new neighbours and was concerned about meeting them, having to say what had happened to T. Inevitably, if we met, they would have to ask, 'Do you have children?' That simple question was now one that I worried about. I was worried about the shock THEY would experience with my answer; and I worried about their attitude – I knew of course that some people disapprove of those who die by suicide, I knew of the stigma of suicide.

'This filtered into my concern when conversations with groups of friends lead to discussion about children, how to treat them, how to educate them. I had very strong views that children should not be smacked, for example. And about the need for equal education. But I was very aware that I should be wary of offering opinion as some may think I was not qualified to do so, since my son had ended his life – that is, perhaps my child rearing had come into question.

'My psychotherapist had helped me prepare for this encounter which went remarkably well.

'I had invited my neighbour in with her five month old daughter. I was offered the baby to hold and she was beautiful,

gazing at me and cooing. At this point, the mother said, "Have you got children?"

'It was as if the baby, who continued to "talk" and coo, was helping me with the answer, and the baby's mother was very gentle and understanding and we have since become good friendly neighbours. Mostly, if I have been asked the 'Have you got children' question, people have been very supportive. But I am always aware that, for them, it is not easy and of course unexpected.'

What J wanted was for someone to say, 'How are you?' She was desperate to tell people how she was, but people didn't want to hear. Her son died about a year after she returned to the home she had let out for eleven years, while working elsewhere, so she no longer knew her neighbours very well.

'The most supportive local friend was someone who had cancer, and she lived for only three years after T died. I think that because she was living on the edge, worrying about dying and leaving her husband and three grown up children, she was more tuned into me and my sadness than most. She would say "How are you?" not in a breezy way, it was a genuine enquiry and I would say, "Terrible but all the better for seeing you." It lifted me, I felt she was present to my sorrow, so I could be quite cheerful, and knew I could cheerfully start saying how dreadful I felt. Because I was invited to talk, and because she tuned into me, I didn't feel such great need to talk. I also knew it was important not to overburden her. There was a comfortable balance between us as with no one else. No one else would ever say, "Do you want to talk about how you're feeling?" I was very aware nevertheless that people were worried about me, even if they might not say very much.

'I had a very close friend, a psychotherapist, and she said "I'm not going to be a psychotherapist, I'm going to be your friend."

I was glad she said that; she was always there to listen. I think if you know someone would be there you might not need it so much.... I probably did talk to her. ...we would talk of many things. I went to visit her and her husband, her husband said, "J how can you bear it? What's happening. What's life like for you?" I told him it was rare people asked and he said his sister who had recently lost her husband told him "Thank goodness someone's said his name. His name seems to have disappeared entirely." It seems a double loss. You've lost them because they have died, and you further lose them because people will talk about anything else but the loved one. It is as if they think you may have forgotten what happened, and if they refer to the death, if they name the one you've lost, you may be suddenly be reminded and have a relapse!!!'

J felt the same,

'I remember people not saying "How's T'" and so you don't hear the name. They can't say "How's T?" any more can they? It's just one of those things. Which is why it's good if people can find something to say that would enable them to say T... But I was aware that no one said, "Do you want to talk about it? About T?" It seemed such a natural thing to say. Mostly of course we meet people in the middle of their lives, on the street, just in passing.

'Once, at a close friend's, there was a gathering, including a man who had recently had a stroke. Talking about education, he suddenly said to me, "That would have suited your son, wouldn't it, that sort of education?." I happily responded, glad to talk of my son but various people said "No, no shhhhhh, no" and looked alarmed as if the subject were forbidden. I felt quite cross – and anger wasn't something I felt during this time – and I told them I liked talking about T but they didn't seem to hear. There were quite elderly, a little older than me.

'I was recently at a wedding, the groom was the age my son was when he died. Of course, these occasions have a poignancy for me. But I was genuinely able to be joyful for the bride and groom. I feel of course that I carry T with me in some way; it is as if all the sorrow I felt in my heart, my mind and body, suffused into something which stays. T is always around me, I can never be surprised by anyone mentioning him. A wedding guest who I know, though we are not close, and who knows what happened to T, suddenly said, "How is this for you? We should be aware". I reassured her I was all right and thanked her for her words as that brought T to life, into the scenario, through her. I felt better for it.

'T's friends from university and A level days were much more helpful at the time of his death, and willing to say his name, and talk about him. They had known him well, post university, and more recently, than her friends and relations, but they were a long way away. Sheffield, Orkney, Sweden, just one or two locally.

'Now, and for the last three years, an ex-girlfriend of T's and another male friend, his best friend, talk to me every three or four weeks on Skype. They live in Orkney and Gotland in Sweden. Prior to that I wasn't sure how and how much to make contact. I did long to speak to them. They had known him in his grown up life, and cared for him, and I wanted to be close to them for that. I knew they had suffered greatly at his death. They were in their early thirties when T died. They are maturing and there has been some healing with time. There are three others I am in touch with but only tentatively, irregularly. Now, because I have ventured onto Facebook we sometimes talk there. One of his friends recently wrote a book and dedicated it to T. I have spent a lot of time longing for more contact. I am settled to what I have now.

'I haven't had a memorial for T – there hasn't been an obvious place. Everything seemed fragmented. When he died one of his friends said 'we should put his ashes in the firebox at the first firing of 35006 at Toddington'. This is an engine T had been helping to restore – P and O Engine no. 35006'. She said we could do it in ten years. Ten years will be in two years. I have discussed it with one of his friends – we are beginning very slowly to plan it now.'

J had not found the voluntary bereavement counselling helpful. She began it in the first year of bereavement. She described the counsellor as a 'nice lady.'

'When I suggested I felt guilty (for not realising T had been so ill, or for not interpreting/understanding what he had said in the last weeks) she would say, "I hope you're not blaming yourself". So it felt like I couldn't say what I needed to say regardless of whether it was 'true' or not and which I couldn't say to family and friends in case they were upset. I remember struggling to get round it, just to get it out, saying "Well I'm acknowledging things." She interpreted that as self blame and wouldn't allow me that luxury even for a moment.....she could have gently tried to discuss it, but no. Yet I needed to talk and blame myself for not seeing that T was unwell. Preventing me from doing so felt hugely frustrating. It was such a bombshell I was trying to fathom – T's death. I remember one of her gestures – she put her hand up to her face, as if hiding her eyes from what I was saying. She obviously couldn't bear what I was saying – I thought she must have heard this self-blaming from others that day – she was the only counsellor there who worked with those who'd lost someone from suicide. She couldn't take any more! I was having to consider her. Frankly, not being able to express guilt (and I don't think it matters whether it is rational or irrational guilt – it

needs to be voiced) felt as if my words were being stuffed back down my throat!

'I had to pretend that was OK and carry on.... I had been very hopeful when I first went, relieved to have the chance to TALK to someone, but it was disappointing.'

This counsellor had suggested she join a group of others bereaved by suicide to share their experiences, but

'I felt myself going into counsellor mode myself, and I wasn't feeling that I wanted to share this experience with them, although I wanted to support them. One was a woman who had had counselling for a year – she was now able to say, "It isn't my fault". I think the counsellor thought this would be of help to me. She didn't know that "getting better" wasn't what I craved. At that stage I just needed to talk and talk about T's death and all the previous sorrows of HIS life – a volatile father, school bullying, etc. – as all these things reared up after his death. I couldn't see anything else. Was I blaming my self? Was I going to kill myself? Those seemed to be the two most important things to her.

'It was only after I saw a psychotherapist five years later that when I could air these things over and over, that I could remember or picture positive things in T's life. But then, he had twenty years experience, was teaching psychotherapy, was a consultant and had worked with victims of torture. Knowing this and meeting him I thought, "Ah, now I don't have to worry about the therapist!"

'A friend had suggested I join a group, Compassionate Friends, for bereaved parents. They have a magazine and conferences. But I wasn't keen to talk to others bereaved. The friend, whose son died in a sporting accident, said she'd attended a Compassionate Friends conference but felt overwhelmed with sorrow by all their stories. I thought I might have more in common with someone

who hadn't necessarily had that experience but who was just good at conversing with me – I couldn't be sure.

'My family, my siblings (Birmingham, Knutsford, Pembrokeshire) seemed unable to provide much support. Psychotherapy taught me we're a somewhat disconnected family and yet have often been close. I do feel close to them. I see one sister a few times a year and we regularly chat. Around the time T died we had seen less of each other. After his death I'd longed for phone calls. My brother was good at talking, perhaps for about three months after T died; I wanted endless calls from my sister in Pembrokeshire and my sister in Birmingham but that didn't happen and it was hard for me to initiate. I realised later that they were devastated too, perhaps feeling guilty because they hadn't seen much of him in recent years. I don't have those feelings now. At first it was my huge need, to cry together with my sisters, and to praise and miss T, but I couldn't ask for it.

She told me of a friend whose husband had recently died of cancer.

'Her need was for friends to say, "How lovely to see you" instead of a breezy "How are you?" So "How are you?" is fine as long as it is meant; otherwise one feels one's plight is unrecognised.

'When my father died, I felt a unique loss – he died very suddenly of a heart attack. T (aged ten) and I were staying with him the weekend he died and I remember thinking we don't realise how devastating it can be for grown children. Sympathy, understandably, is directed to the spouse. My mother died a few months after T, having had ten yrs of dementia, and all I could feel was a wistful sadness in amongst the devastating loss I was feeling for T. I didn't feel more than a slight ripple of sadness for my mother. We all sang "You are my Sunshine" at her funeral – I could only think of T. No one would guess this, or if they did, no-one mentioned T to me. I did speak at the funeral about my

mother and T and how she had supported us, but it was muted grief; I couldn't feel for anyone other than T.'

She went on to tell me how music had changed for her, which reminded me of what Caroline said about all her senses being heightened. J said:

'My senses were so heightened for sound, my sense of hearing was heightened. Loud voices – some people have naturally loud voices, would disturb my emotions; birdsong – and T died in April – sounded like taut, stretched, rusty wires – a screeching that made me cringe.

'When people came to visit, or I stayed anywhere, I didn't want music, or TV or films.

Music – we listen to be emotionally stirred and that is good. But when the emotions are already stirred with bereavement, any music coming in can additionally and uncomfortably make the feeling worse. Sometimes friends would offer music, thinking it might soothe. Music didn't soothe, it caused an uncomfortable emotional response.

'Lyrics could be difficult too. "Amazing grace – I'm blind and now I see" – would remind me what I had not grasped about T's needs in the last weeks of T's life. No matter how simple the words, they would resonate. And yet eight months after T's death, deep in grief, I joined a choir. This is a contradiction isn't it? Though I couldn't listen to music, I could sing in a choir. I thought it would be soothing to use my voice, my whole body.

'I lived alone. I could cry as much as I liked. I found myself crying a lot, sobbing. I found it eventually physically hurt me in the diaphragm. I had to find a way of stopping. And I thought the singing might help that, sooth that area. And concentrating on the harmony – having some control, was therapeutic, a kind

of distraction. *So I could sing but I couldn't listen to music! I went to another choir in another town, Stroud, for four years, staying overnight with various friends, which was therapeutic in itself. The choir leader knew of my loss, as did a few of my friends there, but I didn't otherwise share it – it wasn't the right time to do so. That worked for me. I loved that choir. It became a kind of drug for me, and therapy.. .very much so. Right at the end lights were put down and we would sing 'all shall be well' in harmony. The leader was a caring person, she had been a counsellor with Winston's Wish. For years I took two buses and walked up a hill to stay with friends. You just hear those harmonies, that helps, you are doing something, you are using your voice.'*

I said it sounded that she had found her own therapy.

'It certainly soothed me, I think it soothed some inner tenderness, but importantly it gave me some distraction from pain and some company overnight with friends: these friends were ready to talk about T. I was very lucky having these friends who had had similar experiences so could relate to me. Though we may not always have talked of T, I knew they were aware this awful thing had altered me. I felt them with me.

'The real key to my healing was a psychotherapist in the same town as the choir, whom I saw for two and a half years. I would go to the choir and next day see the psychotherapist. There was a great difference in how I felt being at home, alone with my sorrow, and those overnights with friends. After a year or so of therapy, I wanted to see how well I coped being at home, without the choir. Prior to the choir, staying at home, I had a lot of anxiety. always needing to distract myself reading science, knitting, map reading/ walk planning.

'So I stopped going to the choir and began visiting the psychotherapist direct from my home, rather than through the filter

*of my friends. I now found I no longer needed the radio on for
24 hours. Some anxiety had dissipated. The psychotherapy was
helping. I had told the psychotherapist I couldn't 'go home without
my sorrow', words from a Leonard Cohen song. The therapist
quietly said, 'you can leave it here, can't you?' At first I thought
that impossible. I thought leaving it there would choke him. But I
figured it could seep out of the walls and windows. So gradually I
began leaving my sorrow there. I wrote a poem about it.*

*'To say something about knitting: I needed the knitting to
help with anxiety, not depression. With depression I would be
too lethargic to knit, but it helped with anxiety. If you have to
follow a pattern, it can helpfully occupy part of your mind. If
I did nothing, there was just too much to process in my mind.
If I could knit something, feel the lovely wool and have a small
finished product, it was helpful'. Handling beautiful wool was a
need. It helped when so much of me was hurting.'*

After an excellent lunch I asked J if she had anything she would
like to add. She first said not, then she told me of a rose she had
shown me in her garden.

*'Someone bought me a rose – she said she thought I'd want
something "that would grow". But I didn't want anything that
would grow , I didn't want to dig the earth or to pull weeds
up. I didn't have any interest in growing. A friend came and
encouraged me to dig, but it was emotionally painful, digging
into the earth. Nor could I pull weeds up, it seemed as if I was
destroying something as I felt the roots tugging so I didn't want
to pull anything out, and I didn't want to plant anything. In the
last year or two I've felt comfortable, relaxed enough to go and
dig out weeds, and plant a few things, I've enjoyed it. I noticed the
difference; over time and with therapy that changed.'*

I asked if anything else had changed in that way:

'As well as not being able to listen to music, I wasn't able watch deeper meaningful films, nor read novels. No story could be of interest, or have any impact at all, except what had had happened to T. But for distraction, I read science – huge complicated things like astro physics, or about microscopic atoms. This was wonderfully distracting. I read about evolution and found it amazing... it could distract my mind just enough.' These were books that had won the Royal Society for Science Book Prizes for scientists who can write well for the ordinary reader.... I loved Your Inner Fish by Neil Shubin. I realised only a couple of years ago that I still wasn't reading nor watching films, now, simply because it had become a habit not to do so.

'So I made an attempt to find books and films – and they are nourishing now, perhaps more than they ever were. Perhaps the deeper issues, tragedy has more resonance now. Shakespeare really does make sense now. I sometimes listen to Beethoven Sonatas. I go to a film society. My feelings are settled so I can watch a harrowing film.

'Just after T died I couldn't understand why anything lived. How could a weed in the gutter still have life? Or an old man still shuffle along.'

Lear: *No, no, no life?*
Why should a dog, a horse, a rat have life,
And thou no breath at all? Oh, thou'lt come no more,
Never, never, never, never, never.
(Shakespeare)

Acknowledgements

Grateful thanks to the following:

First, and most important, my heartfelt thanks to all the contributors: those 45 lovely people who were willing to have conversations with me, sharing your often personal, sometimes infinitely painful thoughts, ideas, insights. I am deeply grateful to you all: this is your book.

To Kate and Lee for their encouragement and support.

To Peggy Seeger for permission to use 'The Joy of Living' by Ewan MacColl, reproduced by kind permission of Ewan MacColl Ltd'.

To Iris Dement for permission to use 'Let the mystery be.'

To Libby Purves for permission to use her son's poem 'The silence at the song's end'

To Bill Caddick, Rough Music, for 'John O' Dreams'

To Faber and Faber Ltd. for permission to quote from Dennis Potter's 'Seeing the Blossom' and from Philip Larkin's 'The Arundel Tomb'

To Lee Gunn for permission to quote the poems 'Just Cope with it' and 'The laws of Biology End Here' by Yanna Gunn

To Ellen for the poem 'My Magic Box' by her son T.

To Lilli May for her poem 'There is an elephant in the corner'

To Caroline for her poems 'Thank you', 'The Grieving Ground', 'Soothing Me', 'The Qualities you had', and 'The Night he Died'.

To J for her poems 'Limb' and 'Going Home'

To Elizabeth, Mick and Jack for their poem 'The Door', inspired by Miroslav Holub.

Bibliography

Adam, D. (2006) *Celtic Prayers*, Bristol, Tim Tiley.

Aitkenhead, D. (2016) *All at Sea*, London, Fourth Estate.

Alborn, M. (1997) *Tuesdays with Morrie: An old man, a young man, and life's greatest lessons*, New York, Doubleday.

Aries, P. (1962) *Western Attitudes to death: From the middle ages to the present day*, Baltimore, JHU Press.

Astley, N. (2002) *Staying Alive: Real poems for unreal times*, Tarset, Northumberland, Bloodaxe Books.

Astley, N. (ed) (2003) *Do not Go Gentle: Poems for Funerals*, Tarset, Northumberland, Bloodaxe Books.

Bailey, R. and Hall J. (eds) (2008) *The Book of Love and Loss*, Bath, Belgrave Press.

Barnes, J. (2009) *Nothing to be frightened of*, London, Vintage books.

Barnes, J. (2013) *Levels of life*, London, Jonathan Cape.

Becker. E. (1973) *Denial of death*, New York, Free Press.

Bellingham, L. (2014) *There's something I'm dying to tell you*, London, Coronet.

Bialosky, J. (2115) *History of a Suicide: My Sister's Unfinished Life*, London, Granta.

Bowlby, J. (1953) *Child Care and the Growth of Love*, Harmondsworth, Pelican.

Bragg, M. (2008) *Remember me*, London, Hodder and Stoughton.

Brayne, S. (2010) *The D Word: Talking about dying*, London, Continuum.

Brayne, S. and Fenwick, P. (2008) *Nearing the end of life: A guide for relatives and friends*, London, Continuum.

Brown, N. (2013) *Spirituality without Structure: The Power of finding your own path*, Winchester, Moon Books.

Chalmers, A. (ed) (2008) *Farewell my child*, West Wickham, Child Bereavement Charity.

Childs-Gowell, E. (1992) *Good Grief Rituals*, a healing companion New York, Station Hill Press.

Clayton, I., (2010) *Our Billie*, London, Penguin.

Clough, A.H.(1974) *The Poems of Arthur Hugh Clough*, second edition, London: Oxford University Press.

Didion, J. (2005) *The Year of Magical Thinking*, New York, Knopf.

Diski, J. (2016) *In Gratitude*, London, Bloomsbury.

Donne, J. (1997) *No man is an island*, London, Folio Society

Doughty, C. (2015) *Smoke gets in your Eyes*, London, Cannongate.

Dying Matters, (2010) *Dying to Know,* London, Hardie Grant Books.

Eliot, T.S. (1936) *Collected Poems 1909 – 1962* London, Faber.

Extense, G. (2013) *The Universe versus Alex Woods*, London,Hodder and Stoughton.

Fenwick, P. and Fenwick, E. (2008) *The Art of Dying*, London, Continuum.

Fergus, D. (2018) *I Let Him Go*, London, Blink

Frankl, V. (1946) *Man's Search for Meaning*, Boston, Beacon Press.

Gawande, A. (2014) *Being Mortal*, London, Profile books in association with the Welcome collection.

Gibrain, K. (1926) *The Prophet*, Harmondsworth, Penguin.

Gould, P. (20120) *When I die: Lessons from the death zone*, Little Brown.

Gunn, Y. (2016) *Late at Night with Razors*, Coventry, Chapplefields Press.

Gross, K. (2015) *Late Fragments - Everything I want to tell you (About this magnificent life)*, William Collins.

Heiney, N. (2007) *The silence at the song's end*, Songstead books.

Holden, A. and Holden, B. (2014) *Poems that make grown men cry*, London, Simon and Schuster.

Hughes, T. (1998) *Birthday letters*, London, Faber.

Ironside, V. (1996) *You'll get over it: The rage of bereavement*, Harmodsworth, Penguin.

James, C. (2015) *Sentenced to life*, Basingstoke, Picador.

Johnson, W. (2016) *Don't You Leave Me Here, My Life,* London, Little Brown.

Jung, C.G. (1933) *Modern Man in Search of a Soul,* London, Routledge and Kegan Paul.

Jung, C.G. (1963) *Memories, Dreams, Reflections,* London, Collins and Routledge, and Kegan Paul.

Kübler-Ross, E. (1969) *On death and dying,* New York, Macmillan.

Kübler-Ross, E. and Kessller, D. (2000) *Life Lessons,* New York, Scribner.

Kübler-Ross, E. (2005) *On Grief and Grieving: Finding the Meaning of Grief Through the Five Stages of Loss,* London, Simon and Schuster

Kumar, S. (2002) *You are Therefore I Am,* Totness, Devon, Green Books

Lacoute, P. (1969) *God is Silence,* London, Quaker Books.

Larkin, P. (2003) *Collected Poems,* London Faber and Faber.

Lazlo, E. and Peake, A. (2015) *The Immortal Mind,* Rochester, Vermont, Inner Traditions.

Lewis, C.S. (2015) *The Great Divorce,* New York, Harper One.

Levine, S. (1984) *Meetings at the Edge: Dialogues with the Grieving and the Dying, the Healing and the Healed,* Bath Gateway Books.

Levine, S.(1997) *A Year to Live: How to live this year as if it were your last,* London, Thorsons.

Macdonald, H. (2014) *H is for Hawk,* London, Jonathan Cape.

Marsh, H. (2014) *Do no Harm: Stories of life, death and brain surgery,* London, Phoenix

Mccormack, J.H. (2005) *Grieving: A beginner's guide,* London, Darton, Longman and Todd.

Motion, A. (2009) *The Cinder Path,* London, Faber and Faber.

Moorjani, A. (2012) *Dying to be me,* London, Hay House.

Norwich, J., (1998) *Revelations of Divine Love,* London, Penguin Classics

Nuland, S.B. (1994) *How We Die,* London, Chatto and Windus

Oates, Joyce C. (2011) *A Widow's Story,* Fourth Estate

Pearson, P. (2014) *Opening heaven's door: What the dying tell us about where we are going,* London, Simon and Schuster.

Picardie, R., (1998) *Before I say Goodbye,*London, Penguin.

Porter, M, (2015) *Grief is the thing with feathers*, London, Faber and Faber.

Potter, D. (1994) *Seeing the Blossom*, London, Faber and Faber.

Purves, L (2009) *Shadow Child*, London, Hodder and Stoughton.

Quaker Quest, (2017) *Twelve Quakers and Death*, London, Quaker Quest Network.

Reanney, D. (1991) *The death of forever: A new Future for Human Consciousness*, Longman, Cheshire PTY (Australia) UK Souvenir Press 1995.

Schwalbe, W. (2012) *The end of your life book club*, London, Hodder and Stoughton.

Servan-Schrieber, D. (2011) *It's not the last good bye*, London, McMillan.

Stanford, P. (2011) *The death of a child*, London, Continuum.

Titmuss, R. (1970) *The Gift Relationship: From Human Blood to Social Policy*, Harmondsworth, Penguin

Tolle, E. (2003) *Stillness speaks*, London, Hodder and Stoughton.

Tolle, E. (?????) *The power of Now*, London, Yellow Kite

Towes, M. (2014) *All my puny sorrows*, London, Faber and Faber.

Tutu, D, (1999) *No Future Without Forgiveness*, London, Rider.

Underhill, E. (ed) (1970) *A book of Contemplation the which is called the Cloud of Unknowing, in the which a soul is oned with God*, London, Stuart and Watkins.

Ware, B. (20011) *The top five regrets of the dying*, London, Hay House.

Worth, J. (2010) *In the Midst of Life*, London, Weidenfeld and Nicolson.

Yearly Meeting of the Religious Society of Friends (2008) *Advices and queries*, London, Yearly Meeting of the Religious Society of Friends.

Websites

Care not killing – www.carenotkilling.org

Centre for death and society (University of Bath) – www.bath.ac.uk/cdas

Child Bereavement Charity – www.childbereavement.org.uk

Compassionate Friends – www.tcf.org.uk

Cruse – www.cruse.org.uk

Death cafés – deathcafe.com

Death on the (Edinburgh) Fringe (lectures, accessed 20/12/15)–
deathonthefringe.wordpress.com/

Dignity in dying – www.dignityindying.org

Dying Matters – dyingmatters.org

Exit – exitinternational.net

Good life, good death, good grief – www.goodlifedeathgrief.org.uk

Grave Talk – churchofenglandfunerals.org/gravetalk

Hospice UK – www.hospiceuk.org

Living and Dying Well – www.livinganddyingwell.org.uk

Living Well, Dying Well – www.lwdwtraining.uk

Marie Curie – www.mariecurie.org.uk

Maytree – www.maytree.org.uk (Carol O'Brienon on the Maytree – www.
independent.co.uk/life-style/health-and-families/features/sanctuary-
for-the-suicidal-9749564.html)

Natural Death Centre – www.naturaldeath.org.uk

Not Dead Yet – notdeadyetuk.org

Organ donation – www.nhsbt.nhs.uk

PAPYRUS – www.papyrus-uk.org

Samaritans – www.samaritans.org

SANDS – www.uk-sands.org

Society for old age rational suicide (SOARS) – www.soars.org.uk

Soul Midwives – www.soulmidwives.co.uk

Survivors of Bereavement by Suicide – uk-sobs.org.uk

The Compassionate Friends – www.tcf.org.uk

The Conversation Project – theconversationproject.org

The Forgiveness Project – theforgivenessproject.com

The Silence of Suicide – www.mansfieldchambers.co.uk/the-silence-of-suicide

Winston's Wish – www.winstonswish.org.uk